C000279576

'*Walking into the Void* by Agnes Horvath and Arpad Sz[...] beautiful and fascinating books ever written on walki[...] much more than a means of transportation, or an acti[...] *experience*; an experience that intensifies our aesthetic relationship to the world, hollowing that essential void out of which forms and meanings become ordered. In this book, the most archaic conditions of our culture are the subject of investigation, at the same time as the transgression of modernity is exposed as a disaster.'

Frédéric Gros, Professor of Political Philosophy,
SciencesPo, Paris, editor of the Collège de France
lectures *of Michel Foucault, author of* A Philosophy of Walking.

'This book is a tour de force; a beautiful, poetic, scholarly and sensitive archaeology of walking in human history that builds upon the authors' experience of walking together and their combined theoretical and methodological body of work - a meeting of historical sociology and political anthropology to walk the reader 'back towards ourselves'. A must-read for all interested in walking as experience, practice, method, art, and pilgrimage.'

Maggie O'Neill, Chair in Sociology/Criminology,
University of York, UK.

WALKING INTO THE VOID

The book starts by discussing the significance of walking for the experience of being human, including a comparative study of the language and cultures of walking. It then reviews in detail, relying on archaeology, two turning points of human history: the emergence of cave art sanctuaries and a new cultural practice of long-distance 'pilgrimages', implying a descent into such caves, thus literally the 'void'; and the abandonment of walking culture through settlement at the end of the Ice Age, around the time when the visiting of cave sanctuaries also stopped. The rise of philosophy and Christianity is then presented as two returns to walking. The book closes by looking at the ambivalent relationship of contemporary modernity to walking, where its radical abandonment is combined with attempts at returns.

The book ventures an unprecedented genealogy of walking culture, bringing together archaeological studies distant in both time and place, and having a special focus on the significance of the rise of representative art for human history. Our genealogy helped to identify settlement not as the glorious origin of civilisation, but rather as a source of an extremely problematic development. The findings of the book should be relevant for social scientists, as well as those interested in walking and its cultural and civilisational significance, or in the direction and meaning of human history.

Agnes Horvath is a visiting research fellow at the Centre for the Study of the Moral Foundations of Economy and Society, University College Cork, Ireland. She has a Doctorate in Law (ELTE, Budapest, 1981), an MA in Sociology (University of Economics, Budapest, 1988) and a PhD in Social and Political Sciences (European University Institute, Florence, 2000). Horvath has published books and articles in English, French, Italian and Hungarian, including *Modernism and Charisma* (Palgrave, 2013), *Breaking Boundaries: Varieties of Liminality* (Berghahn, 2015, with Bjørn Thomassen and Harald Wydra) and *The Dissolution of Communist Power:*

The Case of Hungary (Routledge, 1992, with Arpad Szakolczai). She also co-edited a special section on 'The Gravity of Eros in the Contemporary' in the December 2013 issue of *History of Human Sciences*, and co-edited a special issue on 'The Political Anthropology of Ethnic and Religious Minorities' for *Nationalism and Ethnic Politics* (Routledge, March 2017). She is one of the founding editors of the peer-reviewed academic journal *International Political Anthropology*.

Arpad Szakolczai is Professor of Sociology at University College Cork. His books include *La scoperta della società* (Carocci, 2003, with Giovanna Procacci) as well as *Max Weber and Michel Foucault: Parallel Life-Works* (1998), *Reflexive Historical Sociology* (2000), *The Genesis of Modernity* (2003), *Sociology, Religion and Grace: A Quest for the Renaissance* (2007), *Novels and the Sociology of the Contemporary* (2016), *Permanent Liminality and Modernity* (2017) and *Comedy and the Public Sphere: The Re-birth of Theatre as Comedy and the Genealogy of the Modern Public Arena* (2013), all published by Routledge. He has published articles in the *American Journal of Sociology*, *Theory, Culture and Society*, *Cultural Sociology*, *Current Sociology*, *History of the Human Sciences*, the *European Journal of Social Theory*, *International Sociology*, the *British Journal of Political Science*, *East European Politics and Societies*, the *European Sociological Review*, the *British Journal of Sociology* and *International Political Anthropology*.

Contemporary Liminality

https://www.routledge.com/sociology/series/ASHSER1435

Series editor:
Arpad Szakolczai, University College Cork, Ireland
Series advisory board:
Agnes Horvath, University College Cork, Ireland
Bjørn Thomassen, Roskilde University, Denmark
Harald Wydra, University of Cambridge, UK

This series constitutes a forum for works that make use of concepts such as 'imitation', 'trickster' or 'schismogenesis', but which chiefly deploy the notion of 'liminality', as the basis of a new, anthropologically focused paradigm in social theory. With its versatility and range of possible uses rivalling and even going beyond mainstream concepts such as 'system', 'structure' or 'institution', liminality is increasingly considered a new master concept that promises to spark a renewal in social thought.

In spite of the fact that charges of Eurocentrism or even 'moderno-centrism' are widely discussed in sociology and anthropology, it remains the case that most theoretical tools in the social sciences continue to rely on taken-for-granted approaches developed from within the modern Western intellectual tradition, whilst concepts developed on the basis of extensive anthropological evidence and which challenged commonplaces of modernist thinking have been either marginalised and ignored or trivialised. By challenging the assumed neo-Kantian and neo-Hegelian foundations of modern social theory, and by helping to shed new light on the fundamental ideas of major figures in social theory, such as Nietzsche, Dilthey, Weber, Elias, Voegelin, Foucault and Koselleck, whilst also establishing connections between the perspectives gained through modern social and cultural anthropology and the central concerns of classical philosophical anthropology, *Contemporary Liminality* offers a new direction in social thought.

Titles in this series

1. **Permanent Liminality and Modernity**
   Analysing the Sacrificial Carnival through Novels
   Arpad Szakolczai

2. **Power, Legitimacy and the Public Sphere**
   The Iranian Ta'ziyeh Theatre Ritual
   Amin Sharifi Isaloo

3. **Walking into the Void**
   A Historical Sociology and Political Anthropology of Walking
   Agnes Horvath and Arpad Szakolczai

WALKING INTO THE VOID

A Historical Sociology and Political Anthropology of Walking

Agnes Horvath and Arpad Szakolczai

Routledge
Taylor & Francis Group

LONDON AND NEW YORK

First published 2018
by Routledge
2 Park Square, Milton Park, Abingdon, Oxon OX14 4RN

and by Routledge
711 Third Avenue, New York, NY 10017

Routledge is an imprint of the Taylor & Francis Group, an informa business

© 2018 Agnes Horvath and Arpad Szakolczai

The right of Agnes Horvath and Arpad Szakolczai to be identified as
authors of this work has been asserted by them in accordance with
sections 77 and 78 of the Copyright, Designs and Patents
Act 1988.

All rights reserved. No part of this book may be reprinted or
reproduced or utilised in any form or by any electronic, mechanical,
or other means, now known or hereafter invented, including
photocopying and recording, or in any information storage or
retrieval system, without permission in writing from the publishers.

Trademark notice: Product or corporate names may be trademarks
or registered trademarks, and are used only for identification and
explanation without intent to infringe.

British Library Cataloguing-in-Publication Data
A catalogue record for this book is available from the British Library

Library of Congress Cataloging-in-Publication Data
A catalog record for this book has been requested

ISBN: 978-1-138-21448-4 (hbk)
ISBN: 978-1-138-21449-1 (pbk)
ISBN: 978-1-315-44592-2 (ebk)

Typeset in Bembo
by Swales & Willis Ltd, Exeter, Devon, UK
Printed and bound by CPI Group (UK) Ltd, Croydon, CR0 4YY

CONTENTS

List of figures   *xi*
Preface   *xii*

Introduction   1

PART I
Walking into sense   **5**

1 The experience of walking   7

2 The language and culture of walking   27

3 The dilemma of representing the void: Michel Foucault
   and Frances Yates   37

PART II
The flourishing and demise of walking culture   **49**

4 Chauvet: the cave of wonders, or representation
   as transgression   51

5 Pergouset: the cave of monsters, and its aftermath   62

6 Natufian settlement: technology, representation,
   standing reserve   86

7 Göbekli Tepe: sanctuary as trickster bestiary,
   or the revival of transgression   102

8 Çatalhöyük: the culmination of settlement   114

9 Tassili: incubating transformation, or a training
   ground for the magi   127

PART III
Returns to walking   **147**

10 Walking in philosophy and religion   149

11 Walking in mountains: the vocation of losing oneself   161

12 Experiencing walking   172

    Conclusion   184

Bibliography   *186*
Glossary   *197*
Name index   *200*
Subject index   *204*

FIGURES

5.1 Palaeolithic trickster metamorphosis   74
5.2 Taking the form: Palaeolithic trickster jumps in/after a bovine   75
5.3 Accelerating movements for transformation   77
5.4 The void, or the shadowed state   78
9.1 The Great God of Sefar   133
9.2 Artificial uterus or the egg motif of transformation   140
9.3 The successful metamorphosis   142

PREFACE

Fermati o passagger
la testa inchina
alle madre di dio
del cielo regina

Stop oh wayfarer
and bow your head
to the mother of god
who is queen of heaven

Inscription on a Florentine tabernaculum, where Via Giramonte
and Via Passo all'Erte meet in San Miniato

This book focuses on a special kind of walking, a walk into the *void*. In a way any genuine walking – not an hour-long casual strolling, but a sustained effort, lasting for long days, even weeks – is a walk into the void, in the sense of going into unknown places. Yet again, we take the 'void' to mean something more; not simply the unknown, but also a literal nothingness: a special one, bigger than us, an enormous emotional charge. Even further, it is here, with the void, that science and religion, supposedly separated with modernity, suddenly meet again, as while the void is the basis of Newtonian science, it is also literally in the void that man can recognise the divine. In fact, the existence of the void, just as the symbolisation of infinity is a thorny problem, and can be simply tied as if on a Möbius strip to the similarly thorny problem concerning the 'existence' of the divine. In still other words, through and with the void the Newton-Kantian transcendental encounters the religious meaning of transcendence.

Still further, the book focuses on a very particular kind of walking into the void: the late Palaeolithic practice of walking into caves, filled with paintings of immense and incomprehensible beauty on their walls, as centres of 'pilgrimage'. These caves, however, represent an emergence and not origin, in the sense that their novelty, the birth of representative art, is not simply the glorious origin of culture, but also the source of representation *as a problem*. Representation is literally 're'-presentation, the bringing into presence of something absent, thus a kind of magic, which furthermore requires technical means, thus generating the art/magic/technology complex, with all its problems. Representative art is thus transgression, as Plato understood it so well.

The end of cave art also coincided with the rise of settlement, around the end of the Ice Age. Thus, the book is also about the opposite of walking culture, which is settlement. A central part of the book is devoted to the question of why people stopped walking and settled. It treats settlement again from a genealogical perspective as an emergence and not an origin; a singular break in history, not the superb rise of civilisation. Yet again, it will not offer a dualistic perspective – 'walking is good, settlement bad' – as *once* humans settled, the rules of the game of life changed, and walking among the settled can be treacherous, even trickful.

Settlement was one of the most momentous changes in human history, bringing about not simply 'civilisation', but also violence and rituals of sacrifice. Philosophers and social scientists over the ages have spent enormous efforts, ink and passion on the question of whether man is violent or not in his nature, but archaeology has long since conclusively resolved this debate, even though prejudices, animated by vested interests, are slow to disappear. There is simply no trace whatsoever of human violence against fellow men before around 11,000 BC; however, just around that moment, clear evidence suddenly burgeons. The reason is also simple: people who are part of a walking culture have no reason to fight: if any problem emerged, they could simply take different roads. This solution became impossible the moment settlement emerged, and thus another transgression appeared: man killing man.

The question of walking, its abandonment and a return to a walking culture are thus issues of enormous significance, literally covering the origin and meaning of our life and history. We can only barely scratch their surface.

INTRODUCTION

> Man perceives in the world only what already lies within him; but to perceive what lies within him man needs the world; for this, however, activity and suffering are indispensable.
>
> *Hofmannsthal,* Book of Friends *(2008)*

In actual fact, nothing is more trivial than walking. This is why so little is written about it, in sociology and philosophy; and this is why it is increasingly forgotten in our everyday life as well. Walking is a 'pedestrian' activity, and the adjective 'pedestrian' quite a while ago gained a negative connotation. Still, walking is the foundation of our being human. Thus, beyond being a crucial indicator of how, why and where we moderns are going, it can also be considered as a royal road of taking us back to where we started. This is indeed the central aim of this book: offering a historical sociology and political anthropology of walking to help us back towards ourselves – together with those increasing numbers that are walking the Camino, and other roads. We could have said, 'back to reality'; however, what reality is cannot be defined, not even philosophically, as it was centrally recognised by Plato. It simply *is*. It is only the deviation from reality, its alteration, or the 'unreal', which can be put into words. The aim of this book is to capture this first alteration, the rise of representation in cave paintings, which eventually undermined walking culture and resulted in settlement, and the firsts of the successive steps of adaptation to such unreality.

It can perhaps best be seen by looking at walking from the reverse angle, considering how many thousands of years humans spent in such an activity. This proves the genuine reality of walking, and not simply facts about how many people are walking, or starting to walk, today. Perhaps; but, at any rate, we invite our readers to think about not years but thousands (and hundreds of thousands) of years of bipedality.

This book is written by two social scientists whose background, education and interests are fundamentally rooted in the contemporary world, but who are using material that mostly belongs to archaeology, anthropology and the history of religions. Yet this is not due to a radical reorientation. The book is closely connected to two central questions about our reality: was the rise of the modern world not the outcome of a clear, inevitable and ultimately beneficial development, rather a peculiar and quite problematic turn taken at a certain moment, and in very distant history?; and, is it possible to do something to redress this state of affairs? Over the years for both of us it has increasingly become evident that the answers to both questions are closely connected, if not identical.

It increasingly seemed to us that both the problems of this road taken, and their alleviation, have much to do with *walking* – an activity closely related to the 'road' metaphor. Our studies, on the one hand, became focused on archaeology, coming up with the suspicion that the civilisational dead end of which modernity is – evidently – the culmination started with a 'stop', taken a very long time ago: stopping walking and starting to lead a settled existence. On the other hand, we discovered a respite from the hardly tolerable tensions of modern life through going on long-distance walking pilgrimage trips. Eventually these two purposes became joined, and this book is the outcome of this event.

For social scientists, engaging on a very long-term historical project needs a strong methodological underpinning. We can offer, as a background for the book, three basic such methodological considerations. To begin with, our work, going back at least to our joint 1992 book about the collapse of communism, follows the genealogical method, as explored by Nietzsche, continued by Max Weber and his closest 'disciples', and given new lease by Michel Foucault. It is based on a simple guiding principle: history can only be understood as it was made, thus starting from the remote past and moving towards the present, and not from the present, by anachronistically retro-jecting present concerns and values into the past, motivated and justified by the quite untenable modernist belief according to which we 'moderns' represent something like the unprecedented height of evolutionary progress. Thus, genealogy is interested in tracing the emergence of a difference, and not the glorious origin of a now established practice, that became saturated with self-justifying 'rationality'. Of course, the pursuit of such a genealogical perspective is easier said than done, as it is very rare that there is a self-evident starting point for such a historical reconstruction; one is rather continuously pressed, and forced, to move further and further back in the time horizon, while a similar kind of endless work is to be performed on the conceptual tools one is using. Yet the need for such a genealogical perspective, and its basic principles, is quite clear.

The second major methodological perspective involves the use of anthropological concepts. Here again the central issue is to go beyond, or overcome, the perspective of modernism: the issue is not to use anthropological findings gathered through the application of modern concepts and theories, but rather to make use of those anthropological concepts that were developed in the field by some of the most sensitive and perceptive scholars who realised the shortcomings of their own formation and managed to developed concepts that captured their experiences while doing fieldwork in non-modern contexts. Such concepts centrally include liminality (van Gennep 1960; Turner 1967, 1969; Szakolczai 2009; Thomassen 2014), imitation (Girard 1977, 1989; Wydra 2015), trickster (Radin 1972; Horvath 2008, 2010) and schismogenesis (Bateson 1958; Horvath and Thomassen 2008). It is since the long years that, together with the group of scholars around the journal *International Political Anthropology*, we are attempting to develop the framework for such an anthropological perspective, and that we also systematically combine this approach with classical philosophy, in particular the thinking of Plato (Horvath and Szakolczai 2013).

However, for the purposes of this book perhaps the third methodological perspective is the most important, which can even be called a 'meta-methodological' principle: the idea that man has been never different, and therefore we all can, from the here and now, understand our distant ancestors, who felt and thought, flourished and declined, like us. Behind their fully modern face, which looked entirely like modern man, they possessed a sensitive and knowledgeable mind, from a time horizon of at least 800,000 years, the distant roots of the Atapuerca *Homo antecessor*, exactly as we did.

Our concern is not to offer a general interpretation about the history of civilisation, but only to explore liminal times from the point of walking or, more precisely, the giving up of walking in liminal situations. Any crisis situation drastically changes the mode of living, even the character of those undergoing it. If the forces of liminality are at work, people adapt new character suggestions in the long run; it is in this way that transformations are accomplished and crises are solved (about such circular adaptation in politics and culture, plunging us further and further inside unreality, see Argyrou 2013; Boland 2013; Szakolczai 2017a; Wydra 2015). This logic of subordinating the concrete for the general became codified in transformative rites, but the role of the transformative and transcendental agent of the liminal, the trickster, was never really theorised in them.

The trickster is a genuine engine of replacing character with adaptivity. Its liminal elusiveness renders it capable of playing the role of both the imitator and the imitated with quick and confusing switches between the two roles. It can take any form, thus can assume a form through which it can be accepted. It is impossible to catch: whenever you feel like you have a hold on it, it is no longer there, as it has changed shape; the trickster defies any definite specification of time, place and character (Détienne and Vernant 1989). However, at the same time, it lives for attention, it perceives, absorbs and retransmits emotions, it plays with words and images, miming intentions and deep feelings, and so gradually alters every original piece of reality into an empty, closed, cold, rigid, ritualistic and legalistic construct by reversing values and creating a new personality composition, using with particular fervour rituals of sacrifice, but also rites of initiation. This new person, called hybrid by Deleuze and Guattari (1987), lacks the former bonds and borders of natural and mutual restraint, animated by authentic principles, and consequently – being empty – the trickster's existence can grow and expand infinitely. Similar figures of the void populate the films of Werner Herzog, from *Stroszek, Woyzeck* or *Nosferatu the Vampyre* through *Cobra Verde* up to *Grizzly Man* and *Lo and Behold*, with some of the central films capturing the message in their striking titles, like *Aguirre the Wrath of God* and *Every Man for Himself and God Against All*. As a genuine liminal character, it is far from being a creator in any sense, being unproductive, even sterile; instead, it is a maker that fabricates artefacts from already existing elements, imitating pre-existing forms and so trans-forming them to secure its own survival and growth (see also Hyde 1999).

The trickster can only produce something new by taking apart things that exist, and combining them in new and unprecedented ways. This is why the trickster acts at the point of intersection between art and technology: designing something new, from the elements, and then making this fake design into reality. Such eventual productivity of the trickster was rendered possible by a crucial innovation, preced-ing the invention of knowledge: the invention of representation. Representation through images was the precondition of representation through written signs; thus, the separation between words and things. We'll discuss it through Chauvet and Pergouset caves, while the same point is made by Herzog in *Nosferatu*, focusing on the vampire as a parasite on human desire. Through representation, characters deprived of their own selves turn towards acquiring the forces of others. This game of subversion eventually grew into an acquisitive universalism, where it stimulated a spirit of conquest, while inculcating an insular community spirit, amounting to a siege mentality, at the expense of others, and also a search for satisfying escalated individual desires. The power of subversion entrapped and accumulated energy, which eventually had to be oriented in an aggressive manner towards the outside. It is an acquisitive force, coming to dominance in a changed reality.

With a series of successive cases we attempt to show the emergence of lin-guistic and visual representations, the manner in which representation helped to alter walking into settlement; how through pure representations the absent, the non-being became the cornerstone of a newly formed reality. With speech, there is always somebody talking, so the human element is present – but an image or a written sign exists even in the absence of such a presence. The first such absence was represented with the first cave paintings, most probably with Chauvet cave, and whatever was the original intention, the fact that a representation was created entailed the possibility of forgetting to look after yourself, to give up your inde-pendence, which culminated in settlements and domestication, or the giving up of walking through the domestication of man.

PART I
Walking into sense

1

THE EXPERIENCE OF WALKING

The earth, that is sufficient,
I do not want the constellations any nearer,
I know they are very well where they are,
I know they suffice for those who belong to them.
Walt Whitman, Leaves of Grass, *'Song of the Open Road' (1990: 121)*

While our interest, over the past three decades and even beyond, was always centred on the modern world, its modality certainly had a decisive change, which can be indicated by a shift from the 'question' of modernity to the *problem* of modernity. Growing up beyond the Iron Curtain, in the grim world of 'existing socialism', trying – always or eventually – to ignore it, escape it, consider it as if it did not even exist, one needed some kind of stable reference point; and Western, liberal-democratic modernity, with its presumed or evident freedom and well-being, seemed to offer such a standard. However, the values of such an 'existing modernity' increasingly proved to be mirages as well, and not merely because of the original, certainly exaggerated expectations.

We started to walk not as part of a research project, but rather as a deliberate effort to get respite from daily life. This is why we did the Camino de Santiago in 2011, completing it in – by the hour – 30 days exactly, and repeating the experience in three long-term pilgrimages in the three following summers. The idea worked perfectly, but we found much more than we were hoping for: we realised that such walking trips, when done properly, do not simply offer a possibly unparalleled mode of good feeling. Walking is to return to be guided by our own heart (Szakolczai 2017b), the most physical and metaphorical essence of our being, so we have to do nothing else but start walking, and continue it, for quite some time. It *is* indeed so simple; and those of us humans who cannot walk can also be helped by those who returned to walking.

The significance of walking is increasingly realised by a number of people. Two of them have a special importance for this book, and will be used as our main guides: Frédéric Gros, a French philosopher and an editor of Michel Foucault's lectures at the Collège de France, who recently wrote an international bestseller on the 'philosophy of walking', offering 'a dense reflection about the transformative experiences of walking and the peripatetic sources of being' (Roman 2014: 59); and Tim Ingold, an anthropologist with an interest in archaeology, who similarly pioneered a sociology and anthropology of walking.

Walking, understood as a mode of moving by foot, in our world is primarily considered as an obsolete, archaic mode of travelling. This is borne out by the most appropriate and strongest form of 'empirical' evidence: changes in the use of language. The most basic term used for 'walking', or using our feet to advance, in English, this most modern of languages – both in the sense of being, together with Russian, the most recent of languages, but also being the language of the flagship countries of advancing modernisation, England and the United States – is 'to go'. However, by our time, the basic meaning of this term became identified with travel, in the sense of 'changing place', and as most of us 'moderns' do not travel by foot, the term capturing such an activity became 'walking'.

Yet, strange as it might sound, there are considerable forces in modernity that promote a shift of attention to walking as an activity. Two examples will be evoked right here, at the beginning. The first is a relatively sudden and certainly unanticipated and unexpected reappraisal of walking that happened in England, just about 1775 or at the moment identified as the *Sattelzeit* or threshold instant of modernity both by Michel Foucault (1970) and Reinhart Koselleck (1988), which can be further-more associated with the first self-conscious modern movement, the Romantics.[1] The second takes place in our very time, with an again relatively quite abrupt, surprising and steadily increasing popularity of long-distance walking pilgrimages, in particular – but not limited to – the Camino de Santiago. Thus, while walking is the non-modern form of travel par excellence, there seems to be a paradoxical *return* to walking with the onset of modernity, and exactly by some of the protagonists of high modernity, in contrast to 'early modernity' or Foucault's 'classical age'.

The situation is quite similar concerning the link between archaeology and modernity.[2] Given that modernity is usually identified with the contemporary and the 'new' (see German *Neuzeit*), any reference to archaeological evidence, especially the Old Stone Age, seems profoundly out of place in any effort to come to terms with the modern world. Yet again, the very possibility of a serious study of archaeological evidence was only rendered possible in modernity; and in such sensitivity and interest there is even something profoundly modern – though it can be traced to the Renaissance. Thus, in an interest in archaeology, just as in walking, there is something modern beyond modernity – not in the sense of the post-modern running further ahead, which is only a version of hyper-modernity, but in the sense of going 'ahead' by going back, to history and traditions, and *thus* seriously overcoming the excessive obsession of modernity with the 'absolutely new' – a kind of 'anti-modern modernity'.

Finally, while any concern with religion, spirituality or the divine is certainly the radical opposite of secular modernity, there is something profoundly, even disturbingly modern about 'religion' as well – at least, certainly concerning Christianity. This concern is again not new, but particularly 'modern', and in the best sense of 'anti-modern modernity', going against the early modern/classical age/Enlightenment age concerns, to be connected to the ideas of Max Weber, the single most important classical founding father of sociology. According to Weber, the source of modern capitalism, and modern culture in general, is not merely a (presumably, supposedly) secular Renaissance, but rather a religious revival promoted by Protestantism. The point can be made even stronger by rendering explicit the evident and arguing that modernity, even modern secularism, is a peculiar consequence of Christianity, a point that was made in the strongest possible sense by Nietzsche. Modernity indeed is not multiple, though of course it has several modalities, but rather singular: it is a 'post-Christian' modernity, paradoxically produced by a Christian 'renewal', Protestantism – thus, the possibility of another religious renewal, from within the same sources, can never be ruled out. Indeed, the most 'modern' of countries, the US, is at the same time one of the most religious of countries, and even the source of a 'fundamentalist' renewal, again for better or worse. The idea of 'multiple modernities' is an ideological point, attempting to minimise the importance of Europe, just as the 'axial age' concern, in spite of all its importance, had a similarly evident and similarly untenable attempt to question the epochal significance of Christianity.

The significance, and exact modality, of this issue will be discussed throughout the book. While this cannot be anticipated here, and while of course no final solution can be envisioned concerning such ultimate matters, a fundamental point of clarification can be offered here. The issue is not to assert, positively, the foundational significance of Christian faith, at any level – though neither will this be questioned or 'bracketed'; rather, it is to positively problematise – and emphasise the significance of – the rejection of the Christian sources of the world in which we live, and thus of our own identity. We became what we are, for better or worse, through our own Christian culture. Denying this amounts to a paradoxical self-negation and self-hatred. It is our responsibility and task to draw the consequences of this fact – but this, as a start, assumes that we cannot ignore the profound responsibility of 'Christianity' for modernity, nor the higher existence.

The modern scientific vision of the world, and methodological perspective, however, is problematic not simply because it cannot capture a concrete event and experience in its singularity, but also because science can only deal with whatever really exists in this world, what is part of some empirical concreteness, while the higher existence indeed cannot be empirically perceived – at least, it is generally believed. It therefore has close affinities with non-existence, or the void – which, however, brings in some unexpected affinities between science and religion, as the void is also the starting point and background of Newtonian science.

This issue is quite central for this book, for understanding the practice of walking and representation as its counter-activity also requires entering the most difficult and tricky question of unreality; the issue where, fortunately, Plato in the *Sophist* offers some guidance. The point is that in a way the question concerning the existence of the divine has a similar character to the existence of the void. In one sense, the void most obviously does not exist in an absolute form, but it exists as a conglomeratum of the most fluxional existence of corporality; as an enormous emotional charge.

It is exactly here, where the foundations of the scientific vision of the world are laid down, hoping to exorcise forever any concern with the divine and the transcendent, that the possibility of posing again the 'existence' of the divine reappears. This is because such existence, in a way, can be approached exactly like the existence of the void – even in the sense that the divine can be all but identified with the void (at least as an analogy). This implies, first, a recognition that something like god, or the divine, or supernatural beings indeed do not and cannot exist in the usual sense of bodily objects. Yet, as electricity and radiation are material existences, and just as – and here we enter the point of the *Sophist* – the imagination itself, or any word, impulse or emotion, while not 'real' in the evident sense can become real, and even alter reality the moment we formulate or design them in representations, our being continuously communicates and operates by using these electric or radiating charges.

However, the divine – let's use now this term in a somewhat technical sense, to capture what cannot be captured – has a further characteristic, more closely associating it with the void, and it is that it is not simply of our own making, but somehow is 'out' there, outside us, without 'really' existing, in the sense of being part of our world. Such affinity between the void and the divine is indicated by the fact that appearances of the divine – epiphanies, hierophanies or theophanies (Eliade 1989; Giesen 2006) – often take place in a void, through a void or due to the void. The most frequent places for epiphanies are mountain tops, deserts or – indeed – caves; weaknesses, illnesses or deaths, depression or other liminal places and moments; occasions where stabilities are dissolved and thus replaced by the emptiness of the void.

And yet, it is exactly here that the radical difference of the void and the divine appears. In the void our senses might perceive the divine; or, such presence assumes our ability of perception. But for this to appear, it seems that there is another condition that must be met: the man who enters the void, metaphorically or literally, cannot be completely empty or void, cannot dissolve himself or herself in the liminal void, but must preserve humanness; the loyalty to one's character must remain substantial, or even 'full': fully *present*. It is only if these two presences, the human and the divine, meet in the absence of the void that walking as a significant experience can take place.

The relevance of cave art

Indeed, a central methodological concern, guiding our efforts at understanding and this book, was the recognition of the full force of the fact that the people who painted and used these caves were exactly like us. Of course, it is impossible for us to 'know' why these caves were painted in the late Palaeolithic, or what our distant ancestors felt while they visited them, but we can assume, and indeed we must, that they in a way were just like us. Any other claim or assumption is unacceptable, inspired by one or other ideology; we have the same feet and hands, the same faces, the same eyes and ears. 'In a way' only because they did not have many of our specific modern 'sensitivities' as a baggage, but this does not mean that they were less; rather that they were more, in the sense of not having been 'spoiled' by those ways in which our perception has been altered due to various technological and commercial developments.

The strong personal experiential encounter with these works made us, as no doubt so many other people, deeply aware of such a constitutional identity between 'us' and 'them'. It made us realise that the impact must have been very similar, if only even stronger, on them as well, and so they were capable for a similar appreciation of beauty and grace as us. It also made it clear for us that our identity, and thus our genuine and 'indestructible' essence as humans, lies somewhere here, and not in some kind of 'rational thinking' or self-consciousness, as it is assumed by various modern ideologies. It lies in the capacity of complex experiences, and their adjudication, which we cannot define here, at the start of this book, but which hopefully will become gradually clear as the work progresses.

Given that one of the central aims of this book is to overcome the limitations of being 'modern', it is important to formulate here, at the start, the exact problem of this 'moderno-centrism' at this level and in this sense. Such moderno-centrism means to assume that everybody is fundamentally the same as 'we' are supposed to be – 'rational' maximisers of 'utility' – except that they were not yet able to 'develop' their 'potentials', as we are. While this might seem a straw man perspective, only shared by the most extreme believers of neoclassical economics and rational choice theory, it is quite widely shared by many archaeologists who focus on the 'rational' strategies our ancestors supposedly followed to make ends meet. In fact, the taken-for-granted current academic 'modernist' position is even more problematic, as – while accepting the perspective of such materialist 'rationalism' as 'scientifically' given – the current consensus also proposes that we should not be 'judgemental' about our ancestors, but rather accept their seemingly striking, even bizarre, repulsive practices as just as legitimate and normal, from *their* perspective, as ours. Thus, we should simply accept that certain cultures buried their dead under the floors of their houses, decorated and used for display the skulls of their ancestors, or even mingled the excrements of small rodents with human remains.

There is something deeply problematic, or even hypocritical, in this combination of assuming universal 'rationality' at the level of purely cognitive abilities while pretending that other differences are due to mere 'taste'. We think, based on our experiences with cave art, that rather the exact opposite is the case: that what today is considered as cognitive 'rationalism', far from being universal, is the result of a very specific and highly problematic kind of development; exactly the general judgements involving 'taste' have universal characteristics, with the burial practices mentioned being clear signs of a kind of societal development gone wrong, similar to the manner in which Gregory Bateson developed the concept 'schismogenesis'. The cave experience is both a data, a 'given', demonstrating that our ancestors were capable of the same feelings and experiences, thus of reasoning, as us; while at the same time it also demonstrates that such caves were used for training and reinforcing the same, proper modes of right judgement. Thus, ultimately, the caves fulfilled the same role of educating judgement as is the task of the social sciences, according to Max Weber – so there are indeed very good reasons for social scientists to venture into the world of cave art.

Finally, the world of cave art is also fundamentally connected to the theme of walking and its opposite, representation. The caves were not only painted, but also visited, though the exact nature and frequency of such visits is a very delicate issue. Experts, however, agree that the caves were visited with some frequency; and, even more importantly, the most important 'flagship' caves like Chauvet or Lascaux were chosen for their location, so that they could be spotted from a distance, and it was relatively simple to give indications from afar to find the cave. Thus, for example, Chauvet cave was located on the Ardèche River, just where the river cut a spectacular arch into the hill that for many millennia it was circling around; and the original opening of the cave was at a visible spot above the arch. People had to walk quite a long distance to visit such caves – and the aim of such a visit was a descent under the ground, into the dark and deep caves, so a genuine walk into the void to behold its representations.

Science is based on the study of phenomena that are part of our reality, and that are regular and repetitive. Modern scientific knowledge is experimentally based, which assumes that we can have control over how to repeat and reproduce experiments, rarely questioning the representative regularity of such experiments. On the other side, religious experiences, or the intrusion of the supernatural, in whatever form, are always singular and impossible to repeat, except as they are represented. Representation has its own independence in changing reality – but only accompanies changes that take place in reality. This unique, parasitic character of representation is well captured in Weber's 'instrumental rationality', which implies a reduction of human life to a search for business success, in the hope of gaining a sign of salvation, ignoring or overriding the perspective of participants.

Cave paintings touched the heart but also eventually transformed walking people, through the rise of representation as an activity, by suggesting that signs are the main instruments for gaining knowledge of the divine.

The return to walking

The actuality, even striking contemporariness of the theme is evident: from about the late 1980s, thus coinciding with the rise of globalisation and the intensification of hyper-modernity, and also a significant fall of churchgoers in countries that up to that time were the least secularised in Europe, the oldest and longest pilgrimage roads experienced a truly stunning revival, among the old and in particular. strikingly, among the young. This is all the more perplexing as walking hundreds of miles, continuously, for weeks, using the most basic accommodation, and being mostly deprived of the comforts of modern urban life is the exact opposite of what modern youth culture is about. Yet, the aim of this book is not simply to study a new subculture, or an aspect of the return of religiosity, but it will argue that this phenomenon touches the heart of one of the most important themes of contemporary social theory, personal identity or character, and its formation and transformation; even more importantly, it centrally concerns the conscious identity of the modern self. To introduce the perspective of the book, and its selected method – or rather the method that selected itself to complete the study – we need to briefly review the basic facts and the existing literature.

The main pilgrim routes are the Camino de Santiago in Spain and the Via Francigena from Canterbury to Rome, which were also two of the three most important medieval pilgrimage roads, the third being the road through the Balkans to Jerusalem, evidently hardly practicable today. The resurgence of interest even led to the creation of new walking pilgrimage roads (see for instance the Via Francigena del Sud, or the Hungarian Pilgrimage Road from Esztergom to Máriagyűd). When the road was re-launched in the mid-1980s, the Camino de Santiago had fewer than a thousand pilgrims completing the Santiago road in a year. Since then, and not counting the Jubilee years, the numbers of pilgrims reached many thousands by the end of the 1980s, tens of thousands by the end of the 1990s, one hundred thousand in 2006, while in 2016 the road was officially completed by close to 280,000 pilgrims, with an over 175% increase, thus near tripling in ten years.[3] The numbers are lower for the other mentioned roads, but are also steadily and significantly increasing. In the past year the Via Francigena was completed by at least 10,000 pilgrims, and the Hungarian Pilgrimage Road by 1,200.

The revival of pilgrim routes since the mid-1980s receives increasing attention (Doi 2011; Frey 2004; Green 2009; Olsen 2013; Slavin 2003). Apart from description, these studies attempt to offer an explanation of the phenomenon. Such effort includes a fundamental question of perspective: should one insert the practice into the standard, mainstream vision of modernity, dominated by instrumental rationality; or should one take seriously the lasting manner in which the experience of undertaking a long-distance walking pilgrimage challenges such vision of the worldly order at its core? Putting it simply: why do walkers walk?

The dilemma can be presented through a recent comparative study of pilgrimages (Olsen 2013). As the title of both the article and the journal indicates, this is a typical modernist venture, in which pilgrimage is simply subsumed as a religious modality of tourism. And still, in the part of the study dealing with the Camino, the author has to acknowledge, based on the research of numerous scholars, that 'it is difficult to fit those who travel the Camino into neat categories' (48), as the activities and experiences of pilgrims do not fit the ready-made categories of social research (unfortunately, this does not prevent the author from using the label 'New Puritan' for a type of pilgrim undertaking the road (see 50), a label that is particularly inappropriate as walking pilgrimage does not exist in

Protestantism); and thus, 'In essence it is the travellers along the Camino rather than the researchers that are the ones doing the typologizing' (49). The growing literature on the Camino increasingly recognises the centrality of the act of walking. Given that so many experiences were happening throughout the walk, the arrival is very often anti-climactic (see Doi 2011). One can add the opinion that this is even more so on the Via Francigena, where pilgrims who very often had a warm reception in the various parishes, monasteries or pilgrim hostels on the road suddenly become lost among the myriad of tourists and the total lack of concern of the Vatican bureaucracy and its guardians upon arrival in Rome; and so researchers often shift emphasis from the end-point to the road. This is particularly true for the excellent study of Frey (2004), who spent years researching the Camino which he personally undertook, and who argues that pilgrims of the Camino place more emphasis on the way the walking itself impacts on one's being, and not whatever one does at the end, after the arrival.

Similarities and differences

The new popularity of long-distance walking pilgrimage, as shown by the increasing number of people participating in the Camino, speaks for itself. Still, the re-discovery of walking is a stunning phenomenon. While we are happy to be a part of this broader process, we need to mark our differences from aspects of this renewal where necessary.

One important reference point is the popular film and novel *Into the Wild*. While showing close affinities with our undertaking, its spirit is quite different from our book. *Into the Wild* glorifies Christopher McCandless as a rebel, and the rebel is a typically modern character, even if rebelling against modernity – thus, it is even hyper-modern. Furthermore, the hero paradoxically ended up settling on a fixed place, in the wilderness of Alaska, instead of walking. Even further, he was not prepared for the adventure, acting on impulse and lacking serenity and patience, which are central aspects of a genuine walker; thus, what he did was in a way closer to an extreme sport than walking, much contributing to the tragic end.

The situation is similar with *Grizzly Man*, a film by Werner Herzog. Its efforts at recapturing our connection with nature are attractive; however, and even more than *Into the Wild*, the film demonstrates the extreme problematicity of American forms of escapism. Such attempts are profoundly rooted, thus reinforce, the very modes of behaviour and forms of individuality they try to reject. Far from showing humbleness, a sign of genuine character, the tragic heroes of these films are rather primary examples of titanic hubris, arrogance and self-assertion.

Bruce Chatwin's concern with nomads, 'nomadism' and walking, in 'The Nomadic Alternative' and 'It's a nomad *nomad* world', fragments of his never finished and unpublished as 'obviously unpublishable' (Chatwin 1997: 13) book project, of which *Anatomy of Restlessness* is just a pale reflection, also has many parallels with our undertaking. Rooted in his Baudelairean 'horreur du domicile' (1), an interesting pendant of Baudelaire's similar horror of progress and the 'modern rabble' (see Calasso 2008: 93–4; Szakolczai 2016a: 242), it is a prime example of 'anti-modern modernity'. Chatwin also wanted to fit his ideas into a broad histori-cal panorama, going back to distant prehistory, helped by his studies of archaeology at the University of Edinburgh (Chatwin 1997: 12). He also placed his work in a wide philosophical and spiritual context. Among philosophers, apart from the evident reliance on Nietzsche, he drew much from Kierkegaard and – even more interestingly – Pascal, especially his hostility to sitting still (12, 100). Concerning central figures of spirituality, his focus was on great teachers like Buddha, Lao-Tse (whom he considered as shamanistic) and St Francis of Assisi, even founders of religion like Christ and Mohammed (12–13, 104). His commitment to the signifi-cance of walking is visible from the following passage, which could even serve as a motto for the problem created by settlement, to be discussed in Chapter 6: 'The best thing is to walk . . . . If we need movement from birth, how should we settle down later?' (102–3).

Yet the problem with Chatwin's approach, arguably a major reason why the original book project remained incomplete, is the conflation between nomad-ism and walking. While the point that not all nomads are homeless is well taken, still, as even the etymology referred to by him makes it evident, nomads are pastoralists, thus much connected to animal husbandry and different from pre-historic 'hunter-gatherers',[4] and were rarely walking. Due to this conflation, the focus on walking became blurred and his approach became dangerously close to exalting a 'gypsy life-style' (12), already characteristic of Romantics and their precursors like Jacques Callot, who was also obsessed with the void (Horvath 2013a: 93–107; Szakolczai 2013a: 249–51), and so instead of focusing on walking, Chatwin became a travel writer.

Walking as experience

Walking, according to the world vision of mainstream modernity, is fundamentally a way of reaching a destination, or a mode of travelling – and a quite inefficient one at that, given the slowness of our two feet. Such long-term civilisational neglect of walking received a further boost from Darwinism and Kantianism, and the ensu-ing 'scientific' vision of the world, to be traced to Newton and Descartes. This implied not simply a dualism of the 'mind' and the 'body', but a double, at once horizontal and vertical split of the human being. Horizontally, the body was split into an upper and lower part, with emphasis given to hands over feet, arguing that the central point in walking on two feet was to liberate the hands for more useful, productive activity.[5] Vertically, the mind was split from the spirit or the soul, promoting the striking and truly absurd argument that we humans are only humans due to our 'mind', mostly concerned with the 'rational' calculation of our 'interests', or whatever helps to satisfy our individual desires, ignoring not only the more noble impulses of our soul, but at the same time instilling a further vertical split between human beings, resulting in an atomised individualism. Such vertical and horizontal splits were integrated in the techno-scientific, nihilistic ideology of 'rationalism', establishing a direct and exclusive link between the brain and the hands. The brain conceives the plan of action, while the hands execute it. The feet are practically meaningless, to be replaced by more efficient modes of transport; while the 'soul' or the 'spirit' simply does not exist. This is the vision of the human being that our rulers not only try to forcefully impose us, but proclaim as our 'deep inner truth'.

In contrast to this, the recent literature on walking emphasises its vital, foundational significance (Ingold and Vergunst 2008: 3), and its close connection to the spirit, soul or heart. The fundamental significance, even sacredness of the Earth, is recognised in many human cultures across the planets. In modern thought, this was recognised by Carl Schmitt (*Land and Sea*; see Schmitt 2002) and Heidegger ('Building Dwelling Thinking'; see Heidegger 1977) − though perhaps without making it clear that this is quite different from agriculture or property rights. It is our feet, through walking on the ground, that literally ground us in life (Ingold 2004: 336), that root us in lived experience (Ingold and Vergunst 2008: 2); our knowledge about everyday life comes from our soles (Herzog 2014: 5). The ground, as being foundational, through the contact we gain through our feet, extends to the landscape, which through walking we at the same time experience and appropriate, make ours: the landscape is one of our three fundamental sources of energy (the other two being the Earth and the heart; Gros 2014: 105); even our footprints are parts of the world (Ingold 2004: 333).

Walking is also fundamental and foundational because of the kind of experiences it provides us with − the kind of experiences it *is*. In contrast to the technological-alchemic, 'scientific' vision of the world, which artificially and violently splits and separates so that it can re-unite in plastic syntheses, walking establishes, through a rhythm, a harmonious unity between seeming opposites. Walking is a fundamentally solitary activity. Whoever walks for a long distance must keep his or her pace, and preserve one's inner quiet and solitude, and this can be shared at most with three to four other people (Gros 2014: 53–4). Yet, even when walking on one's own, one is never alone, as one is immersed in nature, in its beauty, as being in nature is 'perpetually distracting' (54). Ingold and Vergunst (2008: 1) similarly argue that walking, just as talking, is always 'in the midst of things', thus being liminal and dialogical par excellence, and is thus 'a profoundly social activity'. It is even a source of sociability: 'we are . . . social beings because we walk' (2). For proper walking silence is fundamental, as one needs to hear the voices, even the silence of nature, which every murmur, especially meaningless chatter, breaks and distorts (Gros 2014: 59–63). Yet, walking is also the source of an ongoing conversation between the body and the soul (56–7), and occasion for a proper dialogue, central for the peripatetic philosophy of Plato; indeed, for the Batek, a hunter-gatherer tribe in Malaysia, walking and talking are inseparable (Ingold and Vergunst 2008: 9). This is reinforced by a study of pilgrimage in a contemporary Spanish village, whose concluding section starts with the claim that '[w]alking can be said to be a form of storytelling' (Lund 2008: 101). Thus, walking neither excludes talking nor valorises talking as such, but rather teaches us the right kind of talking.

The same applies to visuality, or seeing. In contrast to the theatrical and tourist-like focus on visuality and optics, central for Cartesian and Kantian 'rationality', Ingold (2004: 327–8) emphasises that walking cannot be reduced to a way to gain 'knowledge' by seeing more. However, seeing is indeed fundamental for walking – or rather the other way around: according to Thoreau and Emerson, and anticipating Rilke, walking is a way for learning *how to see*, as '[b]efore speaking, a man should see' (Thoreau, as in Gros 2014: 62) or, '[i]n the woods, is perpetual youth . . . [where] I am nothing; I see all' (Emerson, as in 84–5). Walking as learning to see is fundamental for overcoming empty chatter and idiotic soliloquy (82), and to learn only things that truly matter. Thus, a morning walk is much more instructive than reading the daily newspapers (101).

Walking teaches us many things; but, most importantly, it makes us realise what is truly elementary. This is one of the most important pieces of wisdom gained by a long-distance walking trip, discussed in detail by Frédéric Gros. One starts by taking with oneself many things that are considered 'useful'; but after carrying all that on one's back, one realises the need to make distinctions, and keep company only with things that are truly elementary. Even further, such a shift from the 'useful' to the 'elementary' has two further, vital corollaries; a negative and a positive. Negatively, one increasingly realises how much the supposed conveniences of modern life are only irrelevant nuisances, which only generate dependence; their supposed benefits and necessities are only illusory (Gros 2014: 4). It is by getting rid of such modern conveniences that we start to regain our real freedom. Thus, we start to gain a new way of measuring things, a '*new economics*', based on the idea that the real value of a thing is not associated with the price we pay for it, but rather 'what it costs in terms of pure life' (89). It is exactly here that the other, positive consequence of learning the difference between the 'useful' and the really necessary comes into play: beyond being concerned with what is necessary, one might reach the stage of simply walking even without the necessary, abandoning oneself to the elements. In such a way of life everything becomes a gift (192), implying a return to the archaic vision of the world *as a given*. Such a mode of living recalls the greatest movements of spiritual revival in European history, like the Franciscans and – originally – the Jesuits; or the central concern in Eastern Orthodoxy with hesychasm (Gros 2014: 214).

It certainly does not seem possible for everyone to follow the way of life of the greatest figures of human spirituality. However, almost everyone indeed *can walk*; and such walking can gain access to experiencing life as a gift, and the world as a given; and thus to some of the most basic truths and realities of human existence. This starts by recognising the value of humbleness. Walking was characterised above as a 'humble art', as it is indeed the simplest and humblest way of moving around (82), the reason for its scorn by arrogant people in arrogant ages. However, humbleness is not identical to humiliation; it is rather associated with the values of simplicity, autarchy and thus genuine independence (200–1), and the recognition that in the world there are powers higher than us. We are guests of a powerful lord where nothing is permitted to be added or removed or taken away, as the motto of our Preface indicates.

Humbleness and humility are even etymologically connected to the earth, the ground where we walk, as both are derived from Latin *humus* – just as the Latin word for 'man' is *homo*, tying further the knots between walking and being human. This is in stark contrast to the opposite of humbleness, arrogant pride and hubris, the main feature of Prometheus, the Titan, supposed enlightener of mankind and inventor of fire (or technology) and sacrifice (or violent, mechanical ritual), choice deity of the Sophists. Hubris is etymologically derived from 'above', thus exactly *not* being firmly rooted on the ground, and is furthermore connected to the German-English etymological source of the word for evil, originally meaning 'exceeding due limits' (Onions 1966: 332). Such obsession with going always beyond, further and above, ignoring our nature, is also captured in another Greek myth about the flight of Icarus, and was brought alive by Aby Warburg, founding figure of modern art history, who in 1923 foresaw the radically problematic character of the modern obsession with speed:

> The modern Prometheus and the modern Icarus, Franklin and the Wright brothers, inventors of the airplane: they are the sinister destroyers of the sense of distance that threatens to push the world back into chaos. The telegraph and the telephone destroy the cosmos. Mythic and symbolic thought, with its attempt to spiritualise the link between man and the surrounding world, create the space for prayer or for thought that instant electronic contact kills.
> *(Warburg 1998: 62)*[6]

Apart from firmly rooting us on the ground, walking is also closely connected to another fundamental and foundational aspect of being human, the source of the unity of the body, mind and spirit, and – after the earth and landscape – the third main source of our energy (Gros 2014: 105), which is the *heart*. Walking helps us retrieve again our own hearts, to recover our essence as a walker, a '*homo viator*, a walking man' (73), and thus – as two great walkers of European culture, Rousseau and Dickens, jointly discovered – helps us tear away the masks of civilised social life, overcoming its pervasive theatricality (66), and rendering evident the corruptness of the contemporary world (7), as once the masks fell, one could return to the heart (76–7). Such a return to the heart, far from promoting sentimentalism, brings together Pascal's reasons of the heart, the rhythm of walking by heartbeat and the impact of the maternal heartbeat on the child to be born.[7] Gandhi has similar ideas about the 'tranquil energy' to be gained by the slowness of walking, its explicit rejection of speed, being 'maternal, feminine' (198–9).

The heart, in every aspect of its meaning, must be kept in motion, exercised, trained, continuously subjected to new and new efforts. This can help explain one of the most paradoxical aspects of walking, experienced by everyone who has at least once in their life completed a long-distance walking trip, that while walking 20, 30 or more kilometres is indeed arduous and tiring, it produces the 'real miracle' of being happy 'not despite . . . but because of' discomfort (4). The difficulty and gravity of walking thus in a stunning way generates the opposite of heaviness: when we become so tired that we no longer even feel it, we reach a state of unprecedented lightness, even grace (181). Thus, by walking, by walking for a long time and continuously, through experiencing pain, we retrieve a joy of existence and 'that childhood eternity once again',[8] the eternal child present inside all of us, that is not searching out for the 'experience' and is not making continuous comparisons, but rather is happy with what is; what one is (Gros 2014: 83; see also Roman 2014: 68–9). It is in this way that, through experiencing walking, we can truly experience genuine states of well-being, pleasure, felicity and serenity (Gros 2014: 139–46). As a kind of ultimate expression of this experience, Gros is using another fundamental pair of terms, also central for Plato, the experience of participation and presence (7, 123). 'Walking gives you *participation*' (96), reaching the 'fullness of being' (139) and the 'absolute simplicity of presence' (67).

Walking also helps us to reassess the value of repetition, so often forgotten in the contemporary search for the always new; a concern also central for the philosophies of Kierkegaard, Tarde or Deleuze. Walking, of course, is repetitive and monotonous, but by no means boring (207). In contrast to the cult of speed, it helps us to valorise slowness in the sense of acquiring a proper *rhythm* in which things are to be done properly (37–8, 215–17). The experience of long walking, and the knowledge and understanding gained through it, is so singular and profound because it offers a perfect balance between stability and change. When we behold a distant view, a mountain, a tower or a city to be reached, it seems so far, and our progress on feet so slow that we think we'll never make it. Yet, after some hours, we arrive; and during this time not only does the target become imperceptibly but steadily closer, but we also continuously encounter new views and experiences, realising that by a quicker means of transport we would have missed all this out. One could even risk saying that walking is *the* proper and natural way of advancing; depending on the kind of terminology chosen, we can say that we were *created* to walk, or that the forces of evolution *formed* human beings to walk. Every other mode of advancing is only a supplement and compensation; the replacement of the natural with something artificial and second-rate; a central element of those tricks and enchantments by which in modern 'civilisation' we are cheated out of our deepest essence.

However, needless to add, like everything that is truly good in life, the experience of walking can also be abused, or turned to excess. Walking is highly liberating, helping us escape the iron grip of the contemporary world and retrieve our true essence; it can help us escape the illusions and preoccupations of contemporary everyday existence, to overcome the continuous pressure for acceleration, which only imprisons (4–5). However, when taken to excess, it can empty and uproot us, turn us into a rebel against the whole world, which – paradoxically – only repeats the basic modern experience of eternal homelessness.

Escaping the suffocating forces of convention, taking off the masks of modern theatricality, recovering the self-forgetfulness of childhood and experiencing the fullness of presence come close to another version of the Golden Age, this time in the form of finding the authentic self. Here we indeed enter the highest stage in the experience of walking, but also its most treacherous part, when one is caught in between the Scylla of modern self-assertion and the Charybdis of self-negating Eastern spirituality. Gros struggles with this dilemma throughout his work, finding a certain balance in the end with his fusion between prayer and walking, through which the walker becomes, in the words of Roman (2014: 67, 75–6), the opposite of yet close simile to the tourist: a 'witness' to the creation of the world through his 'participation in being'. To be sure, the outcome of walking experience cannot be finding an 'identity', in the sense of a fixed and stable self that will forever be the same. The freedom of walking rather implies the opposite, 'in not being anyone . . . just an eddy in the stream of immemorial life' (Gros 2014: 7). Such an experience is close to the central concerns of oriental philosophy, the loss of one's self and identity, a kind of depersonalisation. An ultimate access to such an experience is offered by an extreme version of Eastern pilgrimage, the road to Mount Kailash in Tibet, where at a certain moment, after walking for long weeks and hundreds of kilometres, one arrives at a pass, at the inhuman height above 5,000 metres, an 'absolute omphalos' of the world, from where an incredible spectacle opens at the immensity of the above and the below, crushing the self (123). The experience of such self-destruction through entering the void and becoming a nothing, or a *nulla*, is contrasted with the similarly ultimate experience of the central European pilgrimage, the Camino, where one is always walking towards the West, or the eventually setting sun, and where the aim of renewal and regeneration, the utopia of a cosmic rebirth, the purpose of every pilgrimage, is not to find one's identity, but rather to invent oneself (127, 102).

Such Western self-invention, however, is just as problematic as the Eastern self-annihilation, as they are fundamentally identical, being schismogenic doubles, implying the same alchemic process by which a certain spiritual death, the fragmentation or even pulverisation and liquefaction of one's being, is the precondition for inventing a new self. A balance between these two opposite and yet complementary, schismogenic excesses is offered in an Italian book, written not by a social scientist but a simple walker, in a book with a title almost identical to that of Gros: the aim of pilgrimage is indeed a kind of conversion, but not one shaping a new identity, or simply dissolving us into the void, but a way of re-conducting us to ourselves (Meschiari 2014: 26). Thus, such a walking trip cannot offer a magical metamorphosis, the shaping of a new identity; at its end, we'll be the same as we were before. Except that now we'll be true to ourselves, our essence, deprived of all the noise and garbage contemporary civilisation invested us with; not self-conscious in a Hegelian sense – a false road few if any modern philosopher can escape – but rather conscious of the reality of the real.

This modality of conversion was presented in a particularly striking manner by a great walker, also a greatest modern novelist, Charles Dickens, in *Dombey and Son*. Its eponymous hero, Paul Dombey, is the embodiment of the spirit of modern individualism, as formulated in his time and place, which implies a philosophy of life radically opposed to the culture of walking, according to which

The earth was made for Dombey and Son to trade in, and the sun and moon to give them light. Rivers and seas were formed to float their ships; rainbows gave them promise of fair weather; winds blew for or against their enterprise; stars and planets circled in their orbits, to preserve inviolate a system of which they were the centre.

(Dickens 2001: 2)

He thus places the self – *any* individual self – at the centre of the universe. A series of particularly trying experiences produce a genuine conversion in Dombey, but this does not imply a sudden change, the proclamation of a new creed or a radical change in his status; rather, it enables him to overcome the mask-like socialisation into which his being became encaged, and thus he can rediscover his daughter and return to his true, essential self that he never lived.

Nothing is more simple, more basic and easier than to walk – to start walking and to keep walking. Yet, this simplest of activities can produce effects that go way beyond the shrewdest magic and most sophisticated science and technology, as it can restore truth, unity and reality – exactly what has been destroyed by the various enchantments of modern 'progress'. Walking is before and beyond consciousness (Ingold 2004: 332; Ingold and Vergunst 2008: 1), and yet it can achieve what consciousness fails to do, as ideally it is 'a state in which the mind, the body, and the world are aligned', as if characters in a conversation (Solnit 2001: 5). The fact and character of this unity are again formulated in a particularly concise way by Ingold and Vergunst (2008: 2): 'thinking and feeling are ways of walking'. This statement is also close to one of the most basic shared pieces of wisdom of the major world religions and philosophies, according to which a prime metaphor for the meaning and truth of human life is the road (see Parmenides, Taoism, Buddha, New Testament).

Thus, finally, walking is related to the most fundamental concerns about truth and reality. 'To walk is to experience the real', while the reality of walking, and the reality we encounter while walking, is a proof of our own consistency (Gros 2014: 94). Walking, due to its naturalness and simplicity, through the participation (not fusion or communion) it generates, is a 'proof of reality': it jointly affirms the reality of the world and our own realness, and at the same time confirms the truth and meaning of this reality.

Given the profound unreality of the modern world, diagnosed by a series of most important modern novelists,[9] it is hardly possible to hope for more.

Cave art as experience

Since the moment of their discovery, and repeated at every major such occasion, the paintings of the cave exerted an enormous fascination on most of those who descended to see them, but especially their discoverers, for reasons that are both evident and still not properly understood, even noticed. Such evident reasons concern the quality of the works and the character of the place where they were depicted, and where they can be most properly appreciated, and from where – in contrast to church altarpieces and even frescoes, luckily – they simply cannot be removed, even by modern means.

Cave 'art', it is often argued, is a misnomer, as these paintings were not made for artistic contemplation. It is a phenomenon that must be experienced, and not watched as a mechanically reproduced copy. Their making, and use, were part of 'rituals', no doubt 'religious' in one way or another; and the experiences captured below are comparable to – though also quite different form – religious conversion. They can only be appreciated in the same way as was done by the people who made and used them tens of thousands of years ago; going down under the ground, often walking hundreds of metres, and then suddenly stumbling upon these stunning animal images. Scholars and explorers were not converting to prehistoric deities; rather they were deeply touched, at the very core of their being, by what they saw.

Let's start with the following account, given by the discoverers of the Chauvet cave about their first encounter:

> During those moment there were only shouts and exclamations; the emotion that gripped us made us incapable of uttering a single word. Alone in that vastness, lit by the feeble beam of our lamps, we were seized by a strange feeling. Everything was so beautiful, so fresh, almost too much so. Time was abolished, as if the tens of thousands of years that separated us from the producers of these paintings no longer existed. It seemed as if they had just created these masterpieces. Suddenly we felt like intruders. Deeply impressed, we were weighed down by the feeling that we were not alone; the artists' souls and spirits surrounded us. We thought we could feel their presence; we were disturbing them.
>
> *(Chauvet et al. 1996: 41–2)*[10]

This description, culminating in the simple claim that '[W]e felt immense joy' (52), has manifold and unique values, and we'll soon analyse these in detail.[11] Here it is enough to call attention to the sudden and overwhelming emotional involvement that overtook the discoverers of the cave.

A similarly life-transforming experience overtook the discoverers of Lascaux; an experience that is only comparable to those who had a sudden vision of the Madonna – strikingly, a phenomenon that in modern times was similarly dominated by French cases, as if to compensate for, or nullify, the evils unleashed onto the world by the Revolution. Lascaux was discovered on 12 September 1940, when WWII was in full swing and much of France already occupied, by four adolescents, Jacques Marsal, Georges Agnel, Simon Coencas and Marcel Ravidat (Aujoulat 2005: 262). The fact that they were shaken by what they saw is visible not only in their repeated return to the cave and immediate informing of their teachers, who then notified the authorities, but that they literally mounted a guard, preventing visitors from damaging the cave. According to André Glory, one of the first scientific explorers of the cave, that the visitors 'did not ransack the cave [was] due to the devotion of these young boys' (263).

This was the reaction of the discoverers, adolescent boys. However, the impact of Lascaux did not diminish over the years. Thus, according to David Lewis-Williams,

> Modern visitors to Lascaux are so overwhelmed by the beauty, size and startling preservation of so many of the images thronging the walls that 'scientific' appraisal is apt to be silenced. A prominent American archaeologist, who was granted 20 minutes in the cave, told me that the first half of his allotted time was rather wasted because, overcome by the wonder of it all, he viewed the art through a curtain of tears. Such is the impact of Lascaux.
>
> *(Lewis-Williams 2002: 237)*[12]

It was the same impact that overwhelmed Norbert Aujoulat, trained as a geologist and called in for reasons of preservation, who recently published an authoritative study on the cave paintings of Lascaux. Aujoulat first visited Lascaux cave in winter 1970. He conveys his first encounter with the paintings in the following words:

> We opened the second bronze door, decorated with polished stones bearing floral motifs, and entered into the Hall of the Bulls. Silence replaced the sound of falling water, the slamming of doors and the shuffling of feet. The following half an hour was to have a profound effect on the course of my career.
>
> *(Aujoulat 2005: 9)*

This meant that he devoted the next thirty-five years of his life to studying the cave, which resulted in a magnificent 2005 book, whose main analytical part ends with the following words, capturing in an unsurpassable way the heart of cave painting: 'The iconography of this cave is, above all, a fantastic ode to life' (Aujoulat 2005: 194).

With these experiences in mind, let us now return to the way the discoverers of Chauvet described their first impressions; the first human beings in about 28,000 years who chanced upon seeing one of the most astonishing products of the human mind, soul and spirit. Such an event of course cannot be repeated or reproduced, thus we are completely at the mercy – in the full sense of the term – of those who were given the gift of this encounter, and who certainly formulated their experiences with as much care as possible.

The first thing to notice is that the encounter suddenly and radically displaced the normal temporal and spatial coordinates of human experience, replacing them with a game of zero and infinity. There was space under the ground and within the cave, but after passing through the often narrow and tight thresholds and channels, space suddenly became infinite, while time was similarly abolished, and instead of feeling the tens of thousands of years that passed since the creation of these works, they had an experience of immediacy, as if the works were just created. This vertigo was felt as a kind of void experience; the abolishing of time and space, or rather of the *difference* in time and space. But this void, at the same time as it was created, also became filled with power substance; a kind of substance for which the New Testament word *exousia*, standing for power, presence and being as well, seems particularly appropriate: it was a fullness of presence (Horvath 2013a) and of beauty, where the time and space separating them not only from the works but also from their creators were abolished; thus the presence of the works directly implied the presence of their authors, as if nullifying any difference between life and work, author and audience. Yet, even more strikingly, such unity or identity had its disturbing aspects; and here the testimony of the discoverers is particularly precious, as these aspects are so unexpected that even here and now we are struggling for words to capture their meaning: as the discoverers became uneasy, feeling themselves as *intruders* – an extremely weighty word, similar to 'trickster' – as they were disturbing the authors of these masterpieces, or rather their souls and spirits – as it were, not simply the works but the spirits of the authors that were still present there. Thus, the striking feeling of being intruders culminates in the fully mystical claim of encroaching upon the *spirits* of the artists.

Such encounter-experiences can perhaps help us to understand the original reactions of the 'enlightened materialists' against the first discoveries of these works.

Evolutionist hostility to Palaeolithic cave art

The staunch hostility of materialist evolutionists to Palaeolithic cave art at first seems perplexing, but on a more thorough look becomes clinically intelligible. Given that the time horizon opened up by geology and archaeology radically dismantled the – dogmatic, Puritanical – reading of the Old Testament time-line, one would expect evolutionary materialism to welcome the ten thousand years' age assigned to cave paintings. Yet this was not so, as became particularly evident in the debate that broke out about Altamira, discovered in 1879, but recognised as genuinely prehistoric only in 1902. The first notices of the discoverer, Marcelino Sanz de Sautuola, 'prudent as they were', were not only disregarded and derided by contemporary academics, 'from the pinnacle of "official science"', but it was argued that the paintings were outright fraudulent, providing us with a lesson concerning the need for humbleness when facing reality (Beltrán 1999: 8–9, 23–4, 26–7). Most strikingly, some critics argued that they were 'the work of conservative Spanish clerics hoping to defend belief in divine creation', while others asserted that 'the cave had been deliberately created by antievolutionist Spanish Jesuits trying to make a laughing stock of the emerging sciences of palaeontology and prehistory'.[13]

Strange as such resistance to new evidence by the pioneers of progress and science may sound, this becomes intelligible through the upsetting of the evolutionary canon by the sheer quality of cave paintings.[14] The champions of progress denigrated the Biblical reading of history only to be able to proclaim themselves heirs of the Enlightenment, as heralds of the new, unprecedented period of human emancipation and development. From that perspective the distant past had to be devalued as obscure times or dark ages when human beings were only struggling for survival; a perspective incompatible with the stunning qualities of cave paintings. As Picasso expressed after his visit to Altamira, 'none of us could paint like that' (as in Lewis-Williams 2002: 31).

These representations of a worldly order in harmony and beauty, when humans were 'standing in' the representations, absorbing the beauty of images and representing divine essence also implied a certain characteristic substitution with their own character that slowly became more and more significant due to various reasons. Their character became gradually absolved in the images, turning into nothing else but a sign, so images became manifestations to themselves of a curious functionality for gaining union with the divine, and taking profit from that. The centrality of cave paintings for their age could remain a silent mystery, but their meaning is still readable in the desired union with the enormous emotional charge of the void.

Notes

1 See Coverley (2012); Jarvis (1997); Solnit (2001).
2 This is discussed in Szakolczai (2016b).
3 See the sites https://www.followthecamino.com/blog/camino-de-santiago-pilgrim-statistics-2016/ and http://www.csj.org.uk/the-present-day-pilgrimage/pilgrim-numbers/.
4 We will use this term, objecting to the word 'forager', which subliminally transforms a life lived as receiving and giving gifts into 'plunder' or 'pillage'.
5 See in particular Ingold (2004).
6 This has already been advanced by Goethe as 'velociferic' speed in the *Faust* (see Müller 2011: 171; Szakolczai 2016a: 178).
7 For details, see Szakolczai (2017b).
8 Needless to say, this is radically different from modern infantilisation, which is rather the reverse of the Kantian rationalist pretence of 'maturity'.
9 For details, see Szakolczai (2016a, 2017a).
10 See Chauvet, Deschamps and Hillaire (1996) and Clottes (2003).
11 Such joy of existence was connected to walking by Gros (2014), discussed earlier in the chapter, and connected to Chauvet in his review essay by Roman (2014: 62).
12 As he revealed to the *Smithsonian Magazine* (see April 2015 issue), Jean Clottes also had tears in his eyes when he first encountered Chauvet. Seeing Lascaux through eyes full of tears was also a central experience for René Char, whose short poem entitled 'La bête innommable' (*The unnameable beast*; a literal but at best approximate translation) was about Lascaux, in particular how wisdom appeared to him on the frieze of Lascaux, as a fantastically disguised mother, in front of his eyes full of tears. Maurice Blanchot (2002) wrote a short essay on Char's poem, focusing on Plato's *Phaedrus* and the philosophy of Heraclitus. Given that Char was Foucault's favourite poet, Georges Bataille (who wrote a book on Lascaux, to be analysed in Chapter 4 in detail) his favourite contemporary philosopher, and Blanchot his favourite literary critic, each demonstrating a strong interest in Lascaux, thus cave art, Foucault's evident neglect of this entire issue is quite astonishing.

13 The former argument was made by Émile Cartailhac, who later changed his mind and with a 1902 paper played a major role in authenticating the findings, while the latter was made by Gabriel de Mortillet, who died in 1898, still firmly believing that the paintings were fake (Beltrán 1999: 9); both were staunch positivist materialists.

14 For a similar case of evident evolutionary materialist dogmatism, see the recent case of the Côa Valley petroglyphs, dated with great fanfare to the Palaeolithic, but recognised as much more recent, occasionally even twentieth century by Robert Bednarik (1995, 2014). The revealing fact is that the 'discoverers' of Côa Valley immediately jumped to the anyway unacceptable inference that therefore *most* Palaeolithic works of art *had* to be outdoors ('it is the outdoor rock art that must have been the rule and the indoor parietal art the exception'), and be secular and not religious (Carvalho *et al.* 1996: 53–4) – as if the sacred/profane distinction could be so easily applied to the Palaeolithic setting.

2

THE LANGUAGE AND CULTURE OF WALKING

> But while we are confined to books, though the most select and classic, and read only particular written languages, which are themselves but dialects and provincial, we are in danger of forgetting the language which all things and events speak without metaphor, which alone is copious and standard.
>
> *Henry David Thoreau,* Walden, *'Sounds' (1962: 187)*

Walking is not deluding us: it manages to substantiate, and in great detail, that the community of man was born out of play, even of divine play, and of the most joyful, self-abandoned, spirited kind of play which only is capable of creating a discrete, graceful, harmonious order; not some rigid, formal mimetism, prescribed by ritualistic laws and maintained by force.

Given this fundamental significance of walking, it is strange that the terminology of walking in most European languages is particularly problematic, unclear. The title of Gros' milestone book is *Marcher: une philosophie*, where the term *marcher* was rendered in English as 'walking', and in Italian as 'camminare', even though direct equivalents for *marcher* exist both in English ('march') and Italian ('marciare'). This is because these terms over the centuries gained a particular, military connotation, for reasons discussed by Ingold (2004; see also Foucault 1979; Mauss 1973); a semantic change that by the way also took place in French. However, in French it is particularly difficult to come up with a word that would capture the idea of 'advancing on two feet'.[1]

If we try to retranslate into French the translated titles, perplexities multiply. 'Walking' in French is *se promener*, or exactly the type of modern 'bourgeois' leisure activity characterised by Gros (2014) as the opposite of a proper walking, which assumes effort, a work by oneself or a care of the self.[2] 'Camminare', on the other hand, becomes *cheminer*, closely linked to the road (*chemin*).

The English term 'walking' is not particularly fortunate either, though over the centuries it gained a meaning quite different from French *se promener*, or Hungarian *sétál*, as it was selected by Romantics in the late eighteenth century as the term describing the new importance attributed to advancing on two feet – at the same time when the term 'pedestrian' gained its modern, more neutral and not merely denigrating meaning. Etymologically the term 'walk' had a quite different sense, connected to 'invade', or a mode of advancing quite opposite to a leisurely stroll. This new meaning gained around the end of the eighteenth century was necessary, as the meaning of the term originally covering the simple activity of advancing on two feet, 'go', become altered. This is visible both through its noun and verb versions. The noun 'go' originally meant 'the action of going', but became rare. The verb 'to go' originally also meant simply advancing on two feet, but over the centuries it acquired an enormous range of meanings (the OED discusses the various senses in fifteen three-column pages), while its prime meaning shifted from using one's feet to any modes of reaching a destination, thus becoming indistinguishable from travelling.

The OED (1989, VI: 618) definition of the kind of advancing meant by the term 'go' offers further precious hints. It attributes three fundamental modalities to 'going': that it is a mode of advancing *without regard to* its point of departure or destination [emphasis added]' – thus, it truly captures the mere fact of using two feet; that in represents a movement *away from* the speaker [emphasis in original]'; and that, insofar as a direction is involved, it is not where the speaker actually is. The combination of these three meanings is quite peculiar, even perplexing, as it indicates a split or distancing from the self, or at least from the usual place where one is, in the key meanings of a verb that captures one of the most fundamental activities that make us human beings.

As the etymology of the term, just as its conceptual history, is quite problematic, it cannot offer much further clarification. However, the most accepted theory, according to which the term is to be traced to the PIE root *ghi* 'release, let go', further emphasises this strange, distancing component. The Latin verb *ire* shows similar problems.

Etymologies of 'experience'

However, we get more interesting results if we approach the language of walking through the terminology of experience. For this, we need to leave the realm of modern rationalist thinking, in particular the terminological alteration operated by Descartes, as his presumed return to experience, away from scholasticism, only amounted to a gradual reduction of the unity of human experience to scientific experimentation on the one hand and mere sense perception on the other, source of the object–subject dualism codified by Kant as the foundation of modern philosophical 'rationalism'.

The Latin verb expressing the unity of experience is *sentire* 'perceive, sense, feel, know'. The range of its meaning is present even in contemporary languages, where English 'sense' or French *sens* mean a 'reasonable' way of behaving, or simply 'meaning'. Italian *sentire* preserved an even broader range of meaning, including 'hearing' and 'understanding'. The Latin word, however, can be traced to the *PIE root *sent*, simply meaning 'to go', visible in French *sentier* 'beaten path'. It is this same root that in German yielded *Sinn*, meaning 'sense' and 'mind'.

The situation is strikingly similar in Greek, though standard etymology resists the idea. The Greek verb for experiencing is *paskho*, in aorist *pathein*, meaning 'experience' in the passive sense of 'suffer, undergo', while *pathos* means 'what one has experienced'. *Patein*, on the other hand, means 'go, walk', thus *patos* the 'path, the trodden way'. While etymological dictionaries deny any connection between *pathein* and *patein*, their reasoning is often strange: thus, the Brill Dictionary claims that 'it is not evident that "way, path" would yield "to tread", an action which focuses on the individual movement of the legs', which is far from convincing (Beekes 2010: 1157); while English *path* is etymologically connected to Greek *patos*.

The connection between experiencing (in its original unity) and walking receives independent confirmation from Hungarian. There 'to understand' is *ért*, while 'to feel' or 'to sense' is *érez*, both to be traced in the same basic root *ér*. This root still has a number of everyday meanings, including 'creek' and 'vein' as nouns, 'to mature' and 'having a worth' as verbs, but it original meaning is 'to reach', connected specifically to reach a destination during a trip. The second Hungarian word used for experience, on the other hand, offers a striking confirmation for the link between Greek *pathein* and *patein*. The term is *tapasztalat*, etymologically rooted in the twin onomatopoetic roots 'tap' and 'pat', existing in the exact same manner and with very similar meaning in English as well. As 'tapping' or 'patting' is the same noise emitted by hands which the feet emit when they 'pad' ('pad' and 'pat' are also minimal pairs), all these seem to be closely connected and embodied in Greek *patein*.

In Hungarian, however, even the standard term for 'walking' or 'going' has strikingly relevant and interesting connotations. Given that Hungarian is a non-Indo-European language, it might be helpful for offering a novel angle. This might all the more be the case as Hungarian is an archaic agglutinative language that, due to the large number of vocals it contains, especially the seven long vocals, etymologically separate from short vocals, has a particularly robust structure, resisting changes over time, which was furthermore helped by the isolation in which Hungarian developed, or rather was preserved.

Going Hungarian

The Hungarian word for 'go' is *megy*,[3] a highly irregular verb, suffering an inflexion with 'n', for e.g. in the infinitive (*menni*), in the past tense (*ment*), and in plural (*mentek* 'you go', *mennek* 'they go'), and also an inflexion with 'sz' ('you go' in the singular is *mész*). The most important feature here is the *megy-men* connection, which will be analysed in detail later.

Concerning basic meaning, two of the three Hungarian meanings are strikingly close to two basic modalities of English 'go': it similarly implies a mode of advancing *away from* the speaker; and if a destination is involved, it is not where the speaker is found. And while the Hungarian dictionary does not place emphasis on movement in contrast to origin and destination, rather focusing on the destination, in line with the fact that in Hungarian the word 'megy' implies a stronger emphasis on success than English 'go', concerning the etymology and conceptual history of the term, the original meaning was connected to the road, for example in the sense that one went where the road 'went' – here, quite close to the Italian meaning of *camminare*.

This short review of etymology and conceptual history offered two basic points. First, walking or going has a crucial, passive experiential component – not passive in the sense of being subjected to some kind of hostile external influence, but having a kind of care-free, cheerful and playful aspect, where one can let oneself be guided by the road which knows well where to take the pedestrian – close to the manner in which Don Quixote, inspired by Ignatius of Loyola, just let his horse decide where to go. This passivity is close to the original, passive aspect of human experience, based on a fundamental unity with oneself, in contrast to rationalist dualism. Second, however, at the same time walking or going also implies movement away from where one is; thus, a kind of distancing.

The contrast between walking as a passive experience of being at one with oneself and the divine world, and walking as a distancing and moving *away*, is particularly intriguing from the central perspective of this book, which claims that walking, especially long-distance walking, is central for securing a basic experience of being-at-home-in-the-world in a joyful contentment.

Home and Dasein (*being there*)

In practically every European language the experience of being at home is expressed by a word closely connected to the house (see French *à la maison*, Italian *a casa*, Russian *domoj*, German *heim* or *zu Hause*). This is because these languages, here assume settlement; thus, arguably, developed taking settled existence as granted. Hungarian is different: 'being in the house' in Hungarian does not at all mean being at home.

The Hungarian terms for 'home' are *itthon* and *otthon*. The two words are very close, twins, but with a significant and most meaningful difference. *Itt* means 'here', *ott* 'there'; while *hon*, today meaning nation and fatherland, originally most probably was the interrogative pronoun 'where', which today is rendered as *hol*. Thus, *itthon* literally means 'here where', and *otthon* 'there where'. This distinction can be understood through the dual experiential meanings of the term 'go' (*megy*), implying a difference between the place where the speaker is, and the direction of his or her walking. In Hungarian one can only say that one is 'at home' (*itthon*, or 'being here') when one is literally in the area considered as home. If one is not 'at home', the home is expressed by the twin term *otthon*, being 'there', somewhere, not here, thus almost exactly meaning 'being there' in the Heideggerian sense of *Dasein*. The current, modern use of Hungarian has become corrupt, so the two terms now colloquially are used almost interchangeably.

The Hungarian word for 'go', through its peculiar inflexions, however, alludes to a series of further hints about the centrality of the experience of walking, in its connection to the very 'being human', substantiating the conjecture of Ingold that thinking is a way of walking.

'Man' as the one who walks and thinks

Here the first point to note is that the Hungarian term for 'go', now taking the word through the 'n' inflexion as *menni* 'to go', or *ment* 'went', has a close structural affinity with a series of Indo-European words for the same activity, including Latin *meo* (etymologically connected *moneo* 'forewarn, tell' (see 'menace'), and *monstrum* 'monster', but also 'show'), Old Church Slavonic *minoti* 'to pass', as well as various Slavic words (de Vaan 2008: 373–4, 387; Ernout and Meillet 1959; Pokorny 1959). In fact, according to Pokorny, this is one of the main meanings of the important PIE root *men*.

This same root, however, has a series of other, separate meanings – separate in the sense that Indo-European etymology, due to the striking irrelevance of vocals for these languages (Alinei 2009), cannot distinguish between them; but also that, therefore, it is possible to connect them, once a good reason is found. Here, as a start, we need to note that the *men/man* roots are closely connected; just as the *men* and *mei* roots. The primary meaning of the root *men*, according to Grandsaignes d'Hauterive (1948), is the idea of a 'movement of the spirit'. It is from here that a series of crucial words, capturing the heart of human experience, like memory, thinking, mind and meaning, are derived, including, most importantly, the German and English words for 'men', *Mann* and *man/men*. However, similar terms are also central for capturing either the human being, or particularly significant, founding historical figures in a number of other and quite different historical and mythological contexts. It is enough to evoke here Minos, first king of Minoan Crete, the first Hindu lawgiver Manu, or the first Egyptian pharaoh Menes; or even the Phrygian moon-god Mēn, worshipped all around central Asia Minor, and having a particularly famous shrine in Cabeira, represented with a Phrygian cap and often with a cock, being a central figure of authority especially in villages (Mitchell 1993, II: 9–10, 24–5, 46). But one can add the word 'shaman' itself, of Tungusic (or Evenki, possibly connected to Turkish) origins, and with a disputed etymology (Mair 1990: 36); or the *muni*, figures of the Rig Veda who were possessed by the gods. Even further, beyond these names there is a root going beyond the Indo-European language that denominates the human being as a spirit, soul or thinking being. This can be seen in most Indo-European languages (see Sanskrit *manuja*, Greek *menos*, English man, German *Mann*, Celtic *mano* and similar terms in most contemporary European languages), but also in languages as diverse and distant as Egyptian *mau*, Malaysian *manusia* or Tahitian *manao* (Cherpillod 1998: 277–8).

It is here that Hungarian again can be brought into the picture, not simply by the evident connection between *ember* 'man' and *emlék* 'memory', but rather by the connection between *megy* 'go' and *magyar/megyeri/mansi* 'Hungarian'.

At one level, this is a trivial result: in many languages, the word for 'man' and the self-identification of the ethnic group is identical. The interesting point is that Hungarian defines itself as one who walks; and that it has affinities or echoes in several other languages.

Huizinga's anthropology of culture as con-testing and re-presenting

Language has little autonomy in itself, as whoever is talking is always a person. It rather accompanies changes that take place in reality. Language is almost identical to representation, as Huizinga has shown it in a masterly way, taking this connection further, into play – though only insofar as the personal and thus potentially experiential component is present, as whenever something is written down or drawn, the possibility of depersonalisation, or words and images detached from concrete persons become a possibility; a problem centrally discussed by Plato, main source of inspiration behind Huizinga's work. Play for Huizinga is fundamental, indeed foundational: we are humans as we play; we are *Homo ludens*, and not *Homo faber*, not to mention *Homo economicus* and similar senility. The claims about *Homo economicus* are signs of senility, produced by a culture that through devotion to exchange and substitutability resigned itself to adaptation to anything, as it has lost its sense of reality. The core of Huizinga's position is contained in his ideas about two basic 'higher forms' of play, 'a contest for something' and 'a representation of something' (Huizinga 1970: 13), rooted in the 'two ever-recurrent forms in which civilization grows in and as play', which are 'the sacred performance and the festal contest' (48). Contests traditionally were not only playful, but also had a strong festive component. Their meaning can be best understood as 'con-testing', or joint testing, where emphasis is neither on struggle, nor the selection of a winner, but rather the maintaining of relationships in a mutual state of respectful, dialogical tension. Representation is a ceremonial bringing into presence, thus again re-presentation, first of a representation of the divine, which means actual involvement and participation. Participation is real: it involves our passing through our own life; the concrete events, the lived experiences, our character by which we become what we are. A play, however, is staged or representative: it follows a pre-arranged scenario in which the actors and the audience, whether they are separate or identical, go through a series of pre-established motions; where everybody knows at the beginning what is going to happen at the end. Still, this participation always risks faked imitation; but how?

This happens, first of all, through a key word, already mentioned: 'real'. A proper divine performance must evoke the experience of contentment, and even if what we see is a performance, not a real event, our experience of good feeling immediately makes it real, by spiritually transfiguring the staged scene into a piece of reality; even into a reality of higher order than 'mere' everyday life. It is always a transformation. The encounters with enormous emotional charges are always moving; in extremis, it moves us to tears, making tears of joy, beyond laughter, into the most characteristic human gesture expressing merriness, though it is also a further possibility for altering the authentic.

Second, however, a divine representation also has another, different and just as important connection to reality: in its original form it is not artificially invented, but is rooted in an original event; and an event of particular, cosmogonic importance (14–15). Huizinga's comments on the exact nature of this representation are so important that they must be quoted in full: 'The word "represents", however, does not cover the exact meaning of the act, at least not in its looser, modern connotation; for here "representation" is really identification, the mystic repetition or re-presentation of the event' (15). It is just as experiential as the original event was.

Huizinga starts with another crucial recognition: a central component of the archaic experience of the divine is seizure, or the feeling of 'being seized on, thrilled, enraptured' (16). The participatory aspect of play can only work if participants are literally 'captured' or possessed during performance by enormous emotional charge, meaning that they manage to feel as if they were present at the original event itself. This also implies that this event must have involved the same kind of experience. Furthermore, Huizinga emphasises contentment or good feeling, decency. The origins of divine experiences and their performance – thus, the origins of representation – cannot be reduced to the victimage mechanism and rituals of sacrifice, no matter how important this particular case was in history, though given the nature of the process of representation, it can easily develop into this dramatic, ritualised phase. But the basic, truly original, authentic and very different kind of religious experience – positive, not negative; uplifting, not lethargy-generating – by which 'something invisible and inactual' took magnificent, graceful, ennobling form: this was the original experience of a divine presence by those who actually witnessed it, and who then continued to reproduce it in their visual representations; a particularly clear and important example being the Palaeolithic.

The proper evocation of an original event involves something more; another basic characteristic of man, another anthropological fundament: imagination (129–30). Imagination is required both at the level of the singular intellect, putting the feeling into form; and at the level of participants who manage to re-live imaginatively the experience. The link between play and imagination is one of the basic tenets of the type of 'fundamental anthropology' promoted by Huizinga, further illuminating the central, joint meaning of contentment and participation.

The liminalisation of man: Bakhtin and Propp

The same point can reached by different means, through studying the origins of folktales and novels, though here an almost imperceptible shift takes place towards an increasing focus on liminality. Here particularly good guides in understanding are Mikhail Bakhtin (1984), concerning the carnival, and Vladimir Propp (1968), concerning folktales, in particular the way the hero is immersed in troubles. Not surprisingly, both are witnesses and survivors of the disaster of communism; and, perhaps more strikingly, both are Russian. Thus, given their close study of historical and ethnographic evidence, and given the close affinity between the climate of the Russian steppe and Palaeolithic France, they might have discovered survivals of Palaeolithic practices. As further evidence pointing in the same direction, we can note here that shamanism, increasingly used to explain Palaeolithic practices (Clottes and Lewis-Williams 1996), is originally a Siberian term; or recall the striking similarity between two relatively mass-produced objects, the fawn spear thrower, made of antler or wood (first discovered in Mas d'Azil, but later various copies were also found, among others in Bedeilhac and Arudy); and Scythian golden stags, found in various places in Russia (one, from Kostromskaya, is in the Hermitage of St. Petersburg, while another, formerly in the collection of Patti Birch, was sold at an auction on 1 June 2012 in Paris – this latter is particularly intriguing as, while made of gold, it imitates wood or antler incision, in its tail closely recalling the Mas d'Azil spear thrower, while its neck is similarly overstretched). The specific feature of both objects is that the animal's legs are folded over under its body. For the original spear thrower, this was functional, to prevent the object from breaking; in the goldsmith work, it just became a convention.

Furthermore, the central themes of the studies of both Bakhtin and Propp were quite closely connected to talking and origins – not concerning the origins of language, but the remote sources of storytelling; an activity that can be connected to walking not only through the walking–talking connection, mentioned before, but also through both being literally linear, in the sense of proceeding along lines, rendered theoretically relevant recently by Ingold's comparative historical anthropology of the line, starting with the simple yet profound question: '[w]hat do walking, weaving, observing, singing, storytelling, drawing and writing have in common?' (2007: 1; see also McNamee 2012).

Bakhtin is struggling to integrate the novel and the folktale, even though it is not immediately comprehensible why he is happier to discuss the connections between the carnival and the novel than to integrate the discussion of the folktale and the novel, though the link seems evident. In particular he makes no reference to the work of Vladimir Propp, his exact contemporary, even though the affinities between the two analyses are remarkable and important. Maybe this is due to Propp's presumed associations with formalism and structuralism (all such labelling is misleading, but this one particularly so), together with the fact that Propp's work was published just when Bakhtin was exiled, which might have contributed to their mutual ignorance.

The affinities between the concept 'liminality' and Bakhtin's account on the history of the novel are multiple and self-evident, even beyond the carnival, having a significant corollary. To start with, every single one of the main types of the novel identified by Bakhtin (1986) can be considered as capturing a liminal situation. This starts with the first form of the novel, having as its theme the travel, and continues with the second, closely related type, the novel of ordeal or trial. The identification and sequential ordering by Bakhtin is of considerable significance, as it captures the two most basic, archetypal kinds of liminal situations, walking pilgrimage and rites of passage. Rites of passage assist an individual or a community to navigate a successful transition between two different stages in the life cycle or the cycle of seasons, with rites of initiation serving for Turner as the par excellence kind of rite of passage, the central moment of such rites being a kind of testing, trial or ordeal. Pilgrimages, on the other hand, as they also came to be analysed prominently by Turner in his later stages of his life-work, are not staged, but rather real-world 'rites of passage', involving a travel with a specific purpose, and the question of their primacy is an important theoretical problem, having significant corollaries for the history of culture and civilisation. It has relevance concerning the question of the primacy of a forced or artificial setting of rites of passage, which is associated with metallurgy (Horvath 2013a); and also for the genesis of rituals of sacrifice, widely associated with the origins of culture and society (Mauss, Durkheim, Girard, Calasso). Bakhtin's intuition, related to a completely different context, thus in this sense 'unbiased', reinforces the primacy of walking pilgrimage over fixed rituals.

However, and even further, this entire line of thought receives further corroboration from the work of Vladimir Propp on the origin and nature of folktales. Propp offers a vital introduction to the state of mind and spirit that walking represents, where one leaves behind the accustomed and familiar and enters the unknown, which is dangerous and challenging. According to Propp's analysis, which is based on a comprehensive study of a large number of Russian folktales, travel, thus walking, is indeed the first and foremost theme of folktales, but in a very specific manner. In the first place, they start not by the hero embarking on a trip, but by figures of authority, mostly parents, leaving the home (because of some kind of danger). Then, after the hero fails to keep a certain inhibition, or limit, imposed by the parents when they temporarily left, much of the story, at its most basic structural level – and where, to the greatest surprise of Propp, his analysis led him to the stunning idea that all folktales follow *one* single model – involves a long travel of the hero, away from and then back home, the central component of which is an ordeal or trial, in the form of a fight with forces of evil, usually a monster of a dragon kind, and involving the liberation of a maid.

Propp's work offers three important points for this book: first, that the fundamental problem, the liminal situation, told and retold by folktales in manifold ways since time immemorial,[4] is a liminal void generated by an absence of authority; second, that the central narrative of the folktale has the character of walking, moving even beyond the perspective of pilgrimage, focusing on risking, losing and retrieving the *home*, evidently a most important concern of human existence; and finally, that it is into this walking framework that the rite of passage kind of ordeal can be properly situated, reinforcing the primacy of walking as an open practice over rites of passage that are artificially staged and follow a pre-set sequence of acts, well captured in Turner's programmatic book title about a ritual *process* – a practice that, on closer look, reveals itself to be too much pre-fabricated to be primary.

Thus, walking, even pilgrimage, is not a transformative rite of passage; this is only a later, modern addition to their meaning. Walking does not change one's character, only reinforces it, even though it is linked to liminality, as this is the most simple and indeed natural and normal human activity and reinforces involvement in a higher order.[5]

Conclusion: the walker's arrival

After a walk, even a walker arrives. But this does not and cannot mean a definite settling down. This is captured in an again unique manner in Hungarian, where 'arrive' is *érkezik*. *Ér* is the most important Hungarian root, source of a series of words, including 'mature' (*érik*), but originally meaning 'reach'. *-Kez* is a postfix indicating repetitive or continuous action, just as *-ik*. Thus, 'to arrive' means to reach the destination, again and again. Thus, the word that in a settled context stands for the completion of an action in Hungarian is formed to indicate continuity and repetition. One becomes mature if one arrives repeatedly – which also implies that it also starts again; just as Ulysses at the end of the *Odyssey*.

Notes

1 One of the authors of this book still remembers his astonishment when in one of his first French lessons, at the age of about eight years, it proved all but impossible for his French teacher to come up with a proper French translation of the simplest Hungarian expression that somebody 'went' somewhere, with the Hungarian word *ment* 'went' eventually rendered by the expression *se dirigeait vers* ('directed himself towards') – an expression whose focus on consciousness and command now can be understood as particularly revealing but also strange and problematic.
2 This helps to explain the affinities between the last period of Foucault's work, much focusing on the 'care of the self', and Gros's interest in walking.
3 It is to be noted that in Hungarian 'gy' is a single consonant, to be pronounced similarly to English 'd' in 'due' or 'during'.
4 On the extreme antiquity of the folktale as analysed by Propp, see also Alinei (2009: 431).
5 Neither 'natural' nor 'normal' imply rigid conformity to a strict rule. This is only the modern, rationalist and clearly inacceptable layer of meaning on these basic terms. 'Natural' is what is required for the fulfilment and transmission of life; while 'normal' is what accepts the given, taken for granted, as a gift.

3

THE DILEMMA OF REPRESENTING THE VOID

Michel Foucault and Frances Yates

> The picture has no other content in fact than that which it represents, and yet that content is made visible only because it is represented by a representation.
> *Michel Foucault*, The Order of Things, *'Representing' (1970: 71)*

Walking is a human experience. Our entire life, both physically and metaphorically, is a walk. So obviously it is three-dimensional. Yet, at the same time, walking is also a central source of stories, narratives, the origin of the folktale and the novel, thus it proceeds alongside a line, or has a one-dimensional character, as when somebody walking is dragging something behind, which draws a line.[1]

While all this is simple enough, walking is also fundamentally connected to the other two dimensions of human life – two-dimensionality and the zero. Here we touch upon the impossibility of representing the void. As, about 37,000 years ago, out of the long, complex and still little-known interaction between Neanderthal and Homo sapiens, an evidently unprecedented modality of walking would emerge; an emergence, not an origin (Foucault 1984): when man started to walk not on but *under* the ground, going into caves, thus encountering darkness itself, or the *void*, to see some images, which similarly emerged, as an apparition (Foucault 1994, II: 143), out of nothingness, on the surfaces of the caves, and which, as images, even if making use of aspects of the surface, had a fundamentally two-dimensional character. This brought something evidently new into the world: the idea of representation, or bringing something into presence in a disembodied, yet permanently objectified manner; in images on cave walls. In his 2010 film *The Cave of Forgotten Dreams* Werner Herzog recognised the significance of cave painting for the problem of representing the void. This problem was a central preoccupation of Herzog since his first films. In fact, an early film, *Play in Sand* (1964), about children playing with a cockerel, in front of the camera, became so frightening due to the emotions the camera brought out that Herzog even prohibited its circulation. Herzog understood that representation itself is the danger, as it can easily become real, altering reality.

The uniquely special and highly problematic (problematic, as implying the alteration of character, starting a slow process of making man settled, not moving and thus more easily pulled forcefully, or dragged along to thinking or feeling for a given purpose, say pulsating for the void, or for being domesticated, forgetting to look after oneself, giving up walking) class of this phenomenon has been analysed with particular perceptiveness by two books published almost simultaneously half a century ago, *Les mots et les choses* by Michel Foucault and *The Art of Memory* by Frances Yates.

These writings are particularly helpful to understand what happened with Chauvet (the events might have taken a few weeks, decades, centuries or even millennia; data are scarce, though precious; rare gifts, which don't allow more precision), as they analyse a quite similar type of reality: the situation of Europe, right after the collapse of the Renaissance. The images of Chauvet, just as Renaissance paintings, did not try to make a 'realistic' copy of something really existing; as we have already indicated, such an undertaking does not make any sense, and is self-contradictory. They both rather wanted to evoke, recognisably, things that exist, to transmit to anybody beholding them a vision about the graceful good feeling of the world around – a contentment that simply cannot be put into words. *This* is what is meant by the origin of art; and this is the same reason why the art of Renaissance Italy simply has no equivalent elsewhere in Europe, or in other parts of the world, as even the feet and eyes of 'mere' tourists testify it, year after year after year.

However, this invention was problematic, a danger that was brought out with particular clarity with two excellent recent books who made what would seem to be the most absurd and anachronistic claims about Palaeolithic art: that it was theatrical (Montelle 2009) and cinematic (Azéma 2011). The cinematic qualities of Chauvet were already recognised by Werner Herzog in his film – and he certainly knew what he was talking about – due to the striking manner in which images, especially of lions, as if capturing the animals in movement, even though such capturing of movement represents a first step towards domestication, as it is a freezing of moving into an image. Such characters were brought off with particular force in the distant past, in the flickering light of torches or oil lamps. The possibility of theatrical rituals performed in the cave, on the other hand, was indicated by certain human traces left inside, just as the enormous, amphitheatre-like character of some underground caves.

The authenticity of Chauvet images in this sense was already immediately validated by the reactions of the discoverers who had no competence in Palaeolithic art way before Jean Clottes would arrive on 29 December 1994 to pronounce his judgement: Chauvet makes genuine people cry with tears of joy. They succeeded to 'bring into presence' even themselves, as again the discoverers testified, after about 37,000 years. But they also created the possibility of drawing something as a mere realistic image; then, a mere image; and finally, a 'playful' image that evokes beings that do not even exist. We now have to make sense of, and evaluate, this possibility of evoking unreality out of reality by representation, as it is explained by Foucault and Yates how and why it happened after the Renaissance.

Foucault: the paradox of representation as knowledge

The central problem Michel Foucault addressed in this book is shown by the original French title: *Les mots et les choses*, or 'Words and things'. It concerns the separation between words and things that happened in European culture after the Renaissance. Up to the Renaissance, words and language were part of reality; after its collapse, words became reduced to a mere instrument of gaining 'knowledge'. Foucault's aim is limited to documenting this change, without offering an interpretation. He had good reasons for doing so. As his central aim was to deny the presumption that discourse has no independence, but only accompanies changes that take place in a reality presumably outside language, he could not offer a metatheory reducing changes in discourse to mere 'reflections'. More problematically, at that moment he was captivated by a certain avant-garde heroisation of the independence of language, taken from Nietzsche and Mallarmé, close to what Calasso (2002) would later call 'absolute literature', and which was a schismatic reaction to the instrumentalisation of language.

However, based on Foucault's work two interpretative points will be offered here. To start with, knowledge gained through an instrumentalisation of words, comparable to Weberian 'instrumental rationality', which implies a reduction of human life to a search for business success, in the hope of gaining the 'sign' of salvation (Weber 1992), can be defined as non-participatory knowledge, meaning a kind of knowledge that presumes a point *outside* social life and nature, ignoring or overriding the perspective of participants. The second concerns the collapse of the medieval vision of the world, to be consummated with the technological, reductionist knowledge proposed by the 'scientific revolution' and 'rationalist' philosophy. Foucault's work touched upon the heart of this transformation, identifying it with the rise of representation as an activity, and the sign as the main instrument for gaining such knowledge.

The separation between words and things thus had two aspects, the focus on the act of representing, and the instrumentalisation of language as mere sign. The relationship between these two aspects contains a central message in the book. The separation of words and things is part of the dissolution of the medieval world order, the 'great chain of being' where things were connected with each other, and harmoniously. Such collapse of order inevitably leads to searches for solution. This was offered through the idea of representation, which – by reducing words to signs – constructed an artificial order in the form of a systematic arrangement of signs, representing things in presumably universal taxonomic tables.

Representation

The single most important idea of this extremely significant and influential book which created a sensation when it was published, making an overnight celebrity out of Foucault, is the claim that the fundamental novelty of the classical[2] episteme is not the use of mathematics in science, or quantification, or even mechanisation, but the act of representing as foundational for gaining knowledge (Foucault 1970: 63). In spite of the success of the book, the radical novelty of this idea has hardly been recognised – perhaps because it was forgotten even by Foucault. It certainly sounds an overstatement: how could representation be more important, for the history of knowledge, than the other innovations mentioned above?[3]

'Representation' refers to a word or an image 'standing for' a thing, implying the problem raised by Magritte in his painting 'This is not a pipe'.[4] This, however, as we have already seen through Huizinga, is by no means the original meaning of the term. 'Re'-presenting means to bring into presence, into concrete reality, the actual here and now something which is absent. Even further, the medieval use of the term referred to a human being 'standing in' for other human beings, in particular in an assembly. This was the basis of medieval politics, as analysed in classic works by Gadamer, Kantorowitz, Voegelin or Pizzorno, having theological roots in the Eucharist. The term 'representation' also implies substitution, in the sense of denying and undermining concreteness, as a 'representative' is not present in his concrete being, only as a substitute for other being(s) who for some reason cannot be there. Substitutability, however, is not only a central principle of the market and exchange, but – as Roberto Calasso repeatedly emphasised – also of sacrifice. 'Bringing the absence into presence' furthermore has a magical and transformative aspect; it is a metamorphosis or transmogrification. Thus representation, far from being just an innocuous way to gain knowledge, is a potentially highly dangerous act.

Finally, and still before the term acquired its dominant modern meaning, representation was used for theatrical performance. The primary importance of such use at the end of the Renaissance is revealed by John Florio's 1598 Italian–English Dictionary, the first such comprehensive undertaking, where *rappresentare* is translated as 'to represent, to resemble, to shewe, to playe comedies or enterludes', and *rappresentatori* as 'players, comedians, enterlude-players' (Florio 2013).[5] Strikingly, Foucault shows no interest in the theatrical aspect of representation. The word is only mentioned a couple of times in the book: on its very first substantive page, after the introductory chapter (Foucault 1970: 17), where it serves, as a 'theatre of life', and in pair with the idea of 'mirror of nature', to characterise the state of affairs *before* the rule of representation; an allusion to Bacon's 'idols of the theatre', which is also little relevant for the concerns of his book (51–2); and in another characterisation of the late Renaissance, which – through its fairs and focus on show and spectacles – is perceptively but somewhat anachronistically characterised as 'the age of the theatre', replaced by the arrangement of things on a 'table' (131). The reason is thus clear: Foucault shares the downplaying of theatre, characteristic of modern thought, in spite of Nietzsche's pioneering hints.

Sign

The central means of representing, in the modern sense, is the *sign*. Not surprisingly, given the importance of representation for the book, the definition of a sign, and of the activity of representing, takes up the central and most difficult part of the book, where Foucault's thinking enters a series of spirals and contortions that are almost impossible to follow. A sign in the 'classical episteme' not only must stand clearly and unambiguously for things – a project already voiced by Bacon – but also must demonstrate with the same clarity that it is nothing else but a sign, has no independent reality; that it does nothing else but represent; a condition that such knowledge could be arranged unambiguously in huge and comprehensive 'tables'. This is captured by the idea of 'duplicated representation [*représentation dédoublée*]', title of the fourth section of chapter 3, entitled 'Representing', thus unambiguously the core of the book, where the sign is first defined as 'a duplicated representation doubled over upon itself' [*le signe est une représentation dédoublée et redoublé sur elle-même*] (65; 1966: 79). As if feeling that such a definition stretches the limits of intelligibility, on the same page Foucault offers four further definitions, or characterisation, of the sign. Something is a sign not simply because it is related to something else, but 'because this representation can always be represented within the idea that is representing'. Furthermore, third, a representation in its 'essence' is 'perpendicular to itself'; this means that, apart from having a relationship to an object, it is also a 'manifestation of itself' (Foucault 1970: 65). Fourth, the attempt at further explicating the point yields a particularly cryptic sentence, containing the term 'represent' in three different grammatical forms: 'the sign is the *representativity* of the representation in so far as it is *representable*' [italics in original]. These four definitions are not only contained on the same page, but within nine lines. A few lines below comes the fifth and last: '[w]henever one representation is linked to another and represents that link within itself, there is a sign'.

The point is by no means to charge Foucault of playing pre-postmodern linguistic games. Foucault made a stunning discovery concerning the centrality of representation for the 'classical age'. He is desperately trying to understand the significance of his own discovery, and transmit it to his readers. Yet, he evidently did not succeed – the mysteries of duplicated representation remained impenetrable.

The actor and the sign

The main difficulty Foucault was facing in clarifying his ideas about 'duplicated representation' was that a sign could only function as a 'mere' sign, or even 'pure' sign, nothing but a sign, if it could not only 'represent' something, but at the same time also indicate the act of representing. It almost amounts to attributing human characteristics to the sign; ideally, they should be able to speak to us, saying that 'sorry, I'm not doing anything else but representing; I do not exist' – which is almost the reverse of Descartes's meditations.

But this is exactly what actors do. An actor only plays a role; the role of a stage character; and even the stage character is not real, only imitating some or other figure of real life. Even further, actors – not only in our times, but already in the Stuart period (see Agnew 1986) – make all kind of asides, when on stage, calling attention to the fact that they were not what they represented, thus exactly performing the function Foucault would like us to understand concerning signs. This is by no means accidental. The order of dictionary entries should be taken seriously: the idea of representing knowledge, through signs, came after the word 'representation' was applied to the theatre, as the theatre indeed was model for the modern organisation of knowledge. The early modern theatre mimed medieval politics, while modern 'rational' knowledge mimed the theatre.

An actor who plays the role of Richard III on stage is certainly *not* Richard III; yet, he 'represents' Richard III, so has to make us believe that the king, Shakespeare's hero, is present in front of us, otherwise the illusion does not work. Yet, at the same time, the actor *is* an actor, must demonstrate that he or she is an actor, so that we would not get the false impression that an actor playing the police chief on stage is the actual chief of police. Thus, by using this analogy, we can easily understand the complicated, invisible foundations of this edifice that Foucault attempted to unravel.

Fortunately, there was a thinker who did proceed further, and in a classic book published in the same year as Foucault's. This author is Frances Yates, and her book is *The Art of Memory*.

Yates: artificial memory, theatre, knowledge

Frances Yates (1899–1981) was one of the most important historians of science in the past century, having been engaged in a life-project that was in many ways similar not only to that of Michel Foucault, but also Eric Voegelin, Lewis Mumford and Franz Borkenau, her exact contemporaries: trying to reconstruct the Nietzschean *pudenda origo* of modern science. At the same time she had a connected interest in the history of Elizabethan theatre.

Yates offers a good introduction to her project in a Preface she wrote in 1974, thus at the age of seventy-five, to the Paladin edition of *The Rosicrucian Enlightenment*. She starts by voicing a 'profound dissatisfaction with the world of today', felt by many, and rooted in a 'distrust in science', based on the recognition that instead of being liberated and empowered, one 'has become imprisoned in technologies, reduced in status as a human being, enslaved by unforeseen results of applied science' (Yates 1975: 11). This often led to a search of escape in esoteric values. However, such attempts fail to realise that modern science grew out of just such esoteric contexts, with a particularly great role being played by the Hermetic tradition, promoting magic and alchemy, having affinities with Gnostic Neoplatonism, and becoming combined with Cabala, producing the Renaissance mage. A particularly important tool of alchemy, 'always called a Hermetic science', was the *Emerald Table* (*Tabula Smaragdina*), the 'bible of the alchemists', as it gave

Hermetic philosophy a 'mysteriously compact form' (16). The idea of empowering man to dominate nature was central to such an undertaking, so '[t]he Renaissance magus is the immediate ancestor of the seventeenth century religious scientist' – a thinly veiled allusion to Newton (14).[6]

According to Yates, the modern vision concerning the role and modalities of knowledge has roots not only in esoteric undertakings, but also in the theatre. Here a central role was played by Giulio Camillo Delminio (c.1480–1544).

Camillo and his theatre

Camillo was not only a contemporary of both Raphael (1483–1520) and Martin Luther (1483–1546), thus locating him at the liminal fracture line between Renaissance and Reformation, but also Dr Faustus, who was similarly born around 1480 and died around 1540. His life-work and its reception (Bernheimer 1956; Bolzoni 1984, 1995; Turello 1993; Yates 1992) fits into a type crucial for genealogical studies. His contemporaries held him in the highest esteem, hailing him as 'divine Camillo'. He was a professor of Bologna with extraordinary eloquence and erudition, and Francis I, the French king who previously had Leonardo da Vinci as conversation partner, financed his memory theatre project for years. In sum, he was 'one of the most famous men of the sixteenth century' (Yates 1992: 135). His book left in manuscript, 'The idea of the theatre', was considered a unique treasure of knowledge, published in 1550 both in Florence and Venice, and frequently reprinted in the century and the following. By the eighteenth century, however, his reputation was dwindling, and then his name fell into complete oblivion. From a genealogical perspective, the type is the trailblazer who – at a crucial liminal moment – performs a breakthrough, but once the results, in a transmuted form, become taken for granted, the figure is forgotten as becoming a liability for his indirect heirs.

The novelty introduced by Camillo was a peculiar combination of knowledge and theatre that on the one hand today sounds completely odd, and on the other is stunningly similar to some of the most cherished ideas of the Enlightenment and modernity. Its aim was to produce, in the form of a theatre, a 'total encyclopaedia' (Turello 1993: 3), which would render visible, for a single all-encompassing glance, all the knowledge about the universe, its very order, thus amounting to a divinisation of man. To appreciate the novelty and significance, and the eventual effects, of this idea, we have to follow Yates in situating it in the history of the arts of memory, or 'mnemotechnics' – a shorthand for a 'technique of impressing "places" and "images" on memory' (Yates 1992: 11).

This technique, which in his last years was also studied by Foucault, is traced to Simonides of Ceos, who miraculously escaped the collapse of a roof during a banquet in Thessaly, but – due to his memory device – was able to perfectly reconstruct the seating order of the guests (17–18). Simonides was a rather peculiar figure of Greek poetry, having a great reputation during his lifetime, called 'the honey-tongued' due to the 'sweetness' of his poems, excelling in the beauty of its imagery.

However, hardly any of his poems survived, while he also had the reputation of being the first to ask for money for his poems (42–3). He also became famous for his peculiar linking of poetry and painting – an idea that, according to Yates, has importance for the invention of the arts of memory, while later would become central for Lessing's attack on the classical European culture of beauty, helping to launch the aesthetics of the sublime. Thus, while belonging to the Presocratic age, Simonides could be considered a proto-Sophist. Such a characterisation seems all the more appropriate as memory techniques were one of the central tools of the Sophists, which they taught for money, perfected in particular by Hippias of Elis, a major target of Platonic dialogues, leading Yates to suggest that the hostility of Plato against the Sophists might have been due to his hostility to such 'superficial memorization of quantities of miscellaneous information' (45). Similarly to his opposition to the theatre, Plato's hostility should not be taken lightly, as memory was a central concern for Plato, discussed as a 'gift' in the *Theaetetus*, fundamental for forming a personality capable of right judgement, helped by sense percep-tions, through which man can accede to the higher reality of the ideas. From this perspective artificial memory interfered with one's personality, possible source of losing one's coherence, substance, identity, soul – worse than poison. It is no doubt due to such interference that mnemotechnics was always more than a simple learn-ing device, and rather a 'very mysterious subject' (20).

For Augustine, similarly, memory represents, with understanding and will, the three main powers of the soul, together constituting the image of Trinity in man (62). The Church shared Plato's hostility, paralleling their joint hostility to the theatre, thus by Carolingian time artificial memory simply had disap-peared in the West (66). Memory techniques, however, survived in Sophist teachings, which became dominant in Byzantium for educating the imperial administration, and were transmitted into medieval Aristotelian scholasticism. Among such devices a central role was played by tablets, or written pages for memorisation (40–1).

The great innovation of Camillo was to combine at the liminal moment of the early sixteenth century three areas that previously were quite separate: the art of memory; the project of an universal science, conquering nature, based on the burgeoning interest in occult forms of science and knowledge; and the theatre, reborn at the time and place where Camillo was living: in Padua/Venice, in the first half of the sixteenth century. The combination, as a peculiar witches' brew, had a tremendous impact; and though it disappeared into oblivion, its effective legacy was massive.

Camillo's life-project was to construct a wooden theatre in which instantane-ous knowledge could be gained about the very order of the world. As he stated in the early pages of his work, his aim was 'to give, so to speak, order to the order' (Camillo 1990: 64), or to reproduce the very order of the universe in a manner that is even more ordered than its order. This was to be done through a series of truly ingenuous ideas, or rather tricks.

To begin with, in line with the idea *theatrum mundi*, a theatre should be built in which all the knowledge about the world could be gathered and 'represented'. This theatre, built of wood, was supposed to have seven rows and seven columns – forty-nine, or seven by seven, being a most significant alchemic number – where, under various labels, knowledge should be collected, classified and placed in huge boxes. The idea was to fix pieces of knowledge into concrete places, to visualise them, and thus imprint their order on memory. The central instrument of Camillo's memory theatre was the *sign*: as it was conveyed by Viglius Zuichemus, a correspondent of Erasmus who was guided through the theatre by Camillo himself in Padua, Camillo

> pretends that all things that the human mind can conceive and which we cannot see with the corporeal eye, after being collected together by diligent meditation may be expressed by certain corporeal signs in such a way that the beholder may at once perceive with his eyes everything that is otherwise hidden in the depths of the human mind.
>
> *(Yates 1992: 137)*

Such signs included images, symbols and words; but as Camillo was steeped in rhetorics, the central role was played by words, in the form of written speeches stored under the various images, thus Camillo 'had hit upon a new interpretation of memory for "things" and "words"' (148–9); links which are necessary, as they correspond to the ontological structure of the real (Turello 1993: 152). The correspondence between words and things, as a 'method' (Yates 1992: 147), was based on the idea that everything 'means' something else, or stands for something else, or a universal principle of substitutability (146–7), also at the heart of Calasso's (2010) anthropology. Thus, to give one example, in the Jupiter series of the Theatre (as there were series for each seven planets), the Three Graces under the sign of the Cave meant useful things, while under the Sandals of Mercury, benevolence. The aim of such series was to 'represent the universe expanding from First Causes through the stages of creation' (Yates 1992: 145); or to offer, through the eyes, thus in a snapshot, but dynamically, a comprehensive 'vision of the world and of the nature of things' (148). The theatre was supposed to reveal the truth, and nothing but the truth, by rendering it visible (Camillo 1990: 60; see also Bolzoni 1995), thus making it open to the public, in contrast to the previous efforts to keep it hidden for the initiates; it thus had the character of an initiation into knowledge (*initiazione sapientale*) (Turello 1993: 83).

The second great trick was that in this building the spatial logic of the theatre was to be reversed, with the spectator brought onto the stage (Peters 2004: 187), who from there could contemplate the way the order of the universe was represented in the theatre, in the rows where usually the audience was sitting. Thus, instead of an audience of spectators looking at a stage, as in a normal theatre or amphitheatre, we have the scholars (*studiosi*), placed at the stage and thus transformed into spectators (*spettatori*), looking at the 'world' around them, as a 'spectacle' (*spettaculo*) (Camillo 1990: 64).

The corollary of this device is significant, and fits fully in line with the late Renaissance speculations of Ficino and especially Pico. By being transformed into spectators, the scholars also become divinised: '[m]an's mind' thus becomes a 'direct reflection of the divine *mens*' (Yates 1992: 150), releasing new powers within the psyche (174). According to Bolzoni's analysis, for Camillo 'rhetoric, alchemy and "deification"' are three aspects of a single transformative process through which man becomes God' (see Turello 1993: 164, referring to chapter 1, 'The art of metamorphosis: eloquence and alchemy in *De transmutazione*', in Bolzoni 1984, esp. 5–6).

Transforming men into gods implies a magical action. The access to the divine is produced by a 'magically activated imagination'; through Camillo's Theatre, '[t]he art of memory has become an occult art, a Hermetic secret' (Yates 1992: 161; see also Peters 2004: 180), the key of the theatre being that its images are magically effective (Turello 1993: 24). In commenting Bolzoni Turello also specifically insists on the transformative aims and capacities of the Theatre: the focus of Camillo's theatre is transmutation, as eloquence, alchemy and deification, its three central focuses are 'the transmutational arts that the Theatre "represents and at the same time renders possible"' (as in Turello 1993: 58; see again Bolzoni 1984: ch. 1).

The promise offered by Camillo's memory theatre was practically unlimited. It offered access through a single glance to a knowledge penetrating the very order of the universe. It suggested a simple, technical means to create such knowledge, by combining the rediscovered architecture of Vitruvius, the images of mnemotechnics, and rhetoric – through the infinite, unending project of collecting all the knowledge in the world, but arranged in a unitary structure. Finally, in this way, he promised to realise an old dream of mankind, to become, through knowledge, equal to God – a dream resurrected by the ancient Gnostics, and evidently preserved and transmitted, throughout the centuries, in the obscure undercurrents of the Byzantine 'sages'. While Camillo failed to deliver his theatre and did not even publish his book, the effects of his work were considerable, perhaps even foundational for modern technology and science. Central figures in this chain of transmission were other Renaissance magi, in particular Giordano Bruno, who misread a passage in Aristotle, interpreting thinking as a speculation in images, leading to an 'overwhelming speculation with the imagination', particularly evident in his last work (Yates 1992: 279–80), and stamping on the history of European thinking the 'compulsion for system-forming' and the 'intense striving for method' (296), two aspects already central in Byzantine Sophistic; but also through Ignatius of Loyola, whose focus on the showing and manipulation of images was rendered possible by Camillo (Turello 1993: 92–3, 171–3).

Notes

1 This is again captured in Hungarian *vonal* 'line', from *von* 'drawing or dragging something behind'. This word, together with the word *ér* 'reaching', but also 'maturing' (as a fruit), captures in a nutshell the central point in Ingold's (2013) book about the link between drawing lines, compared to 'the trails left by two people walking abreast', making and growing, in contrast to the focus on image, object and conscious projects (20–1).
2 Foucault defined the 'classical age' as the period between about 1650 and 1800, combining the rise of modern science and the Enlightenment.
3 Arguably, Bataille's ideas on transgression were central for Foucault's discovery.
4 The trivial, yet vexing point is that the painting of a pipe is not a pipe (Foucault 1994, I: 635–50).
5 On Florio, see Yates (1964).
6 For obvious reasons, Newton was a taboo for Yates: '[a]bout Newton, I have nothing to say' (Yates 1992: 368).

PART II

The flourishing and demise of walking culture

4

CHAUVET

The cave of wonders, or representation as transgression

> The efflux of the soul is happiness, here is happiness,
> I think it pervades the open air, waiting at all times,
> Now it flows unto us, we are rightly charged.
>
> *Walt Whitman*, Leaves of Grass, *'Song of the Open Road' (1990: 124)*

It has been repeatedly stated, by those in official charge, that Chauvet cave is 'the best dated site of rock art in the world' (see for example Clottes and Geneste 2007: 12). The claim encountered some dissent, though this was rather limited to a small group of experts (Paul Bahn, Paul Pettitt and Christian Züchner; see Pettitt and Bahn 2003, 2015; Pike *et al.* 2015), some of whom had a long-standing conflict with the ideas of Jean Clottes, connected to the linking of Palaeolithic art with shamanism,[1] and this dissent seems rooted in a particularly dogged, dogmatic vision of linear materialist evolutionism.

After a very recent study (Quiles *et al.* 2016), conducted by a number of highly classified experts of a most varied background from France, Germany and the Netherlands, opposition to the dating of Chauvet is no longer tenable. We need to gain a clear idea concerning the meaning of such dates, a point that goes to the heart of a fundamental methodological issue in the social sciences, the meaning of facts, or rather data, which are 'given'. The stunning, truly mindboggling age of these paintings must indeed be accepted as something given; a true gift. The real question concerns the meaning of such facts. While the dating of the paintings is a matter of science *tout court*, and the entire complex is a patrimony of mankind, understanding the meaning of these paintings requires the efforts of all social and human scientists.

This first requires us to become familiarised with the dates as established recently. While the difference is minor, the new dates are slightly even older than the previous (Quiles *et al.* 2016: 4672–4). The cave was frequented by humans in two basic periods. The first ranges from about 35,000 to 31,000 BC.[2] This was the period in which most of the paintings were made; and in this period the cave was visited by humans and cave bears. This ended when a major boulder rockfall partially blocked the entrance. Cave bears stopped visiting the cave; however, after a gap lasting for several thousand years, man again visited the cave from about 29,000 BC to 26,000 BC, probably adding a few paintings. At that time, another rock falling happened. Blocking was still not complete, as some animals kept visiting the cave, but no sign of any human visitation could be ascertained. In about 21,500 BC and 19,500 BC (Quiles *et al.* 2016: 4674) there were two further rockfalls, after which the cave was completely sealed off for any but the smallest animals.

This is the age and sequence of visitation we must make sense of – concerning the specific purposes of this book.

To begin with, such further receding in the dating of Chauvet makes even more evident the need to situate cave art in the context of an interaction between Neanderthal and Cro Magnon cultures. This question is particularly relevant for this book, as Neanderthals did not produce images in caves. All that matters is to give proper consideration to the transgression evidently present with the new appearance of images on cave walls – as it implies a bringing into presence by something which itself is absent, empty, being a mere image, even just a sign. As a starting point, we suggest taking up the considerations of Georges Bataille on Lascaux. Apart from the evident value of Bataille's ideas, there is a good methodological reason for doing so. Bataille was an early and most important French student of Nietzsche, interpreted by Michel Foucault as such, thus offering a genealogically sensitive perspective.

While Bataille was evidently wrong in assigning a primacy to Lascaux, one can simply shift the arguments to Chauvet, and the same thing could possibly be made for any future discovery. However, without excluding such a possibility, the explanation has to take into account the specific features of Chauvet, which altogether extend to a period twice as far back in history as Lascaux, and which renders it quite unlikely that a centre comparable to character and importance to Chauvet could be discovered as belonging to a much more distant past.

Let's now make sense of Chauvet as the start of a 'walking into the void'.

Bataille on Lascaux and the birth of art

To begin with, Bataille characterises Lascaux as a place of *birth*. The term, given Bataille's closeness to Nietzsche, immediately evokes *The Birth of Tragedy*, Nietzsche's first book; and furthermore, given the closeness of Foucault to Bataille, who wrote a Preface to Bataille's *Complete Works*, just when he was writing his milestone essay on Nietzsche and genealogy, also brings in Foucault's genealogical method. This intimates that for Bataille Lascaux is as important for our origins as theatre is for Nietzsche – except for Bataille adding that Lascaux was the birthplace of three things at the same time: apart from art, also of religion, and even of humankind (*l'umanité*, see Bataille 1970: 9). It is this triple birth that he repeatedly characterises as a *miracle* – a miracle only comparable to Greece; a sense of miracle that accompanies these works since their first discovery (11–12, 14–16).

Given that Bataille connects this miracle to the difference between Neanderthal and Cro Magnon man, or *Homo sapiens*, which he repeatedly contrasts with *Homo faber*, and is even inclined to call, after Huizinga, *Homo ludens*, the shift from Lascaux to Chauvet only makes the point stronger. Even further, given the Castelperronian character of Chauvet, it makes the genealogical character of the break even more marked, though adding Bakhtin to Foucault: the novelty is not simply the absolute difference between Neanderthal and Cro Magnon cultures, but rather was produced by the particular transgressive link between the two.

The miracle of the cave is not limited to the 'rise' of art, but is triple, concerning at the same time art, religion and mankind. It is in this sense that the change marked has a both *decisive* and *incommensurable* value (13; our emphasis): very weighty words indeed. Concerning the origins of art, the change is undeniable and radical, and Bataille uses a particularly significant term: Lascaux (or Chauvet) 'created *out of nothingness* (de rien) *this world of art, where begins the communication of spirits*' (emphasis in original, 12). It we interpret this nothingness as the void, in particular the emptiness by which one is surrounded in the darkness of a cave, then this is exactly the problem we pose and try to solve in this book: why did humans started to walk into this void, and how did the incomparably wonderful paintings emerge out of this encounter with the void? Bataille argues that the intention of these artists of remote times escape us, and this is certainly the case, as we can hardly hope to 'interview' them; yet, we argue that from the perspective of walking we can gain some possible insights. For this, we have the incomparable beauty of these paintings; in fact, the very word 'beauty' fails us, not sufficient to render the experience. 'Beauty' here implies the Platonic vision of *the* world *as* beauty: beauty not as a matter of 'aesthetics', an 'autonomous' sphere of knowledge, rather as an overwhelming *thaumazein* experience (see the *Timaeus*). This is clearly the sense implied by Bataille, through his similarly Platonic evocation of love and friendship: 'Is not beauty what we love (*nous aimons*)? Is not friendship (*l'amitié*) the passion, the ever resumed interrogation, to which the only response is beauty?' (13). Another given is the humbleness of these artists, the lack of any arrogant pride on their part (16), even though they created art, a representation of the recognisable, based on a tension of desire, evidently out of nothing.

Here we move from art to religion. The key term is *presence*, in particular a 'sense of presence – of clear and burning presence' (13); a presence evoked by enormous emotional charges, and linked to friendship – a term which in French, just as in Greek, and – etymologically – even in English, evokes the feeling of high emotions. It is also connected to contact with the divine, established in particular through divine animals, those which are assumed to possess, or facilitate, such a contact (76), a phenomenon still present in shamanism. Animals manifest in the images their intact dignity, linked to the widespread belief that their capturing and death could not happen without their consent, entailing a ritualised behaviour that survived almost to the present (Bertolotti 1991; Frank 2008).

It is also here that Bataille locates the rise of humankind – though here we should be careful, as for two major reasons he cannot be fully followed. First of all, and most evidently, neither the humanity of Neanderthals nor of their ancestors, even back to several million years, can be denied. The footprints of Laetoli (Tanzania) are 3.6 million years old and are not different from the footprints of modern man: they have an elegantly raised arch, their big toe is large and aligned with the second toe, thus are characteristically identical to those of modern man.[3] Their toes grip the ground like our walking feet do now. Modern man was walking on earth 3.6 million years ago. A central aspect of the shift from Lascaux to Chauvet was exactly the reallocation of cave art from the novelty of *Homo sapiens* to the dubious contact between Neanderthals and *Homo sapiens*. But there are problems with the way Bataille conceived the character of this break, connected to his philosophy of the limit and transgression (here expressed on pp. 39–42; see also Foucault 1977); a problem to be located with the Hegelian concern with the primacy of consciousness.

Bataille traces the difference between human and animal existence to the emergence of prohibitions (*interdits*; Bataille 1970: 31–9), concerning death and sexuality. In his view this lifted man out of the darkness of 'larval existence', already in Neanderthal times, which for him was '*a time of the night*' (*le temps de la nuit*, emphasis in original), and which is connected to the use of hands (the *Homo faber*), and the rise of intelligence (32). The problem is that this framework accepts as taken for granted the kind of neo-Kantian neo-Darwinism that, as Ingold and Gros argue, ignores the reality and significance of walking, overplaying the importance of the hands and the mind. This allows Bataille, in spite of his closeness to the Platonic concern with recognising beauty as central, to focus on the dualism of prohibition (or the Law) and its transgression, identifying the rise of cave art with the transmutation of prohibition through the rise of play and art into the transcendence of the Law, and placing special emphasis on the feast, combining play, sacrifice, feast and transcendence in a singular unity (39–40).

This interpretation is untenable, a confusing mixture of quite distinct elements, as there are no signs of sacrifice in the Palaeolithic (the first evident signs are in Çayönü, with some previous indications in the Natufian), just as the first trace of feasts can only be followed to the Natufian (Balter 2010b; Dietrich *et al.* 2012; Munro and Grosman 2010). Still, the central point of connecting the novelty of cave art to a giving of order to the previous system of prohibitions is well taken; and even the modality of how this happened is identified in a way. Cave art, with Chauvet, indeed emerged out of nothingness or *nulla*; this *nulla* was the encounter with the void in the depth of the cave (see Horvath 2013a); and this was rendered possible by a genuine 'walking into the void', as part of a play, combining Huizinga's senses of 're-presenting' and 'con-testing'. Through this, Bataille is right in arguing for replacing the idea of man as *Homo faber* with Huizinga's *Homo ludens*; but his Hegelian focus on the conscious mind must be replaced by Kierkegaard's and Nietzsche's recognition of the formative significance of walking.

Central for Bataille's argument is the recognition of the unique, path-breaking importance of cave art, and its literal emergence from the void – if not out of absolute nothingness, given that important aspects of human culture, which he connected to prohibitions, existed before. So far it was claimed that most of his argument could simply be lifted from Lascaux to Chauvet. However, the question now concerns whether new discoveries concerning the 'background', compared to which Chauvet/Lascaux made the difference, can be harmonised with this argument.

We cannot offer here a detailed account of the background against which cave art emerged. Only one aspect will be singled out for attention, uniquely significant in itself, but particularly so given its evidently timeless connection with long-distance walking: Atapuerca.

Atapuerca: the origins of language and culture, c.430,000 BC

Atapuerca's name, and its significance, is still little known by social scientists. Though the site was visited, even by major archaeologists, since the start of the twentieth century, its systematic exploration only started in between 1972 and 1983 (Arsuaga et al. 1997b: 109–10). While human fossils were already found in 1976, the true significance of the site was only realised in 1989, when the first in-site bones were discovered. The new campaign of excavations until 1995 found more than 1,600 human remains, from at least thirty-two individuals, making it 'the world's largest known human repository of fossil humans from the Middle Pleistocene' (Arsuaga 1997a: 105). As only a relatively small portion has so far been excavated, it remains 'a site for the twenty-first century' (106).[4]

There are a series of reasons for the unique significance of the site. To start with, it illuminates the way Neanderthals emerged in Europe. The analysis of seventeen skulls, now traced to at least 430,000 years ago, conclusively showed that these distant ancestors should be considered not as belonging to the *Homo heidelbergensis* group, but rather as representing a major Neanderthal type. As the Atapuerca fossils 'are now the oldest reliably dated hominins to show clear Neanderthal apomorphies' (1361), Neanderthals considerably extend back in time. Furthermore, the site also revealed the presence of mortuary practices and the separation between the dead and the living (Arsuaga et al. 2014), considered so fundamental by Bataille. Investigators found no trace of humans living in the site, while the character of the deposits made them consider the accumulation of bones as being due to intentional deposits, thus perhaps burials. This idea received strong confirmation by the recent finding of a particularly impressive, carefully crafted and beautiful handaxe, nicknamed 'Excalibur', which according to the investigators was intentionally deposited and not accidentally dropped into the cave (Carbonell and Mosquera 2006), tracing the origins of mortuary practices, and thus symbolic behaviour, back to almost half a million years ago.[5]

Even further, it is argued with increasing conviction that these distant ancestors of ours talked. Given that our ancestors walked millions of years ago, this is also natural – in fact, what is surprising is the idea that man walked without talking; an evolutionist residue. While until recently even the ability of more recent Neanderthals to speak was hotly debated, the exceptionally well-preserved remains – including a fully intact skull – of Atapuerca enabled investigators to all but prove such capacity in such an early stage. Skull remains not only contained hyoid bones, central for the capacity of speaking, but also mid-ear bones, rendering it possible to distinguish between various sounds, necessary for hearing (Carbonell and Mosquera 2006: 156–8; Fitch 2009; Johansson 2013; Martínez *et al.* 2008a). Recent studies argue that the sound power transmissions for modern humans and the Atapuerca skeletons are all but identical, and very different from those of chimpanzees (2013: 97–9; 2008b: 4180–1). These findings 'are consistent with other recent suggestions for an ancient origin for human speech capacity' (Martínez 2013: 94; see also 2008b: 4181). From the Atapuerca fossils (Gran Dolina) a totally modern face emerged, that belongs to the present, in spite of the many thousand years of distance.

The significance of such findings gains further weight by taking into account that Atapuerca is not simply in Northern Spain, about 100 miles equally from Altamira (to its North), and Ekain (to its East), but is right on the Camino de Santiago, so much so that – not the cave, certainly, but the nearby township – is a leg in the Camino, with several pilgrim hostels. This offers another clear indication that pilgrimages are renewals of extremely old practices, which furthermore are fundamentally and foundationally connected to the oldest mankind, to our past.

The Chauvet effect

We have to assume that readers are familiar with the images from Chauvet cave. They are today accessible freely on the Internet. At any rate, there is no point in reproducing them within the limits of this book, in small black-and-white photos. They should be consulted in the widely available album-size books (Chauvet *et al.* 1996; Clottes 2003); or, if possible, by watching the masterful 2010 film of Werner Herzog, *The Cave of Forgotten Dreams*, preferably in a cinema, and in 3D: for this film, the technique truly works. We call attention in particular to the frieze of horses and of lions, each about 10 metres long, producing an impact, even in a good book reproduction, that cannot be described here in words. In his film Herzog keeps showing them on and on, for long minutes, moving back and forth, left and right, up and down, as if he could not turn his attention away. In fact, 'the clear certainty that you are facing an awe-inspiring presence' comes through simply by watching his film (Roman 2014: 64). We can only convey the impressions of the discoverers, the first human beings who saw them, on Christmas Eve 1994, after a time that is beyond comprehension, some 26,000 years at least – a full Platonic year; whose first reaction to the frieze of lions 'was a burst of shouts of joy and tears. We felt gripped by madness and dizziness. The animals were innumerable' (Chauvet *et al.* 1996: 58). In his film Herzog interviewed Julien Monney, one of those allowed regularly inside the cave, who would have to stop visiting the cave for a time, as he would be saturated with intoxicating dreams about the animals in the paintings, revealing the contagious character of images (see Roman 2014: 64). We can magnify the same many times for those who saw them for the first time – or who made them. If Lascaux was rightfully compared to the Sistine Chapel, Chauvet, not simply due to its age, but due to its sheer character lies beyond any parallel – it is truly incommensurable.

The making of Chauvet

These paintings were made for people to 'use' them; to visit them, in order to have the same kind of experiences we now have if we take the trouble and visit the painted caves – not Chauvet, which cannot be visited, but those others that can be accessed. In one basic sense, these experiences are fundamentally comparable, equivalent.[6] The ideas of Bataille concerning the formative power of such experiences are fundamental, confirmed by the experiences of discoverers and experts, discussed above. The paintings of the most important caves, the experience of visiting their world, emit and transmit a coherent, unique and complex vision of the world, through a set of emotional charges. There can be no doubt that the paintings were made to render eternal such a feeling – to consolidate this way of perceiving and make it available to all future visitors; to help them appropriate and understand this way of seeing the world, and to act accordingly. The heart of this vision is an ode to the beauty of living – the enormous emotional charge present in the void.

The fact that the Chauvet paintings exist, that they were made at that particular moment in history, at an almost unbelievably remote time, and the manner in which they exist, confirm the perhaps metaphorical, perhaps more 'real' assessment of Bataille concerning their character as a miracle. All these data, in the etymological sense of being 'given', genuine *gifts*, mean at least four different things.

To begin with, and most importantly, they exude a royal vision of the world, or a mode of experiencing the world. This vision is transmitted to all who perceive and experience such images, and not only in Chauvet but in all the other prehistoric caves which contain works of art of similar character and quality; and which is so difficult, if not impossible, to put into words. The central issue, beyond trying to capture the exact nature of personal experience, is not simply the 'realism' – rather 'recognisability' – or even 'beauty' – of the images, rather the kind of overwhelming affirmation of life, and the world, that transpires through them. The vision of the world thus rendered evident can only be compared to the most ultimate yes-saying and world-affirmation characteristic of Nietzsche's *Zarathustra*, and so it is not accidental that it was a French follower of Nietzsche, Georges Bataille, who attempted – through Lascaux – to capture the character of this vision of the world as a kind of 'miracle'. However, instead of using highly charged and perhaps misleading expressions, we can rather talk about a quiet serenity, a sense of certainty, a higher feeling exuding contentment with reality that emanates from the experience of beholding these images. There is hardly any frightening image in the caves; even the way dangerous carnivores are depicted combines a sweetness of observation, up to minute details, with capturing the graceful beauty of these animals: we are admiring them, not getting afraid from them. The decisive feature of Chauvet paintings, valid for the entire period of cave art, is that people living at that time were capable of having such a vision of the world. We do not know anything about the 'social' dimensions behind such a vision, who gained it, when and why, and how many people acquired or shared it, only that it evidently existed, as such 'social' dimensions did not then matter; and that those people who had developed or acquired such a vision not simply were not 'primitive' in any evolutionist sense of the word, but rather were exactly *primitive* in the literal, etymological sense, being primary and primordial, *the* firsts, original and foundational, way ahead of us, moderns, so much so that we are hardly able to comprehend and express the vision of the world which they not only possessed, but were able to preserve and transmit, for tens of thousands of years.

This is where we reach the second of our four basic points. The people who had, or acquired, such a positive and life-affirming vision of life eventually also gained the idea of representing it, making it available for others by bringing this into presence, oblivious of the fact that this implied transgression. Transgression, following Foucault (1977: 34), not simply negates the limit but affirms limitlessness, or liminality, the infinite into which it leaps and thus opens this zone to existence for the first time. Chauvet cave was seat and witness of this representation, thus also transgression, as for the first time in human history, man's actions were addressed to the void in such a monumental and grandiose level: it was 'a way of recomposing its empty form, its absence', as 'all of our actions are addressed to this absence in a profanation which at once identifies it, dissipates it, exhausts itself in it, and restores it to the empty purity of its transgression' (30–1). At Chauvet transgression occurred, which recomposed the empty form of the void, artists projected into it their own desires and hopes. Thus, as 'this existence is both so pure and so complicated, it must be detached from its questionable association to ethics . . . it must be liberated from the scandalous or subversive, that is, from anything aroused from negative associations' (35). It had to be a way of registering that at the same time was capable of rendering the vision alive, real and by such animation helping to transmit this experience.[7] It thus had to possess a coincidence of three aspects: the first is registering or recording, leaving a trace, and a kind of trace that would never disappear, becoming *permanent*; furthermore, a registering that did not simply make a copy, a shadow or a dead, mechanical account of this vision, but that at the same time managed to render such a vision alive; and finally, third, which did not simply evoke this vision, but was able to make experiencing the vision permanent, thus teaching this vision in feeling for life – teaching by making an indelible mark – and not by forcefully and trick-fully stamping those receiving this vision-message, but by having them participate in and share the joy of having for their entire life this mode of seeing their reality. Thus, our distant ancestors not only had a powerful and joyful vision of their reality, but were concerned with rendering permanently accessible the eternal perpetuation of such a vision.

Here we reach the third point: they found a quite singular and unique way of rendering permanent registering and transmission jointly possible: on the walls of caves, deeply under the ground. The solution was truly striking, extraordinary, genial – when dealing with the phenomenon of Palaeolithic cave art, one is repeatedly faced with the impossibility of expressing in words the character, modality and amount of experience and wonder – as this mode truly solved, with a single masterstroke, all concerns, offering the best possible solution: underground on cave walls the paintings were well sheltered, away from the potentially corrosive impact of all kind of forces (weather, climate, animals, bacteria, other people), while at the same time, with their darkness and silence, offering the best possible environment for evoking and thus transmitting the emotional charge literally embodied and captured in the images, by transforming caves into artificial wombs. Even further, and in a manner that will require further efforts at understanding, apart from the concrete conditions in which the images eventually could be seen and experienced, the road of access itself contributed to the character of the experience, as visitors first had to walk a long way, certainly often hundreds of kilometres, to reach the caves; and then walk, occasionally hundreds of metres, to come into the presence of the paintings: had to walk into this womb that became impregnated by them; or, symbolically and literally, into the void. Such efforts necessary to reach the destination, to come to the presence of the images were not yet part of a special, trick-ful ordeal, but rather a way in which the overwhelming emotional charge could become experienced and appropriated forever, unforgettably. The difficulty of reaching the images, while contributing to their physical preservation, at the same time enhanced and rendered possible their proper experiencing.

Finally, and fourth, apart from having such a unique, singularly powerful and valuable vision of the world, gaining the idea of transmitting it, and conceiving the evidently best possible way to do so, these people at the same time were also able to execute their ideas, by painting images that artists would not equal until the Renaissance.

The four points, discussed separately above, represent an effort to comprehend how these images could have become possible. But they do not imply that the four concerns were separate, results of conscious, purposeful, sequential deliberation. The phenomenon of cave paintings evidently and profoundly defies scientific identification. The problem can be compared to the origins of language – to identify a sound, or a visual mark, as a meaningful sign, the 'representation' of something, we must have an idea about language as such, as a whole – a single sign cannot create 'language'. Something emerged, suddenly, evidently out of nothing – and clearly out of the void. This is the point we now have to explore in some detail.

The void and its enormous emotional charges: the problem of incommensurability

We know about the vision of the world as expressed by Chauvet or Lascaux because the paintings are still there; anybody who gets a chance can go and see them. We therefore tend to assume that this vision emerged more or less in the moment when the first such pictures were depicted. If this is so, then this state of mind is probably a consequence of the encounter between Neanderthal man and *Homo sapiens*. However, we do not know for sure that this is the case – maybe the vision was already carried by Neanderthal culture and here we only witness a recording of that vision, depicted by others than the original bearers.

At any rate, what we do know now is that this vision soon developed a next copy, dare to say counter-ideology, or a counter-memory (Foucault 1977), expressed most prominently in the Shaft Scene of Lascaux. This is due to the danger inherent in any work of art, which has been formulated with particular zeal by Plato, and is thus at the very heart of philosophy. Any work of art is a copy (art as artificiality) – not simply the imitation of the real, but the copy of the original 'model' or *eidos* of which objects of the real world are themselves copies. Thus, in one sense they are particularly close to the 'real' thing; but on the other hand are subject to infinite imitation, thus giving rise to the possibility of a corruption or alteration of the real – corruption, if the images are repeated endlessly, but of ever lower quality; and alteration, if the images start to develop a life of their own and produce unprecedented and unreal combinations, down into a totally unreal world.

The single exception of human images in Chauvet is not due to similarity with the 'sorcerer' images of the Gabillou or Trois Frères caves, but rather evokes a subtle allusion to the creation of the world – very different from both the physical violence and unbounded imagination unleashed by Pergouset around this theme (see Chapter 5). It also confirms a key and still valid insight of Leroi-Gourhan, his identification of the bison with the female (rather motherly) 'principle'.

The world-vision of Chauvet or Lascaux was immortalised in hundreds of other painted caves. However, many caves also contained engravings on the walls, or on various objects, that express a quite different feeling of the world, and that can be considered as indeed fearful, corrupt or altered images. These images, to be discussed in Chapter 5, are from a number of different places; they are single occurrences or outliers, of which the most important is the Shaft Scene of Lascaux (discussed in Horvath 2013a: 25–35, and Szakolczai 2017b: 160–6). However, there was one particular cave where, at a unique place, such imaginary figures became dominant. This is Pergouset cave, in particular its Room IV, containing the 'monsters of Pergouset', which can be considered as the possible archetype of all the rest.

Notes

1 We cannot enter here into the complex issue of the parallels between rock-art and shamanism. We can only signal our view that if the point is understood in the proper, genealogical sense, considering contemporary forms of shamanism as extremely late, decayed and corrupted form of practices that existed in Palaeolithic times, and not as 'models' by which the past can be understood, and, in particular, if we accept that the artificial stimulants

used by modern shamans, and similar figures, are particularly corrupted modalities of this 'spirituality', then the parallels stand.

2 In the book we will systematically only use 'BC' and not 'BP' dating. The problem is not simply that the shift from the standard 'BC' to 'BP' dating is modernist ideology, absurdly raising the ever-changing 'present' into a stable omphalos of the world, 'present' often being identified with 1950, thus placing the darkest year of Stalinism and the Cold War into the 'centre' of world history, but that the distinction between uncalibrated and cali-brated BP dating is a source of permanent confusion. Given that uncalibrated results are always given in 'BP', archaeologists should have *then* calibrated all data into the universally intelligible, traditional 'BC' form. Instead, as a 'politically correct' solution, matters became hopelessly confused with the unnecessary addition of a third, middle, 'liminal', calibrated BP date.

3 See the Smithsonian website, http://humanorigins.si.edu/evidence/behavior/footprints/laetoli-footprint-trails, accessed 10 February 2017.

4 The main findings of Atapuerca are in a new museum in Burgos, built mostly to house these discoveries.

5 On the significance of handaxe, see also Ingold (2013: 33–45).

6 See Voegelin (1990) on the equivalence of experiences.

7 This point is discussed extensively by Montelle (2009) and Azéma (2011), in comparing Palaeolithic art to modern theatre and cinema.

5

PERGOUSET

The cave of monsters, and its aftermath

> I don't know how they can succeed when they're full of so many monstrous absurdities, because the soul can only take delight in the beauty and harmony that it sees or contemplates in what the eyes or the imagination places before it, and nothing that contains ugliness or disorder can give us any pleasure.
>
> *Cervantes,* Don Quixote *(2000: 440)*

Pergouset cave and its monsters

The cave, located in the Lot region (locally the region is called Quercy), about a 100 km south of Dordogne, was discovered in 1961, but knowledge of and awareness about it are still minimal. This is for two simple reasons. First, the cave only contains engravings, not paintings, and interest in Palaeolithic art, for a very good reason, focuses on paintings. Second, access to the part containing the engravings is extremely difficult, rendering it impossible to enter not simply for visitors, but anyone except most expert speleologists.

As a quite striking coincidence, the significance of the cave only became evident in the middle of the 1990s, when Chauvet and Göbekli Tepe were discovered, and when the more interesting findings in Atapuerca became widely known. As engravings inside a cave cannot be dated, only guesses were made about the age of the images until in 1996, in a place that so far had escaped attention (in a cliff cornice and covered by a layer of silt clod, about 40 cms under Panel I), pieces of charcoal were found. When the laboratories delivered the dating, experts just could not believe what they were told, as the pieces of wood were burned 32,850 (+−520) years ago (Lorblanchet 2001: 35, 167).[1] The 'awakening was brutal', as experts were suddenly thrown outside the 'comfortable chronologies' of Breuil and Leroi-Gourhan, just as it happened, contemporaneously, with Chauvet cave (167).[2]

To understand properly the significance of this dating, we again need to review matters of context. To start with, such a remote date was so astonishing as the character of the images, especially in the first three of the four rooms, were closest to the later Magdalenian, thus were thought to have been made about 15 to 12,000 years ago. In fact, there are two nearby painted caves: Pech-Merle, one of the most important prehistoric caves, with the famous dotted horses, partly dated to 20–25,000 years ago, and Sainte-Eulalie, dated to the late Magdalenian (170). While the images of the first three rooms are closer in style to the paintings at Sainte-Eulalie, Pech-Merle also contains a number of fearfully 'fantastic' images.

To move further, it is now necessary to give a somewhat detailed overview of the context and character of the cave as, according to Lorblanchet, its natural features were central for the way it developed into a 'secret sanctuary'.

The cave in context

To start with, the cave has a particular link to water (148). It was situated in-between, at a time even literally connecting, two different sources of water: the river Lot, of whose bank the opening of the cave is, and which still periodically floods it (Lorblanchet and Sieveking 1997: 37); and an underground river which is reached at the end of the cave, of which the cave was an overflow, the water of which occasionally still surges into the cave. Note that no significant change took place in the physical features of the cave over the tens of thousands of years separating us from its first human users (Lorblanchet 2001: 37, 148).

Apart from the dangers of flooding, on both ends, access to the inside of the cave, containing the engravings, and in particular the last, fourth room, containing the 'monsters', was particularly difficult. From the entrance on the river bank one has to crawl for about 80 metres to reach the first figures, where it is still not possible to stand up, and another 20 metres to arrive at the fourth and last 'room', where in some areas a small person could stand (Lorblanchet 2001: 149; Lorblanchet and Sieveking 1997: 37).[3] Thus, as Ann Sieveking argues, 'it must have been not only arduous but terrifying to penetrate the mud-choked passage – low, constricted and, in places, steep or plunging – equipped only with a primitive lamp which could easily blow out in the prevailing draught. One can imagine that the Palaeolithic explorers crawled into Room IV half terrified, half triumphant at their achievement in reaching such a deeply hidden gallery' (in Lorblanchet and Sieveking 1997: 53).[4]

Room IV, or the monster bestiary

Room IV is the culmination of engravings. The cave continues for another 70 metres, where it joins the underground river; but beyond the rooms there are only few and insignificant marks on the wall. This room, however, is unique and striking both due to its physical characteristics and the features of the decoration – two aspects that are closely intertwined. The previous three rooms contain a number of engraved figures, several of which are of considerable qualities, but not beyond standard late Magdalenian caves.

Room IV is in a bend of the cave where the flat ceiling is higher than anywhere before or after, but is sloping downward, with a niche on the right, in the curve, while continuation on the left is partially hidden behind the bend, creating '[t]he impression . . . of a sloping screen with possible entrances, or exits, on either side' (Lorblanchet and Sieveking 1997: 38). The walls are also relatively straight and flat, though full of cracks, rendering the engravings even more difficult to perceive, while the character of the wall, with natural concavities, depression and fractures, in particular a kind of wall-seat or shoulder, offers frames for the engravings. The artist made full use of such natural structuring devices, thus engravings can be divided into 12 panels,[5] starting from the right-hand wall, moving in a circle, including the sloping ceiling, and returning on the left side wall at the 'entrance'. Even more strikingly, and reinforcing the homogeneity of decorations, the starting and ending panels are purely geometrical, containing both curved and zigzag lines that partly follow natural fractures, and partly are situated between two such fractures, which seems to imply a then commonly shared meaning, like a 'V' sign in Panel I (43, 50–1). The most important panels containing the monsters[6] are on the sloping ceiling wall, thus to see them, from the right to the left, which is the supposed order in which they were engraved, one has to advance inside the cave, a move during which one can perceive that on the right side there is no further cavity, only a niche, while on the left the continuation of the cave opens up.

Panels IV to VII contain a series of striking 'monsters' that progress, sometimes within single panels, towards increasing stylisation and incompleteness (Lorblanchet and Sieveking 1997: 45–8; Lorblanchet 2001: 151). While 'monsters' can also be found in other caves, their numbers and density in Room IV make Pergouset unique (Lorblanchet 2001: 161). As a further singular feature, some monsters are linked by lines, establishing a relationship between them. Some of the animals can easily be identified, while others are more controversial. Where Leroi-Gourhan, who only spent a short time there, perceived the head of a bison, Lorblanchet now identifies a heron; and the bison tails Leroi-Gourhan saw everywhere, due to his theoretical effort to identify the female and the bison, are now considered as not being there (Lorblanchet and Sieveking 1997: 40, 42). However, none of the animals are fully and realistically designed; thus, a doe might have an elegant head, but a disproportionately long neck, a clumsy body and a completely different tail (38). Human and animal features are mixed, with distinction often being difficult – and it must have been even more difficult for anyone inside the cave, *then*. There are heads without body, or bodies without head; or altogether imaginary figures that combine beaks and horns in ways that do not appear in nature, and that must have been particularly scary and terrifying then and there (see for example the head in Panel V; 46). The long, swan-like necks of cervids or horses are a particular trademark of the decoration, remarkable also because of their affinity with the similarly curved geometric lines, present in the opening and closing panels, which – among other things – call attention to the manner in which the design and natural features of the walls are closely integrated.

The most striking image, no doubt, is the last figurative image, on Panel X, thus back to the starting point (49). It is a headless man, with a disproportionate upper body and very small but well-designed legs, between which there is a long and sagging penis. It is also just facing the first panel containing monsters, Panel II, with the almost realistic, only slightly exaggerated horse, the start of the journey moving from the realistic to the unreal (see Lorblanchet 2001: 103, 106–7). The shape of the neck recalls a protuberance on a fox-like image in Panel V (Lorblanchet and Sieveking 1997: 40, 49), which is particularly striking, given the absence of foxes in Palaeolithic cave art; and also because it is just under the heron-like image, thus establishing a link between fox-like and bird-like creatures, central for the imagery of Göbekli and Çatalhöyük. Apart from his head, the image also lacks any extremities of hands and feet, thus being without *any limits*, while the two arms, without hands, are drawn close to each other and extended in a manner that recalls praying figures, characteristic of Egyptian paintings (49), but also the Tassili prayers of the Round Head period (see Chapter 9). The hands of this last figurative Panel furthermore point back, towards the further recesses of the cave, or the void.

Before following the explorers further in their interpretation of this stunning and unique decoration, some comments of a methodological order must be made. To start with, Lorblanchet spent several decades in visiting and reflecting upon the cave, thus his ideas offer an indispensable starting point, and in some sense an unsurpassable horizon. Leroi-Gourhan's 1983 attempt at an interpretation, while containing important insights, was stranded due to it being limited to fitting the findings into his own, preconceived intellectual schemes. However, on the other hand, no matter how unique the knowledge Lorblanchet gained about Pergouset cave, and the caves of the entire region, his knowledge is also limited by the baggage of his own conceptual framework. Here it is particularly relevant to take into account what he could have meant by 'shamanism', and by the pretence of a purely scientific approach, relying solely on archaeological proofs, and not using a poetic imagination (Lorblanchet 2001: 162–3), especially given his spectacular reversal concerning the relevance of shamanism for understanding the cave decoration.

On the one hand, the issue seems to be to connect shamanism exclusively to relatively modern practices, studied by anthropologists, and especially the taking of artificial stimulants, like drugs, plants and mushrooms, to produce 'altered states of consciousness'. It is certainly a valid point that it is unlikely for someone, under the effect of any kind of stimulants, to undertake with any success the extremely arduous journey of descending into that cave. But this does not mean that we therefore must affirm 'rationality' and 'scientific objectivity' as the starting point of our understanding. On the other hand, as Clottes (2002) made it clear in his otherwise positive review of the book, the interpretation offered by Lorblanchet, beyond and outside the 'shamanistic' hypothesis, is by no means 'objective' and 'scientific' – and it is all the better for being so as, concerning something like the 'monsters of Pergouset', the call for 'scientific objectivity' is just an ideological pretence.

'Scientifically', as this is understood today, concerning repeated experiments, hypothesis testing and the like, we can say *nothing* meaningful about the cave. We must try to attempt to make sense of the data, the 'given' that we possess, to the best of our abilities, bringing in as much evidence, and theoretical perspectives, as we can possibly muster – knowing well that our efforts must be recognised by our peers, in the academic – rather than 'scientific' – community, but also that attempts that at one point are considered extravagant, bordering on lunacy, might be judged differently as time passes. Lorblanchet's analysis is interesting exactly because it went way beyond the narrow limits of 'scientific objectivity'.

Returning to the images, the first point concerns a puzzle, and tension, between the attempt to interpret the cave in its wholeness, as a singular entity, and the bringing in of a comparative perspective – a dilemma central for any historical or anthropological analysis. On the one hand, at the end of his long-term famil-iarisation of the cave Lorblanchet came to the realisation that the decorations, at least in Room IV, given its homogeneity, were the product of a single hand and mind, perhaps with one or more helpers, keeping light and assisting in return (Lorblanchet and Sieveking 1997: 42, 49, 53). All the engravings there were done at one and the same time, starting from the right and ending at the left, with the plan of the entire programme being conceived in advance – thus, starting and end-ing with geometric signs, as if offering a frame.[7]

Here, we are still fully inside the 'rationalistic' paradigm, even excessively so, with the idea of a single mastermind behind the entire decoration, preparing everything mentally beforehand. However, at the same time, the artist also made use of even minute cracks and protuberances on the walls, using them as eyes or external shapes, thus performing the decoration being fully immersed in the environment. There was therefore a kind of mutual attuning between man and nature, but how and why in this dark and not easily accessible place? In their article Lorblanchet and Sieveking, evidently together, made a further step, and in line with anthropological studies of rock-art argued through analogy that for such artists the rocks and walls themselves might be 'eloquent', with the wall being 'as meaningful a ritual element as the paint', where 'paintings appear to enter and leave cracks in the wall, are folded into concave right angles, start from convex edges and are fitted into hollows' (49, 52).[8] In her section Ann Sieveking goes a step further and ventures to argue that the central target of ritualistic meaning was the act of creating the images, and not their display; and their visitation might have been extremely infrequent (53).

While the decoration of Room IV is unique, similar motifs do appear in other caves, though they are very few in number (overall, there are fewer than fifty such examples; see Palacio-Pérez and Ruiz Redondo 2014: 259), and restricted to a very few caves. There is also a recurrence of motifs, for example the long and narrow neck. Thus, while the cave may have been only rarely visited, over the centuries and millennia it evidently exerted a considerable impact.

The idea of these images being more important than their display is extremely interesting, but one must be much more specific concerning the exact meaning of such a statement. In our view, this can be done from the perspective of Plato's philosophy, in particular the problem of Not-Being, as exposed in the *Sophist*, which at the same time helps to illuminate Plato's concern with leaving the cave, in the *Republic*. Through Plato, the idea of such designs indeed represented an alteration in the very order of reality, by creating, evidently for the first time, purely imaginary creatures, thus perverting everything that was done before, making Not-Being manifest. Chauvet already represented transgression, as images were without concrete presence; the implications of transgression were brought out openly in Pergouset.

Chauvet was as open and accessible as it was possible, where anybody, even from a long distance, could easily find the opening of the cave above the big arch cut into the hill by the river and then walk into the cave. The entrance of Pergouset was much less visible; however, more importantly, it was all but impossible to reach the rooms deep inside the cave. Thus, for all purposes, the cave was hidden, secret, and its visit was initiatory for the purpose of transformation. Even further, it was probably even a *first* initiation rite, as the visiting of Chauvet did not require such acts; and also helpful for distinguishing rites of passage, which always have a direct collective, public aspect from initiation rites which are more individualistic and might develop a closed, secret character. Here the difference in emphasis between van Gennep and Turner is helpful. For van Gennep, the most characteristic rites of passage were mortuary rituals, and were thus connected to the very order of life. Victor Turner, however, shifted attention to initiation rites, in particular the rites by which young people were integrated as adults into the community. The nature of Pergouset precludes such rituals; it is much more probable that such an initiation, through a *secret* sanctuary, was reserved for people who had special connections with the *void*.

Perhaps one can take a further step by investigating the connections between the 'secret' and the 'sacred' – a link that is not etymological, yet goes back quite a time. The central point concerns the meaning of 'sacred' as 'setting something apart' – a concern already discussed by Durkheim and Eliade in their well-known books on the sacred and the profane, but given a renewed and quite significant discussion by Agamben (1998). For Durkheim and Eliade, the idea is somehow taken as evident, perhaps due to their own background and the resulting acceptance as 'natural' of the world vision characteristic of two special priesthoods, the Levitic and the Brahmanic; but, as Agamben helps us realise, it is by no means so. Whatever is truly divine is connected to contentment, and thus should be easily accessible to anybody, and not the preliminary concern, and property, of certain people who 'set it apart' after they themselves 'set themselves apart'. *This* is the true problem of the sacred, the contrast with the saint and the holy, grace and mercy, and not the contrast with the 'material' or the 'profane', as the idea of the sacred as something to be 'set apart' is indeed problematic.

This can receive further support from the work of Mary Douglas (1970) on purity and danger. According to this, what is set apart in any human community is not the sacred, but rather dirt – something that is truly 'out of place'. In fact, the equation can even be reversed, and from this Douglasian perspective anything that is out of place, due to this fact, becomes dirt, whether it is dirty or not in the usual sense of the term. Pergouset cave and its monster images are clearly 'out of place', and in several senses: they are not corresponding to anything we can find in contentment. Even further, accessing them also implies a direct involvement with dirt, due to the need for crawling for a long time literally in the mud. Thus, through Durkheim and Eliade, but especially through Agamben and Douglas, we can argue that the novelty represented by the Pergouset monster bestiary is the sinister result of transgression.[9]

A myth of creation?

At a first level, while the engravings in the caves were transgressive, they were dedicated to the 'sources of life' (Lorblanchet 2001: 154). Such sources include the water, omnipresent in and for the cave, and the very shape and character of the cave, which recalls the womb, and thus becomes, symbolically, a giant womb of nature. Here, in this particular cave, in the engravings this is expressed in three vulvas (or rather female sexes; see Clottes 2002: 164), which are both extremely realistic and constitute a sequence. One, deep inside the cave, is schematic and incomplete; the middle one belongs to a young woman, probably at the early stage of pregnancy; while the third, close to the entrance, indicates several completed deliveries (Lorblanchet 2001: 154; see also 75, 166). More significantly, this last incorporates a hole of the wall, thus directly linking emptiness and void with the source of life. Finally, the entire cave is 'a universe haunted by creatures, sometimes discreet, sometimes realist and detailed, dissimulated in the rock and in the obscurity of the gallery' (154), thus manifesting the same connection in a grotesque way between animals, animation, life and contentment that is at the centre of the vision of the world contained in Chauvet and Lascaux.

   This, however, is only a first step, as Pergouset goes further, much further; in fact, way too far. The second step concerns a *mythology* of origins (163, 182), which is quite different from a simple capturing of the sources of life. It is a mythology of origins, as it is elaborated into something like a narrative system; a narration that is concerned not simply by presenting the source of life through nature, but extends such ideas into a *speculation* about the *origins* of life. Such a myth of origins is thus identical to a 'myth of creation' (154); or a 'theory about the creation of the world' (165). It is in this sense that Marc Azéma (2011: 54) also argues that the cave itself became a symbol, the 'original matrix (*matrice originelle*)' of the world, as the source of all living beings.[10] Thus we are transported beyond life and the celebration of its sources to something very much removed to it – literally infinitely removed, as it implies a trip back to the original nothingness, the 'darkness (*ténèbres*) of primordial chaos' (Lorblanchet 2001: 182; see also 161), with the waters surrounding the cave transmogrified into the 'ammoniac liquid' of creation (182).

   This, of course, is purely hypothetical, but this is the hypothesis of Lorblanchet. It also assumes something similarly hypothetical, which is the understanding that the designer of Room IV had, perhaps as far back as 33,000 years ago; hypothetical in the sense that how could he have known about the original chaos – except if he received such knowledge as a revelation from somewhere – and who are we to know what did he know and how? So we might be allowed to add a further layer of hypothesis, after the intuition about the sources of life, the mythology of origins and the mythology concerning the creation of life, a hypothetical *substitution* of the designer as a creator – a pretence to create new figures, thus the pretence of *becoming* a joint creator of the world. Such pretence is visible in the most important novelty of the cave, the invention of *metamorphosis*. In Chauvet, just as later in Lascaux or Altamira, animals were not simply realistic but evocative: their artists did not want to 'represent' an animal as it was; rather, they wanted viewers to realise how they can assimilate themselves with the hauntingly beautiful life and nature. They rarely mixed creatures, altering their features, as they no doubt would have considered such an alteration at once horrible and a terrifying offence. The designer of Pergouset thought differently, and 'offered all kinds of transitions and graphic games between human and animal species' (Lorblanchet 2001: 161), thus turning the room into the invention of metamorphosis. We, children of modernity, are bound to consider this as an ode to human inventiveness. But it isn't: it is rather a first step towards technology, the alteration and destruction of nature (Horvath 2015); the creation of an unreality which for previous generations might have been the 'light cloak' to take on as a game, but in which we are now forced to live, as inside an 'iron cage' or casing, giving a Borkenau-Heidegger-Mumfordian interpretation to the ideas of Max Weber.

The pretence of this cave was and is absurd, as swan-necked horses do not exist. Such pretence, however, involved a price, even a dual price, both well visible in the images. The first price is a loss of reality, and a slow rise of fearfulness. The images document a gradual, sequential loss of reality that was different from, and more serious than, the simple assumption of substances producing an altered state of consciousness. Its most serious effect was on the one who made the designs, and which was certainly repeated by those who visited the cave as the source of secret, initiatory knowledge: depersonalisation or falling into the general. Here again Lorblanchet is most perceptive, though does not seem to grasp the full significance of his recognition. Such depersonalisation is captured in some of the most important designs of the cave, headless (acephalous) figures. There are four animals without heads, of which one, a doe, is particularly interesting, as its head is replaced by a symbol, a triangle, which must have had a concrete meaning at that time (Lorblanchet 2001: 93, 163).

The idea perhaps might be taken to a further step and applied to the similarly headless (male) figure that closes the monster bestiary. For Lorblanchet (2001: 166), the image does not simply show a lack, the absence of a head, but rather a 'deliberate will *not* to represent [emphasis added]', a refusal of personalisation. It is indeed a sign of depersonalisation, and – as the last image – perhaps an *ultimate* such sign: a documentation of how the author of the images himself lost his own concrete character in the undertaking. In this sense, it can thus be considered as a most paradoxical first self-image: not the self-representation of the artist as 'pure' artist, an artist who struggled to understand the meaning of art, and of self-portrait, as Velazquez, Tiepolo or Picasso, or only the greatest artists, would do later;[11] and who perhaps understood that an artist can only depict himself as being without a head – as the artist, the more they try to become inventive, and thus personal, the more they deconstruct and thus depersonalise everything around themselves, emptying it of meaning, ultimately including even themself. This is because something else also appears in artistic activity: all human personality disappears there, as dissolved into the void. In other words, the void empties everything, swallowing up or absorbing the persons, generating a desire to become at one with the void. The artist who expressed themself becomes exposed, as if naked, deprived of any stability and background. This might culminate in a pure state of suffering: solitude, hopelessness, distrust; a process of becoming a demon.

From this perspective, a new interpretation can be given of the extending, praying hands of the acephalous image: it is the artist themself who is praying to the void, the darkness behind the end of the room; without their legs, as they stopped walking, only crawled up to the room; without their hands, as they even stopped engraving, having finished the work; and without their head, as in the act of artificial creation, losing the ground, they had lost their personality. It was thus a genuine, though thrice-vain act of self-sacrifice: first, because it was a product of hubris, or vanity; second, because it did not lead to anything worthwhile as a result, not a new created world or even a new life, which any human couple can produce, not by setting themselves apart, but rather uniting in genuine, burning desire, only a series of imaginary figures that one can perceive if one is obstinate enough, just as the first artist, to bring themselves into the room; and finally, because vanity itself is nothing but emptiness, or the void, even etymologically.[12]

Extending hubris into water, after fire

Taking a step beyond Lorblanchet's identification of the cave as depicting a creation myth, we can connect it to the myth of Prometheus. That myth was about the origins of the human mastery of fire; this cave, through its focus on water, pretends something even more, an account about the origins of the world, while also pretending to make humans equal to god, through their ability to create and manipulate images. Traces of this myth can be followed up to the origins of philosophy, as Thales, the 'first philosopher', much connected to Chaldean astronomy, considered water as the origin of all things, while the only surviving aphorism of Anaximander, 'second philosopher' and his direct follower, is about the original chaos (*apeiron*).

Prometheus was punished for hubris, and hubris or arrogant excess accompanies the Pergouset bestiary at every level. It is a hubristic excess to go into such a cave, crawling a hundred metres to depict some images which, as if to make an asset out of a liability, claim to compete with the creator of the world. It is hubristic because such excess effort is unnecessary, as images can be depicted under much different conditions; it is hubristic, furthermore, as it involves a struggle with mud: men were 'created' to walk on the ground and not to crawl in mud under it. We are humans to make efforts, but by keeping balance and not exaggerating them. The idea that something requiring *more* effort is by definition better is quite misleading, a first step on the long, and indeed infinite, road of hubris: as hubris implies the trespassing of limits, and once such a process started, there is no stopping point, as the measure itself is lost. This is also identical to the etymological root of evil, 'exceeding due limits' (Onions 1966: 332), as hubris is indeed evil, which the Greeks again knew so well (Gernet 2001). Somebody who commits a crime or a sin can be punished, and thus might redeem the act, but hubris is worse than trespassing the law: it is a basic character fault; whoever is hubristic is beyond repair.

Excess, or hubris, the drive to extremes, can be perceived in the entire monster bestiary project. At the start the same animals were depicted as in any other cave. Then only a minor change was introduced, subtly followed by further and further 'innovative' displacements, moving gradually away from reality, eventually arriving at the shocking and the terrifying.

Trickster metamorphoses in the Palaeolithic

The centrality of void for cave art and its character is best expressed by engravings. While painting and engraving both imply a certain subversion, they do this with a stunning difference. This difference resides in the character of the artist, as expressed in the different ways they work on the material: a painter with his colorants adds something to the surface of the rock wall, while an engraver takes something away by scratching into the rock, literally generating a void. The first is inspired, driven by Platonic madness, while the second is, at least originally and archetypically, a thief and robber, close to the Sophist, according to Plato, who is keen to take away and not to give, and to sit on and hide whatever he managed to acquire.[13] The paintings are not destructive, riotous, as a lot of the engravings are, as it will be presented now, through Palaeolithic images of the trickster figure. The focus on subversion, of divesting someone of character, offers a new theoretical perspective in the social sciences, an approach integrating insights from anthropology and archaeology. Such an approach, arguably, is crucial, as its focus on origins helps to locate the particular dynamics of subversive practices. This starts by contacting the void, then a set of acts performed to awaken the void, forcing a response from it, and then, by being attuned to the response of the void, releasing the self and giving a place for the void inside the self in a specific manner. Perhaps the term 'trickster' itself is inadequate when applied to a period before its conceptualisation, but this could not imply the denial of the actual existence of similar phenomena; thus we will use the anthropological term, as we can't find anything better (Plato's word *gôes* is just as good). In prehistoric settings, a significant amount of specific and even specialised knowledge had been generated concerning the subversive trickster. The aim of this section is to analyse the untimely appearance of subversiveness through the anthropological figure of the trickster.[14]

The decisive element in the trickster phenomenon is that it is timeless and unchanging. Its central points are subversiveness and the infinite, roll-over continuity of this mode of action. Those things are infinite whose limits are dissolved and who become at one or united with something else, whose individual arrangement and position are modified into another entity. Once started, such a process of exchange, substitution or mutual metamorphosis will go on forever. This particular procedure generates change, though it also releases self-defensive energies, as viewers become touched by the 'irresistibility' of the trickster, and nothing stands in the way of merging into each other.

The trickster is the embodiment of a subversive power or soul-fetching (Hyde 1999; Radin 1972). In his activities, paraphrasing Goethe's *Faust*, business, warfare and piracy cannot be separated from each other, as was already evident in the Greek Hermes. In a way, the trickster of the void is itself the incorporeal, infinite lust for consuming limits. When assessing the relationship of the void to this framework of subversiveness, the works of Aristotle offer particular help. According to him, it is the void that things touch when getting into contact with each other, following Plato who denies that the absolute void exists (Aristotle 1955: 325b29–34), and so become continuous in a way that the void offers no resistance at all anymore: there is 'nothing of the same nature as themselves between them' (Aristotle 1957, 231a23). Concrete individual behaviour, temper, solid, characteristic emotional and mental states are all lost due to the trickster touch and its dissolving of boundaries, and now the disturbed character itself becomes a trickster, who now seduces other characters, perpetuating the game of subversion.

The trickster's presence jointly produces feelings and experiences that are usually opposite: one is paralysis or palsy, the inability to do anything, a resignation to fate; the other a frenetic search for a model that would solve this crisis, soothing the aching feelings. The latter state itself has two opposite animating forces: rational thinking, understood as an intensive purpose-oriented activity of the mind; and imitation, where suggestions that seem to offer a way out can be suddenly followed, alongside a spiral, by an ever increasing number of individuals. These two are connected by the mind being not simply the seat of rational thought, but a machine to produce images, a source of imitation, even etymologically. The presence of the trickster drastically changes the personality and identity of those getting in touch with it (Horvath 2013a). It creates a situation of tension and threat, where one's sense of security quickly, almost instantaneously evaporates. One can no longer rely on one's own qualities (this is what can be called a character), and instead trusts outside structures and personally unknown but convincing-looking 'others', thus in mere objects and sheer numbers, and then, as a compensatory mechanism, attempts to impose this presumed security on others, usually with the help of violence. This is the process that we will describe under 'settlement' in the following chapters. Concrete characters became less and less important, while external goals and desires become dominating. According to Girard (1977), this logic of subordinating the concrete for something else became codified in sacrificial rituals; however, in his focus on the scapegoat Girard does not pay proper attention to trickster, even though for Radin (1972) trickster is the sacrificer. This will gain a crucial importance some thousand years later in Neolithic settings.

Transformation of character: subversiveness

The trickster's artefacts are products of a curious method, which result in an exponential growth, building and rebuilding the elements of reality, activating them and even stirring them up – making them ever more distant from the original. If we say, paraphrasing the German political scientist Heinrich Popitz (2014), that building worlds for others is an artificiality, then this is a modification of what is naturally given, and so fabricating artefacts adds to the previous state of the world an imitated modality, an altered, expanding force which has no natural boundaries, which lacks subjects that are distinct from itself. In this way, we can understand how this artefact in turn exists only as a copy, something that was lifted from its original form and place, and which now became a subject on its own: a transformed being (Horvath, forthcoming). This is the process of subversion: getting the substance and diverting the sensations of concrete persons to another purpose, different from the original, concrete one, while keeping the copy of the form. As a banal example, one can mention the logic by which commercials take up and reorient the basic impulses animating family life, thus destroying the family while presumably glorifying it, using its appeal; as a more complex example, one can refer to the whipping up of emotions in the French Revolution, as analysed by Tocqueville, evoked by Dickens in *A Tale of Two Cities* and more recently discussed in the PhD thesis of Camil Roman.

Needless to say, tricksters' artefacts, the subverted souls are sterile beings, unable to feel freedom for independent action, lacking inner power, close to the other-directedness of David Riesman, also captured by critiques of 'mass society' like Heidegger or Ortega y Gasset. They can easily be subordinated to a generalised external 'rationality', whether by markets or states (in the modern world), as they have been left alone, once reduced to a weak and humble state; or by settlement and the artificial deprivation of horizon, in small and enclosed spaces, as it happened in Natufian villages or in Çatalhöyük. They are unable to reproduce themselves; instead, they need a perpetual crisis situation, the one that made their imitative existence possible. A good example for this is the way every modern revolution culminated in a period of terror, where excess fervour was again and again instigated to keep revolutionary enthusiasm alive, until complete exhaustion and apathy.

The trickster practises this subversive technology in a transcendental situation, where the naturally given borders and orders are dissolved, generating a liquid state or a liminal flux. Ironically, for Newton and Kant this desperate situation is considered as a natural because universal order of the world. The problem is that they fail to perceive that no being exists purely according to universal laws; their obsession with the universal implies a permanent, forced return to the point of absolute origin, where nothing concrete existed, only 'quantities' moving in the 'void' of the 'big bang'; and thus the 'transcendental', in the sense of Kant, is identical to the destruction of all those concrete borders and boundaries that give stability to human existence and that render meaning possible, thus requiring the imposition of external, artificial boundaries by regulatory institutions. This is why the transformed needs to repeat, again and again, the same transcendental situation (crisis or liminality) for survival, as its life is reduced to a struggle for survival; the archetypal political situation of modernity, since Hobbes. The trickster is conflict-ridden: it only lives, as a survivor, in liminality, thus it requires conflict to stay in existence by absorbing conflict-ridden souls. It also requires pulsating sensation, the sensation of separation generating pain and suffering, as only this necessitates the trickster's interference, the situation whereby the trickster is able to take away the soul of others, while infiltrating its own void or emptiness into the others, thus multiplying its own trickster form infinitely through the emptied beings.

But if such synthetic fabrics of the void can now imitate everything, why can't we recognise its tricks and mischievous nature before imitation is actually in place? This supernatural being, to be found in the folklore of many 'primitive' people, is sometimes distinguished by prodigious biological drives and exaggerated bodily parts. Furthermore, it is not only an intermediate being, believed to possess powers to affect the course of nature, but is considered as part of nature, as some Palaeolithic (Magdalenian) engravings show it (see Figure 5.1).

The absorption of the power of fetched souls gives the trickster the possibility to set in motion a peculiar power, a merging with the void. This is possible, as the resistance of the concrete individual person, the self-resistance to intrusion is undermined in liminality. Under extraordinary circumstances of pain and suffering, or in any other type of emotional upheaval, the identity of the self is dissolved. Dissolved entities, persons deprived of their inner power, are ready to accept and tolerate any form that brings them out of the liminal, the state of separation, into a new union with themselves and the community. This is the transcendental moment that helped Eisenstadt recognise the significance of Weber's charisma concept, its link to transcendence and the liminal crisis situation.[15] He saw an empire-building potential in Weber's concept, and not without a reason. Through an instrumental use of liminality, artificial methods for making new identities are gaining increasing ground in politics and society, spanning the new, second power at the price of destroying the first, the personal character. The process of taking on an individual form can be seen in a figurative manner in the following bone incision (see Figure 5.2).

FIGURE 5.1 Palaeolithic trickster metamorphosis (https://es.wikipedia.org/wiki/Cueva_de_los_Casares). Magdalenian stone incision from Los Casares cave, showing the phallic Trickster jumping into another being, into a fish-form

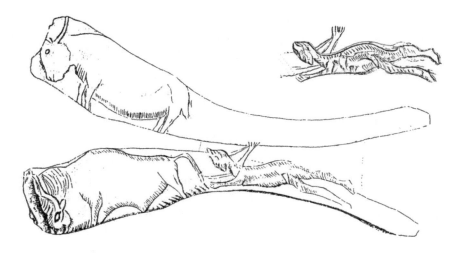

FIGURE 5.2 Taking the form: Palaeolithic trickster jumps in/after a bovine
(Photo: Don Hitchcock, http://donsmaps.com/laugeriebasse.html).[16]
Magdalenian bone incision, showing a phallic trickster catching or rather
infiltrating an auroch; from the Laugerie-Basse cave in Dordogne, which
is also central for prehistoric cinematic animation (see Azéma 2011).
Note also the trickster's repeated focus on flying, and also on crawling, in
contrast to walking[17]

This is a three-dimensional object, so the arm extends beyond the boundary of the two-dimensional rendering, around the bone, taking the image in the
moment of the dynamic movement of catching the form, jumping into it, taking
possession. Note the two sequential phases of the moment: in the first the animal
has a relaxed tail, in the second it is erect, accepting, and the head is turned downwards in a submissive pose. Why is this particular example for the infiltration of
a character so significant? Here reason and observation both play their own part.
The method of the trickster is unchanging: dividing and reuniting, destroying and
re-establishing, and evidently the division is easier if the barriers are broken, when
the individual lost its integrity, its energy, and thus its soul is also lost. With this
ideal in mind, the trickster is able to 'void', to transform anything existing into a
mere, empty unreality.

The trickster's reality is unreal not simply in contrast to the reality of the concrete character, but also due to the way they both can actually exist inside the
world. The point is that the trickster's reality is qualitatively different, due to its
joint presence in reality and the sphere of the unreal (see again Hermes being
in-between two worlds). It is a dramatically altered reality due to its unreal absorption with the void, but it is not possible to say that it does not exist. Even more
interesting is the question of the void: what is it, in fact? One of the cardinal rules
of the transcendental is that there are no preferred frames of reference where it is

'true' and where it is 'real'. In the frame of reference of our reality, the world itself is always stationary; it is the same in all frames of reference. You can only have the void in some frames of reference and not others. If you are in a stable, stationary situation, you are not in the void, rather in the real, but you are not aware of it. It is only through encountering the liminal void that you come to realise what reality is; but only if you succeed in overcoming the liminal, which is unreal, can you truly return to reality. This is how, in ancient thought, retaining yourself when encountering the divine is the proof of a real (pious, virtuous, witty) man, and contentment with this state is the most simple and natural way of truthful reality for the Greeks.

However, there stands the trickster, this void-filled entity that preys on others; the one who cannot overcome – not himself, as Nietzsche stated in *Thus Spoke Zarathustra*, rather the challenge of the unreal, and so can never become real. The trickster is imperfect as a human, but is a perfect hybrid that embodies both man and the super-real in an ever-growing power over nature. Imagine that you have entities without strength: they cannot move by themselves; they are in an apathetic and motionless state. As you begin to accelerate the movements and impulses, emotions and senses, their activity increases. Now we have the conditions for transformation. Eventually, when all these images of activities are travelling around at a high enough speed and intensity, their emptiness will change into a concentration of energy.[18] This is how the transformative power is formed. This concentration will be enough to form liminal figures like the trickster, though in themselves they are empty, without character. If it is true that the intensity of an image will increase as one speeds up its projection (basically the kind of materialisation that happens during sorcery, shamanism and other kinds of magic, just as in modern electronic image projections),[19] this is only due to its character as an image, as a materialised image remains unreal, even though it has now become part of existence. However, it is not just materialised images that affect reality; so do the intensity and pressure of the moment. All three of these are combined into a transformed entity, the trickster's artefact, and it is this entity that determines the subsequent changes in reality (see Figure 5.3).

The movement of transformation took place by quickly rolling the bone. In this manner the two different image-sets, the bovines and the feline-bovine-human figures, collided with each other. An arrow sign is visible on one of the hybrid's thighs, and also two arrows on the body of the bovines, indicating fracturing, the act of changing the form, the break of unity. Their absorption into each other is complete in this way, through pressing the bone down, thus causing the images to move and shifting each into a new form, offered by the other; altering, changing or modifying the original identity into a transformed one. By pressing the bone and rolling it, the images are merging into each other, due to the intensification of movement, as if lessening the strength of their identity and taking each other's forms.

Such effects of sorcery are non-negligible, so the first, diverted reality will be followed by another one in an even more deformed way than the previous one,

FIGURE 5.3 Accelerating movements for transformation (Photo: Don Hitchcock, http://donsmaps.com/isturitz.html). Magdalenian bone incision from Isturitz cave

using the technique of image transformation by miming a new identity into a new layer of character every time: thus subversion is completed. While people are morally bothered by contemporary cloning, the trickster used this technique of subversion already in Palaeolithic times and in several Mesolithic and Neolithic images as well. Such transformations continue even today as well, absorbing characters, making hybrids out of characters, thus emptying characters. At that time, it might have been just an extraordinary event of sorcery but, since the time of domestication and early farming, manufacturing a hybrid, or a domesticated animal, became a recurrent technology of subversion.

It still happens that crops become fabricated by making identical copies of the original, by miming a tissue into the original identity, literally sacrificing the original to make a new character that was taken away from the former. In this way, plant domestication became an everyday example of sorcery, eventually grown into the technological method of cloning.

The softly curved bodies of tricksters shown above are the consequence of observing a distant object, moving in a dimension different from our frame of reference. But if we happen to be this subverted object ourselves, if we happen to become invaded by tricksters, everything whatsoever would appear to change, even the intensity and the extension of the impulses we have. With subversion we become unable to move further, to influence by our own character alone. It generates dependence from the resources of others, equivalent to the never fulfilled desire of shadows for possessing others, as it is illustrated in Figure 5.4.

Subversion implies a serious loss, the destruction of one's character, the unique centre of existence – so how could this lead to an increase of power? The answer

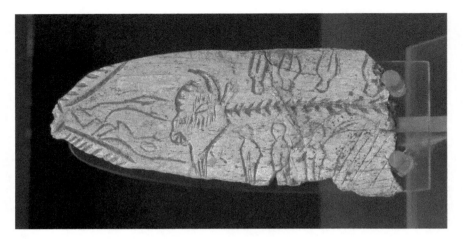

FIGURE 5.4 The void, or the shadowed state. Magdalenian bone incision, Raymonden cave (Photo: Don Hitchcock, http://donsmaps.com/raymonden.html). A dissected bovine, with an upside-down fish bone instead of a skeleton; its dismembered, separated legs lying in front of its heavy head; humans in a row on both its left and right side. It is alive, with open eyes, though its body is in pieces, incorporating the shadows of humans

can be found by tying together the void and transformation, so this can only be done through the paradox of the void. The void is evoked by the crossing and destruction of boundaries, thus the intactness and integrity of characters; but this does not generate an absolute elimination, only a formless mass of various elements that keep and even intensify their emotional charge. The previous, ordered existence is thus replaced by bursting intensity, whether through provoking pain and suffering or inciting pleasure, which possesses an enormous transformative power, especially if such elements are present in large numbers. Le Bon (2009) pioneered the study of crowd psychology and analysed effectively how political leaders emerge, gaining power from moments of distress, from empty situations of high intensity, from hazy fusions of sensualities. Similarly, Max Weber (1968) with his concept of charisma found a spiritually sensitive notion for crisis situations, where everything is ready for transformation and charismatic attraction.

Weber's idea is one of the most widely used concepts in contemporary politics, while the works and ideas of Le Bon are hardly mentioned, and yet the two can only be understood together. Le Bon and Weber were contemporaries, and tried to give answers to the same problems. Le Bon's crowd leaders are nonentities who gained fame and influence solely due to the force of circumstances; while Weber's charismatic leaders similarly only emerge in crisis situations, where one never fully understands whether they have inner, personal qualities guaranteeing the success of their actions, sent by divine powers to solve the crisis; or whether they simply manage to convince people and fool followers under the out-of-the-ordinary conditions. If the latter is the case – and Weber's support for the communist demagogue Eisner, just as the qualification of the political monsters of the past century, like Hitler, Stalin or Mussolini as 'charismatic leaders', strongly points to this dimension – then modern 'charismatic' leaders are mere champions of the crowd by no means dissimilar to the trickster sorcerers of Magdalenian caves, or the Tassili mountains, to be discussed later.

The main problem with such a trickster scenario is not simply its own falsity and emptiness, but its irrepressible, imperialistic aggressiveness. A genuine charismatic person brings lasting solution and peace; a crowd leader, however, especially if moves in a virtual pace, operating through image magic (Szakolczai 2007), must continuously escape forward, maintaining a siege mentality that can only go forward by violence and conquest; that transforms its unformed but massive and intense emotional power into a perpetual aggression. Thus, paradoxically, emptiness produces aggression and imperialism. Not surprisingly, the best analysts of the rise of Empires similarly emphasise that such conquests are never motivated by genuine needs, only by a growing void within, due to internal decomposition (Voegelin 1974, much relying upon Jacob Burckhardt), or a 'leakage of reality' (Brown 1982: 32–40).

Trickster effects: prehistoric theatricality

In contrast to Pergouset, Chauvet cave can be identified through three basic features. To start with, Chauvet produces, even through simple colour representations, an immediate perception of presence. This is particularly strong to those who are physically there in the cave, and for whom such presence is immediately and experientially given. Second, this presence transmits an original recognition, the same recognition that animates as a *thaumazein* experience Plato's philosophy, as formulated in the *Timaeus*, the recognition of the striking beauty of the world as a foundational experience for our being human. Third, such recognition of beauty, and of presence, has no precondition: it is freely and openly accessible to every human being, just as Chauvet – and later Lascaux – was clearly marked and accessible to anybody who cared to go there.

Pergouset, just as the images presented in this chapter, presupposed and evoked a completely different kind of access and experience. In resuming them two books are particularly helpful, offering unprecedented and seemingly anachronistic readings of Palaeolithic art through theatre (Montelle 2009) and cinema (Azéma 2011). Both devoted special attention to Pergouset cave.

In considering prehistoric art as theatrical and cinematic, both books prominently discuss religion and magic. The distinction between religion and magic is a perennial problem of sociology and anthropology, as any clear analytic distinction is fraught with difficulties, yet it is evident that they are not identical. Cave art offers a strikingly fresh perspective. Cave paintings, in particular Chauvet, evoke presence, which is as close to religious experience as possible, yet without any specifically 'religious' character. For this, the 'cinematic' qualities of its art-work, the stunning capacity of the images to capture and evoke motion (Azéma 2011), is fundamental. Chauvet thus evokes a religiosity *before* religion. Pergouset and its possible frequentation, together with other similar caves, however, do something similar yet opposite: it alludes to religious practices *before* the separation between religion and magic. These include rituals, central for religion; yet also efforts to influence powers that rather belong to magic; and finally, as if at the point of inter-section between the two, it is possible to find traces of theatricality, 'intentional liminal behaviour' or 'self-conscious display' (Montelle 2009: 16, fn.1; 1),[20] where not only the borderline between religion and magic, but even between ritual and theatre is porous.

It is this same ambivalence that becomes even more pronounced if we try to capture the character of the figures who perform or lead such rituals. They were called 'sorcerers' or 'magicians', now rather 'shamans', but they also reveal the features of a priesthood, gaining their 'knowledge' by rituals of ordeal (67–8, 84–5, 98–9), which furthermore assume secrecy and darkness (98). The easy access to Chauvet and Lascaux, and many other painted caves, contrasts with the extreme difficulty of access to Pergouset, but also to several other caves similarly associated with monster, hybrid or 'sorcerer' images (see Gabillou, Trois Frères, Marsoulas, Cougnac).

This shift, from Chauvet to Pergouset or the Shaft Scene, is transmitted through the terminology used to describe this new kind of practice, capturing a shift from unity of presence to a break and distance, through secretive knowledge and the-atrical performances. It starts with the very word 'knowledge'. The term is not applicable to Chauvet, but is used to describe the 'message' supposedly coded inside and 'communicated' in the more recent caves (34–57, 162–5).[21] Such mes-sages are no longer accessible to everyone; we can only assume that they possessed some hidden, secret, presumably deep meaning. Montelle uses two particularly sig-nificant expressions, as if taken jointly from Foucault and Yates. On the one hand, the images and the signs together can be considered as mnemotechnic devices or *mnemonics* (5–7, 131–18), defined as 'a technique of memorisation based on classificatory procedures (mnemonic devices) designed to aid the memory' (131); helping recollection, though at the same time also altering one's memory (110–11, 132), when reliance on dreaming is replaced by the alteration of one's imagination through an artificial stimulation of the mind to produce images (see also Azéma 2011: 21–2). On the other hand, while the cinematic images of the Chauvet lions are immediately accessible to everyone, the recognition of a sign implies knowl-edge about the sign *as* a sign.

Montelle's efforts to indicate this novelty not only closely recall Foucault's ideas about duplicated representation, explicitly connecting duplicated representa-tion to theatricality, a point not made by Foucault, but even extend to liminality. Montelle names his approach an 'archaeology of theatricality', and defines it in two crucial sentences, first as 'an archaeology of passage, of transient progressions through layers of fictive realities';[22] and immediately after as 'the excavation of material remains characteristic of a social process where signifying objects are semiotized into signs of signs' (57). The latter definition, closely recalling 'duplicated representation', is later repeated and explicitly connected to theatricality: theatricality emerges out of decoding an incomplete or undecipherable sign where, due to such insufficiency 'the sign is hermeneutically processed as a "sign of a sign"' (83). The space of the cave is thus transformed into an 'organised place', and specifically a space of knowledge, where topography itself becomes meaningful, especially through the transformation of the cave into a place for initiation rites (107–8). Here a central role is played by passages. As the cave has been transformed into a liminal space of initiation rites, such passages are not simply between different physical spaces, but between different *types* of realities, with theatricality mediating such passages in and out of various 'modes of being' (Latour 2013), or the 'passage from one reality into the next' (Montelle 2009: 86).

A crucial connection between sign and theatricality, but even between art, magic and religion, is marked by one of the most conspicuous signs of Palaeolithic caves, the negative handprints; and, in particular, the strange practice of missing fingers. At one level, such fingerprints were only used to mark one's passage (69–70, 82–3, 85). However, the hand, instrument of making representations, gained a special place in the universe of representation, including both images and theatricality, through 'the process of re-allocating the hand as limb (sign) into the hand as the *image* of the limb (the sign of a sign)' (86). This helps us to understand a key feature of the famous Gargas fingerprints, among others, that many of them have missing fingers. While Leroi-Gourhan (1986) showed that probably most such fingerprints were done by simply folding fingers, the actual mutilation of hands cannot be ruled out as a – certainly extreme – way of personalising the passage (85). One can even perceive a certain sequentiality here, where the mere joy of being there, expressed by leaving the trace of a hand, is first transformed into some kind of personal identification, and eventually a mark of making the ordeal, where the seriousness of such an ordeal, in the hands of a presumed secretive priesthood, could be transformed into a practice of mutilation. A possible trick is to cajole people by the mere image of a folded finger to actually cut their own fingers – and once a single person was thus misled (literally seduced), the practice can become 'established'.

At any rate, the final effect of theatricalisation was the radical undermining of the world vision dominating first Chauvet, then Lascaux, Altamira and the other major painted caves.[23] The experience of presence and participation was transposed into schism and fragmentation, signs to be decoded by 'those in the know', implying an instrumentalisation of image in the service of knowledge, to be deployed theatrically, in front of pure spectators (29), with rituals being combined with self-conscious display (1). Apart from duplicated representation, theatricality and mnemotechnics, through an 'interruption of the continuum: a schism or rupture in the quotidian' such instrumentalisation also implied a concern with alterity, or otherness (7), an invitation to transgression through a 'licensed "otherness"' (3). The invitation to transgression included the use of sounds, especially music, in particular the flute, but also the bull-roarer, producing a sound that must have been impressively effective in caves (114–26).[24] The theatricalisation of the cave altered cognition and recognition through its 'intentional construction of otherness' as 'a social response to the uncharted void', with theatricality thus emerging out of a 'hermeneutic void' (154; also 17).

Ultimately, thus implied a basic substitution: the substitution of the source of such creativity with the priest-artist who has successfully undergone all such ordeals as equivalent with the creator of the world. It is this revaluation of values that Nietzsche captured in the *Genealogy of Morals* in the emergence of the ascetic priest.

Conclusion

Subversion only ever produces illusory, ostensible, virtual results. It closes off, blocks and obstructs, making one blind to whatever is left outside and ignores what these others intend to reciprocate. The character, the only token of reality evaporates, fading away, the character's ability that is necessary for living: to look around, to perceive, to comprehend, to investigate, to search for understanding and explanation, ceases to exist. This produces a paranoid vision of the world as will be seen in the following chapters about Natufian culture, and also Jericho and Çatalhöyük, where whatever happens to a person is transmogrified and demonised into something threatening and terrifying, justifying the ever-renewed and necessarily failing efforts to overcome it by external means suited for large masses.

Science, including political science and anthropology, consists mostly of models, concepts, definitions. Such assumptions may correspond to reality, or they may not. The usefulness of particular theories depends entirely on whether they predict observable phenomena and work well with other models that predict events. We seem to assume that the better a theory predicts reality, the closer the model is to how reality actually operates. However, reality is indefinable, given that artefacts – whether technological or artistic, political, economic or cultural – add new elements to whatever already exists, so we only enter an interminable, vicious circularity. The power of altering reality also evokes the power of the void, which is produced by transgressing and destroying the borders and boundaries that define the character of any concrete entity and render possible meaning. The transformative potential of the void has not yet been sufficiently studied, given that modern science has been lured by the empty, universalistic promises of the Kantian concept of the transcendental.

Scientific imagination pretends that everything moving though the rational world has a cohesive or gravitating power. Because of that, the entire notion of the self being centred in the soul is no longer accepted, considered as a hypothesis of Plato that was rendered obsolete by modern science. Instead, forces outside the self are supposed to govern human action, in the overall framework of a secularised transcendental power. According to this, man and nature must be disciplined and regulated as, in themselves, they are a confused, disordered mass, only capable of disobedience, and the charis, contentment component of man's soul became forgotten. The idea of a structure and agency-based second type of power is built on the ruins of the first power and, at best, the fluxional character of power was declared, as in the theories of Foucault. The ability to judge our usefulness or harmfulness in facing reality evaporated, and we became produced by external features that are no part of ourselves; we were even discouraged to use our own capacities. Instead, technological means were deployed to remind of us life, instead of participating in it. Perhaps even Weber's charisma concept belongs here, which offers the appearance of wisdom, being similar to authority based on gift-giving for the utterly simple people into which we developed over time, having emptied our inner power and thus growing into nothingness, subordinating the most beautiful essence of our personhood, the ability to look always upward, to the slavery of impulses.

Notes

1 We should note that this – strikingly – almost coincides with the ending of the first period of visitation in Chauvet cave. Of course, the Pergouset dating would also need more recent confirmation, and it is impossible to secure a proper historical sequence for such remote events, but the closeness of the correspondence is still worth mentioning. Also, while there is no evidence whatsoever that the piece of charcoal was left by those who made the engravings, this makes it clear that the visitation of the cave extends to much earlier times.

2 Strangely, in his 2010 book Lorblanchet stepped back from this evaluation of the dating. We cannot follow here the behind-the-curtain developments of archaeology, certainly not independent of the three spectacular reverses of Paul Bahn, an evidently powerful impresario in the field, concerning the relevance of shamanism, the relative values of stylistic and carbon dating, and the dating of Chauvet in particular. We accept that the Room of Monsters was engraved 33,000 years ago, as the charcoal piece was indeed a torch, and as it was found just under the first engraving of the room.

3 Such matters of size might not be irrelevant, as in Chauvet cave it was possible to identify, through hand imprints, the presence of two individuals, a male and a female, both about six feet tall.

4 While the paper is signed by two authors, the last two sections are explicitly attributed to Ann Sieveking; which thus seems to imply that the rest of the paper is mostly by Lorblanchet. Such detail has its importance, given that Sieveking strongly endorses the 'shamanism' thesis, while Lorblanchet in his 2001 book (though not in this joint article) explicitly distanced himself from such an idea. Note also the importance of the steady draught or breeze inside the cave, central for the 'experience' in the cave (Lorblanchet and Sieveking 1997: 38), recalling the strong breeze inside the 'Shaft' of Lascaux.

5 In his 2001 book Lorblanchet added two panels, containing only signs. As this does not alter our analysis, and as the 1997 article is more accessible, we'll keep the original numbering.

6 The etymology of the word is particularly revealing in this context. The Latin term *mostrum* 'divine omen, sign' originally involved the will of god, showing something as a revelation, but in the specific sense of 'repulsive character, object of dread, awful deed,

abomination'; the verb *mostro* 'to show', without any religious connotation, is only a later development (Ernout and Meillet 1959: 413; see also *Online Etymology*, consulted 24 January 2017).

7 Concerning such striking uniformity of composition, we could mention the distant but important cases of Rouffignac, Knossos or Assisi.

8 Such a link between eloquence, alchemy and magic would become central for Giulio Camillo, according to Yates, Bolzoni and Torello (see Chapter 3).

9 A connection between metamorphosis, imitation and error/sin (*colpa*), even capital sin (*peccato capitale*), was also proposed by Calasso (2016: 119–23), who even offered a particularly striking explanation that fits almost too perfectly with the previous reasoning: '[w]hen pushed to the extreme, imitation is metamorphic' (125), and even draws the consequences concerning 'the latent violence of every imitation' (127). The contagious character of images, as we discussed in Chapter 4, is central for the Chauvet experience. As we'll see later, such potential mimetic violence contained in the image will be unleashed by settlement, thus helping us understand the Biblical injunction about 'graven images'.

10 The etymological source of 'matrix' is the same *mater* 'mother' as for 'matter'. This connection between 'mother', 'matter' and 'matrix' is something absolutely fundamental, understood by prehistoric artists as well as the people who formed Latin, but lies beyond the comprehension of modern 'rational' thought.

11 See Foucault (1970) and Elias (1987), key methodological books of two major social theorists, each having *Las Meninas* by Velazquez as their title image. See also 'Alexander the Great and Campaspe in the Studio of Apelles' by Giambattista Tiepolo, where the artist depicted himself, bewildered, as the Hellenistic painter Apelles, in the act of painting the portrait of Alexander's mistress. This was a central theme in a recent, major Picasso exhibition in the Palazzo Strozzi in Florence ('Picasso and Spanish Modernity', 20 September 2014–25 January 2015).

12 This is again particularly true in Hungarian; see *hiúság* 'vanity'; *hiába* 'in vain'; and *hiány* 'lack, gap, emptyness'; here even recognised by the standard Hungarian etymological dictionary (Benkő 1970, II: 106–7, 122–3).

13 This helps to make sense of the stunning fact that even scraping was carefully collected in recesses of particularly difficult access, intimating that 'special, powerful properties (*des vertues particulières*) were attributed to them' (Lorblanchet 2001: 166–7).

14 In this book we use the term subversiveness to characterise the proliferation of subversion by trickster figures, which eventually can even be taken for granted.

15 See in Weber (1968). Eisenstadt would also soon recognise the importance of liminality, organising a conference together with Victor Turner in 1982.

16 We thank Don Hitchcock for generously making available all images on his site for academic purposes, and in general for maintaining such a useful and excellent site.

17 Here Hungarian is again particularly helpful. The Hungarian word for flying is *száll*; and the same root is used for 'possession' and 'invasion' (both *megszáll*), and settlement (*szállás*). *Száll* as a verb is also used for songs, music being a particularly effective help for 'possession'. 'Possession' even in English is linked to settlement, its etymological root being PIE *sed* 'sit'; see 'sedentary' or 'settled'.

18 According to Bednarik (2015), such transformation happens even with a stone when hammered tens of thousand times, resulting in the formation of cupules with a protective surface. He calls this 'kinetic energy metamorphosis'.

19 Such speeding up of movement is a central characteristic of 'prehistoric cinema', produced for example by a quick repeated flipping over of the two sides of pierced disks (*rondelle*), producing a kind of optical illusion. Marc Azéma considers the invention of these prehistoric 'thaumatropes' (optical toys) just as important as the invention of graphic narration and sequential animation in Chauvet, and traces it to the late Magdalenian Laugerie-Basse and La Vache caves (Azéma 2011: 26–7, 144–55).

20 The second is a quote from Richard Schachner, a main collaborator of Victor Turner on liminality and theatre, interpreting some footprints found in Tuc d'Audubert cave, a cave in direct contact with the Trois Frères cave, where the most famous Palaeolithic 'sorcerer' image was found.

21 It should be noted that the etymology of 'message', both in Latin: *missus* 'a sending', but also 'a throwing, hurling; and Hungarian: *üzenet*, to be traced to '*űz*' chase, hunt, is quite intriguing, as it alludes, behind a seemingly innocuous tool of communication, a disturbing, upsetting, even violent act. Even further, putting these meanings together, we gain the two central aspects of *Homo sapiens* activity: hunting, or chasing animals through spears, or 'missiles'. This ambivalence is centrally captured by Kafka, both through his problematisation of communicating through messages, and letters, and the role played by the 'hunt' or 'chase' in the *Process*. For details, see Szakolczai (2017a: 78–82).

22 See also p. 243, n1, where this definition is verbatim repeated.

23 In our reading Lascaux and Altamira represent a reassertion in the Solutrean of the world image first depicted in Chauvet.

24 Concerning sound effects, see also the three lithophones identified in the Quercy caves of Pech-Merle, Cougnac and Les Fieux by Lorblanchet (2010: 117–18, 305, 330).

6

NATUFIAN SETTLEMENT

Technology, representation, standing reserve

Why did we settle? And where?

Walking offers an Archimedean point to restore measure and limit; and a central aspect of this undertaking is to dislocate the current, evolutionist *voidism* – where from 'nothing' a gradual evolution is supposed to take place, ever better and perfected – from its dominating position. Archaeology is fundamental in this regard; and, indeed for decades, following both a series of milestone discoveries and ongoing reflections, archaeologists have been moving just in this direction – though not without enormous, almost unintelligible controversies.

A central aspect of this debate concerns one of the most momentous changes in the history of humankind, the end of the Palaeolithic, and the eventual arrival of the Neolithic. The dominant perspective was codified here by V. Gordon Childe, who proclaimed that the central reason for this change was technological, the discovery of agriculture. However, a series of recent (and even not so recent) discoveries simply invalidated such a perspective, so much so that archaeologists hardly believe in the idea of an 'agricultural' revolution anymore. But the question remains, and is burning all the more: why did we settle? And why did it happen where it did – in the Natufian; or, using a more familiar name: in the Southern Levant, in Palestine, or even more specifically in Galilee?

Apart from Palaeolithic cave art in the Atlantic, around 35,000–10,000 BC, there is another chronotope central for the history of humankind: this is the Near East, origin of settlement and agriculture, around 12,700–7000 BC, with its beginnings corresponding more or less with the Late Magdalenian flourishing of cave art culture.

The first thing to notice here, again valorising the concept 'liminality', is that this area is the exact opposite *type* of South-Western Europe. Far from being the 'end of the world', where one could not keep going much further, so had to turn around (Lewis-Williams 2002), thus the perfect place for a kind of pilgrimage, the

Near East is a par excellence place of transit, connecting three continents. From Africa, the road towards Europe or Asia goes through the Southern Levant, while it is in the Northern part of the Fertile Crescent, in Northern Iraq and Southern Turkey, that the road towards Europe *or* Asia deviates, and which therefore is also a main road *between* Europe and Asia. This helps us to understand that this region was a birthplace of a very different kind, or rather exactly the opposite: not a centre of pilgrimage, where one arrives only to return, but a place, at the intersection of roads, where some people decided to do the opposite, to *settle*.

Steps towards an answer

As a first step towards answering the question, we must realise that this is an impossible task. Causal explanation is rarely possible in the social sciences, and certainly not possible if liminality is involved. Liminality means flux, transition and suspense, a situation where the 'old' no longer applies and the 'new' is not yet there. We thus must stay as close as possible to the archaeological findings, and try to make sense of them – staying as close as possible to the way those living at that time and place experienced settling down.

In trying to make sense of this truly radical change which meant permanent human settlement, we should again start by avoiding reading it backward, considering it as the origins of civilisation, or even of cities, as it was not, in any meaningful sense. We should rather start by regaining the surprise to be encountered by such an idea – to become permanently tied to a single, limited space, given the immense vastness of the planet, and the various experiences and resources it offers to all; and, even further, to restrict much of our life to living in and sharing a small, walled and covered space that is a house. It is such a surprise that it is restored, artistically, in a film by Akira Kurosawa, *Dersu Uzala*, where the eponymous hero, a Tungusic hunter, is astonished how somebody could live inside a 'box'.

Understanding this perplexing fact first of all requires establishing the exact temporal and spatial liminality involved.

Temporal liminality: the rhythm of coincidences and its sequences

Our understanding of human prehistory is fundamentally shaped, and is still dominated, by the division between the Palaeolithic and the Neolithic, or the Old and New Stone Age. The Old Stone Age is considered the period of wild, untamed, uncivilised existence, when men were brutes and lived in caves, while life was 'brutish, nasty and short', with the New Stone Age representing the start of the advancement of civilisation. While nobody with a minimal awareness about the concrete facts today accepts such a simplistic vision, most of our contemporaries, including many social scientists, still fundamentally think along such narrative lines, and at a very basic level: this is simply *the* modern vision of human history.

To overcome the very foundations of such a vision, we must start by getting the facts right, starting by clarifying the exact manner in which the Old versus New Stone Age dichotomy and its still basically taken-for-granted interpretation is fundamentally wrong.

The idea that the Neolithic emerged due to the rise of agriculture was first questioned by the excavations of Dorothy Garrod in Palestine, finding traces of settlements around 15,000 years ago. After the first site when this new culture was unearthed, a cave near Wadi Natuf, it is called 'Natufian'. At first it was thought that this also represents an early rise of agriculture, but since then it has been established that the rise of agriculture took place several millennia later. The existence of settled communities in such a distant past, however, was confirmed.

Natufian settlements consist of a small number of scattered houses, often only five or six, in Palestine, clustering in particular around Mount Carmel in Galilee (Bar-Yosef 2002: 105–12; Bar-Yosef and Valla 1991). Houses are often partly dug into the ground, with stone foundations, called pit houses. There is some evidence of storage facilities. The centre of the house is the hearth, around which there is plenty of food-processing equipment (Watkins 1990: 343). Simple as this may sound, the entire set-up with its various features together is quite unique: 'no field project outside of the Levant has yet exposed any indication of a prehistoric entity that resembles the Natufian' (Bar-Yosef 1998: 159). The question remains: why did it take place *then*, and *there*; and what was so special about this strange first settlement?

An attempt at understanding cannot start with *assuming* that settlement was a necessary evolutionary step, 'rendering possible' the later development of agriculture, cities and thus 'civilisation'. It must genealogically start from the practices that were in place there before, and which centred around *walking*. So we first of all need to understand the reasons why people *stopped* walking, exactly after a period in which walking, in the sense of a walking into a void containing representations, became particularly intensified. This is a problem also because the first settlements coincided with a warmer and milder climate, though also a fearful one, with pulsating changes in the environment.

Climate change at the end of the Ice Age

The end of the Ice Age was neither a single, abrupt moment of change, nor a long, continuous and gradual shift. It indeed lasted for a considerable period, covering several millennia, but had both its reversals and radical moments of discontinuity. It was also not uniform in all parts of the planet, though – given the truly global, planetary implications of such a shift in climate – the basic changes were quite similar everywhere. Scientists consider the record of temperature changes as preserved in the ice sheets of Greenland as a particularly good proxy for climate change.

Concerning the theme and time horizon of this book, the first important point to mention is that during the late Palaeolithic there was an intensification of cold spells, combined with a fall in the sea levels, culminating around 20,000 BC in the

Last Glacial Maximum. After this, there came a gradual and slow warming-up, with a secular rise in the sea levels, intensifying first around 15,000 years ago. This was due to a relatively intense warming-up period, called the Bølling-Allerød interstadial, lasting from about 12,700 BC to about 10,800 BC (Pirazzoli 1991). In terms of the European late Palaeolithic, this coincided with the Late Magdalenian, which brought about a particular flowering of cave art culture. However, at a different and particularly liminal place of the planet, in the Southern Levant, it was the period when the first settled human communities came into being.

The intense period of relative warming was suspended around 10,800 BC, indeed a few centuries earlier, with the onset of a colder and drier climate, called Younger Dryas, lasting until 9700 BC. At that moment a quite sudden and sustained climate change happened, ending the Ice Age for good, when in a period as short as a decade average temperatures rose by 7 degrees (Mithen 2003: 54). This also entailed a relatively quick and abrupt rise in sea levels; according to some estimates, in less than a century sea levels around Europe rose by about 50 metres, so there was not a few millimetres, but outright half a metre of sea-level rise annually.

Thus, in terms of time, Natufian settlement coincides with the start of a major warming period. The coincidence is literally there, but it is by no means an explanation. This can be best seen if we shortly return to the Atlantic. The same moment when some peoples started to settle in the Natufian, others, in the Atlantic, lived through the highest flowering of Magdalenian art. All that the trivial economic logic tells us is that warmer climate was an opportunity. It cannot explain why this opportunity was used differently in the Atlantic than in the Eastern Mediterranean.

We need to look further.

Spatial liminality: the Northern Africa–Southern Levant links

From time, we need to move into space. The Atlantic was in a very real sense the end of the world, literal *Finis terrae*, preserved even in contemporary names – whatever was their exact moment of origin – as Fisterra in North-Western Spain, or Finistère in Brittany. The Southern Levant, however, was, if not the 'centre' of the world, certainly its 'middle', in the sense of being in-between the three continents.

Being in-between, however, is only a possibility or potential. The question is, what is being realised of this? Being in-between Africa, Asia and Europe, what was the 'significant other' of the Southern Levant at the end of the Ice Age? Evidence indicates that by that time the area had closed its links with the Atlantic, while becoming close to Northern Africa – whatever it could have meant at that moment. But whatever it may have meant, it was certainly relevant for our key concern, the rise of settlement.

As a first step, we need to restate that we are still dealing, at the Ice Age, with cultures of walking. Thus, trivially and evidently, though this is easy to forget, there were no borders to cross, no cities to get admitted to; one simply had to walk from one place to another, if one had to, or wanted to. Of course, there were various natural obstacles, including wild animals, but our ancestors knew well how to deal with them. As explorers and hunters of the past centuries abundantly relayed through accounts of 'natives', and as anybody can realise from YouTube by watching San people handling cheetah or lions, if a man is not afraid of an animal, he won't be hurt. Man could walk anywhere – but where did he walk and not walk around the start of the late Palaeolithic?

Aurignacian and Ahmarian in the Levant

The background, even here, concerns the presence and dominance of Neanderthal. Compared to this, Homo sapiens reached the Levant from two directions: from Africa, producing a culture called Ahmarian; and from Europe, bringing in the Aurignacian (Cauvin 2000: 13–14; Goring-Morris and Belfer-Cohen 2006; Belfer-Cohen and Goring-Morris 2014). The latter arrived later, and was more influential on the Northern part of the Southern Levant, bringing with him the art objects characteristic of the European late Palaeolithic. Thus, connections with Western Europe, the area from where Neanderthal culture radiated, was maintained. The exchange also had a partially mutual character, as Ahmarian influences can be demonstrated in Eastern Europe, through the Danube, up to Moravia (Belfer-Cohen and Goring-Morris 2014: 30).

The connection with Europe seems to have been severed during the Last Glacial Maximum, and especially with the rise of Kebaran culture.[1] This latter has three central features. The first is the increasing use of microliths, intensifying a 'microlithic tendency' (Cauvin 2000: 13) present in the region since the Ahmarian, but now pushing it towards an 'extreme tendency of microlithism' and extending it to the Nile Valley (Huyge et al. 2000: 309). The second point concerns the parallel tendency of geometrisation, which took place in particular after the shift from Kebaran to Geometric Kebaran, around 15,500 BC (Godfrey-Smith et al. 2003), ending with the rise of Natufian around 12,700 BC. Finally, there is the disappearance of objects of decoration and art. Taken together, such 'miniaturisation' and 'geometrisation', out of which Natufian culture emerged, are quite striking, as they offer signs of a significant and long-term process of cultural decline. Parallels are strong not only with the Azilian, but also with the Spanish Levant, in particular the Los Dogoes cave in Castellón; the Grotta dei cervi cave at Porto Badisco in Apulia, Italy; the collapse of Mycenaean-Minoan civilisation; the collapse of the Western Roman Empire and the rise of the Roman style; or the collapse of the Byzantium. All these periods were marked by a radical intensification of violence. This already intimates that settlement was not some kind of 'civilisational progress', the emergence of man out of some kind of 'homeless', 'wandering', 'primitive' life, but rather a sign of a serious civilisational collapse and dead end, which first emerged in the highly liminal place of the Southern Levant, and radiated from there.

This can be rounded up by considering that the connections between broader Europe and the Levant were cut at the same time when, during the Solutrean, at the Last Glacial Maximum, the Atlantic cave art culture spread to Northern Africa, with Magdalenian-style art reaching the Nile Valley. Thus, with Kebaran culture, Southern Levant became, from an open geographical crossroad connecting three continents, a kind of cultural cul-de-sac.

Afro-Asiatic language

The shifting connections during Natufian can be further illustrated from the perspective of linguistics. The areas around the Natufian (from Northern Africa up to the Near East) belong to the Afro-Asiatic linguistic family, which has about 300 million speakers and includes Semitic, Berber and ancient Egyptian, as well as some other languages in West Africa and the Sahel (in particular the Hausa in Northern Nigeria, who are culturally closely related to the Fulani, who carried memories of Tassili rituals up to the 1950s), and in the Horn of Africa (Sudan, Ethiopia and Somalia). The original homeland of the family is much debated, with evident ideological overtones. Recent research tends to favour the Near East as the original place for the language, and in particular the Natufian period (C. Turner 2008, Blažek 2015), the main contention being that, apart from Semitic, all languages in the family are spoken in Africa.

However, if we move from a specialised question of linguistic into the broader issue represented by settlement, and its character, the Natufian origins receive clear support. Settlement clearly represented a radical change, and such a change can easily lead both to a shift in language, as well as the eventual spread of this language to other areas. Several archaeological findings suggest such directionality. One concerns dental morphology, where a clear shift can be perceived in the Nile Valley around the end of the Palaeolithic, with homogeneity both in the previous and in the later periods, but a radical shift in-between which can only be explained by population replacement or large-scale migration (C. Turner 2008: 20–1). The teeth of Late Palaeolithic Nubians are similar to Western Africans, while those of Holocene Nubians are similar to South-West Eurasians, especially Natufians. Such directionality can be supported also from the archaeology of the Neolithic, where in every step in the spread of agriculture the Nile Valley followed Levantine models (Gilbert 2015).

Even further, there are some signs that such movements of populations, techniques and languages were accompanied by eruptions of violence. The most spectacular example concerns the mass cemetery of Jebel Sahaba (Holliday 2015). Discovered in the early 1960s, it is still considered the earliest evidence of warfare. While experts even today tend to perceive this as evidence of the inherent violence of human nature, we get a better perspective if, instead, we consider this as a consequence of settlement and the necessary escalation of mimetic processes characteristic of a narrowing of horizon within a closed space, analysed so well by Girard (1977, 1989). After all, it cannot be accidental that the site is dated to about 11,000 BC (Lahr et al. 2016: 394; Antoine et al. 2013: 68), thus the transition to Late Natufian, where climatic conditions worsened, rendering the maintenance of settled existence ever more problematic. Apart from such 'rational' explanation, focusing on scarcity and resources, settlement also produced its own inner void, which was bound to culminate in external expansion and conflict, a kind of pre-historic empire building on spreading fear.

There are several aspects of the site that support such an interpretation. Jebel Sahaba, now under water in the Aswan Dam, is not that far from the sites where rock-art recalling the European Palaeolithic was found, in Qurta, but also further to the South, near Wadi Halfa (Huyge *et al.* 2007; Huyge 2009). Furthermore, earlier ideas about internecine warfare and intergroup violence are questioned both by the extreme care taken to bury the dead (Holliday 2015), and by recent research that considers the mass killing as the work of enemy archers.[2]

Even more importantly, new findings offer corroborating evidence. According to a paper published in 20 January 2016 in *Nature*, evidence of warfare from 8000 BC was found in the Lake Turkana area in Kenya (Lahr *et al.* 2016). Even here violence was extreme, with women being killed with their hands and feet bound, and young children thrown into a mass grave, together with the adults. The most significant finding was that several obsidian weapons were found near the bodies, though obsidian was not locally available, found in sites that were near neither in place nor time. Though this finding is considerably later than the Natufian, its place coincides with the border zone of Afro-Asiatic expansion, and can be under-stood through the Natufian-Jericho continuity.

For a full interpretation of these findings, we need to present the character of Natufian settlement; in particular, its obsession with burials and death – central to understand how something so outrageous and unprecedented as warfare could have come into existence.

Natufian liminality

The Natufian was not only liminal in time and space, but virtually in all its charac-teristics. Whether it possessed a particular feature or not, it was always an end or a new beginning, always in-between.

Thus, to start with the most basic thing, it was in the Natufian that the greatest revolution in human history happened, settlement, the source of all other revolu-tions and revaluations of values, the major reason why the world is in the state it is now, after receiving its modern spin. For this, it is enough to consider some most basic facts: the planet has existed for about 4.2 billion years; human beings for several million years; settled existence for about 15,000 years; and modernity a couple of centuries.

Settlement was the key innovation and central feature of the Natufian, not agriculture, a development that took place many millennia later. Natufian in this respect represents an end, and literally an end, as it was after the Natufian that the first experiments with plant and animal domestication took place. But the Natufian, together with the Kebaran, also had a singular position concerning art. Art was central for the Palaeolithic, but was absent in the Kebaran (Cauvin 2000: 14), and while small portable art objects existed, especially in the Early Natufian, they were rare (17–18; Grosman 2013: 623), and bizarre (see the small statue of a copulating couple, evidently the first ever explicit representation of a sex act; Bar-Yosef 2002: 122).

There were, however, other 'positive' senses in which the Natufian brought something new. The first was a direct consequence of settlement: the concern with *keeping*. Natufians did not produce food, but collected and stored pulses,[3] nuts and plant seeds, culminating in the strange fact that the first (self)-domesticated animals, after the dog (which is a different and much longer story), were mice and rats, so much so that the presence of such remains is now considered the main criterion for recognising sedentism (Bar-Yosef 1998: 168; Bar-Yosef and Valla 1991: 5).[4] Instead of domestication, Natufians practised selected hunting, killing only the biggest males, but as a result the size of gazelles decreased, rendering food shortage an even more pressing issue (Mithen 2003: 46–7).

Neither animals nor plants were domesticated in the Natufian. This allows us, following hints from Foucault and Mumford, according to whom technological innovations, in particular the invention of the machine, was first experimented on humans, to apply the same logic to settlement: before humans domesticated animals, they themselves 'became' domesticated. Even further, this development can be given a Heideggerian reading. Heidegger (1977) argued that enframing transforms man into a standing reserve, and this was central for the rise of modern technology. This can be directly taken back to the Natufian and not further: it was settlement that first transformed man into a standing reserve.

The single most important other feature, strict correlate and correspondent of sedentism, was a literal obsession with death,[5] resulting in the emergence of a genuine culture of death, where impulses were concentrated, whether for good or bad.

Before reviewing this fact, we need to clarify two general introductory points. First, of course, death is something which every human, in fact every 'genuine' animal, had to face. But death was never the central concern for human existence: it was rather life, and contentment with the world. Sad, gloomy feelings are sporadic, they go up and down, especially when man is continuously in the move, as in walking, when he is gaining always new and different emotions. If the Natufian obsession with death looks so familiar for us, settled moderns, educated through Freud's death instinct or Heideggerian philosophy, this is because we indeed have affinities with the Natufians, but not because this contains a great discovery only we two share. Settlement is an immobilisation, a fixation to a point, a no-escape, a trap for everybody in every age.

Second, as it will be seen, death indeed became here a genuine obsession; unprecedented in every one of its elements, and mostly not followed, though producing, and in various ways, a substantial impact.

Modalities of Natufian settlement

Given the unquestionable significance of settlement for human history, it is somewhat strange that no good explanations are offered for Natufian settlement.

There is certainly a link to climate change, and here a recent, methodologically sophisticated study by Grosman (2013) is particularly helpful. According to this, Early Natufian started around 12,700 BC and lasted to 11,600 BC, without a peak, having rather a plateau, thus indicating continuity. Late Natufian, however, started around 11,100 BC, showing a definite peak around 10,800 BC, and ending in 9500 BC (Grosman 2013: 625–7).

These data lead to a number of significant inferences. The start of Natufian clearly coincides with the Bølling-Allerød interstadial, also started around 12,700 BC, with warmer temperatures rendering Natufian settlement possible. Similarly, the start of Late Natufian also coincides with a significant environmental change, this time the colder and drier Younger Dryas period. This response was quite abrupt. However, instead of returning to the lifestyle they led before settlement, Natufians rather spread from their homeland towards surrounding areas. The response can thus be considered a kind of expansion and conquest.

This idea receives support if we carefully consider the third and most important date, the relative gap between 11,600 and 11,100 BC. According to Grosman, Early Natufian ends around 11,600 BC, but Late Natufian only started around 11,100 BC. Separating core and periphery within Late Natufian renders the analysis even more interesting. According to this, within the core area there was a move towards Late Natufian just around 11,600 BC, but this loses momentum, and only picks up pace at 11,100 BC, or when the temperatures quite suddenly turns colder. However, Late Natufian grows particularly outside the core area, a peak being reached there a century earlier, 10,900 BC (629).

To make sense of these data, in particular the reason and manner of shift to the periphery, we first need to review in more detail the dynamics of Natufian settlement.

Settlement as permanent liminality

Natufian settlement emerged out of commensals, originally seasonal gatherings (Mithen 2003: 44, referring to François Valla), at a liminal time and place: around Mount Carmel, full of caves with a long archaeological record, and saturated with – highly liminal – meanings, being close to the Bay of Acre, a major port, and eventual home to the prophet Elias. Its situation and shape recalls the Cordes Mountains (*La Montagne des Cordes*), with the Neolithic hypogea of Fontvieille, close to Arles and the Rhône delta, but also the Bay of Marseille (Guilaine 2015); a hundred kilometres south of Chauvet and west of Cosquer caves.[6] These gatherings became extended in a series of directions: towards feasting, of which first evidence only appears in the Natufian (Munro and Grosman 2010: 15363); this occasionally could have gone, and certainly went, out of hand. As one such possibility, a 'feast gone wrong' scenario may have resulted in the emergence of sacrifices, with its unique, weird, emotionally highly charged combination of pleasure and pain.[7] In another direction, the scenario of such gatherings may have become standardised over time, leading to ever more formalised rituals. All these developments, in whatever combination and succession, eventually gave rise to permanent settlements: a permanentisation of the temporary (Szakolczai 2000: 215–26, 2009). Settlements then became fundamentally centres of emotional impulses, with pain dominating mortuary activities, but these became combined with the pleasure of eating and feasting, producing a particularly explosive scenario.

While the details of the process, and its sequence, are not known, the central elements of this complex set of activities are captured in a series of Hungarian words, having an evidently common root. The words are *lak(ik)* 'inhabit, dwell', *lakik* (today almost exclusively as *jól-*) 'eat to satiety', *lakoma* 'feast, banquet' and *lakol* 'pay, atone for something'. The etymological dictionary is in evident difficulty, as the root *lak* is part of the oldest layer of Hungarian, yet it cannot fit together all meanings, thus giving the sources of all words as uncertain, 'perhaps' related to *lak(ik)* 'inhabit', and even for this only claims that the ancient origin is 'possible'. No connection is implied between Hungarian and Natufian settlement; it is only claimed that the connections between the four words can be perfectly explained as elements of the dilemma explained above. Settlements in houses (*lakás*) are connected to commensality and eating to satiety (*jóllakás*), which can be extended into full-scale feasting (*lakmározás*) where, if the limit is trespassed, people have to pay for it (*lakol*; -ol being a common Hungarian suffix for making a verb out of a noun). Thus, beyond Natufian correspondences, the Hungarian words even indicate that the sin of settlement-feasting (*lakás*) requires atonement or expiation (*lakolás*).

Natufians, and their successors, evidently did not pay attention to the limit. They may have been intrigued by the possibility, opened up by warmer climate, of keeping the feast forever. The result was a combination of three central features of settled existence: the emergence of *scarcity*, as settled people had to turn to the same sources of food repeatedly; the emergence of *stress*, as people sharing the same limited place inevitably generates tensions; and an entrapping of the pulsating emotions of pain and pleasure due to the same space being inhabited by the dead and the living.

Mortuary practices

Apart from the fact of settlement, the most specific characteristic of Natufian concerns mortuary practices. Here as well, Natufians introduced a fundamental novelty, a novelty even more striking than settlement, and its direct and most immediate consequence: the burial of the dead inside settlements, even inside houses, under the floors, thus mingling the living and the dead (Cauvin 2000; Banning 2003; Byrd and Monahan 1995), at the place where people were living, now permanently: 'Natufian graves were uncovered in all of the hamlets' (Bar-Yosef 2002: 112). The separation between the dead and the living and the observation of certain respect and taboos concerning death were central marks of the difference between human and animal existence, the very emergence of humankind, as Bataille argued; in fact, even animals have an instinctive repulsion of staying where dead bodies are. This was infringed in the Natufian. Thus, while 'we' moderns somehow tend to see in Natufian settlement the origins of 'our' civilised existence, the truth is the exact opposite: far from representing advance, Natufian rather represents a drastic, singular leap aside.

Associated with this negative novelty, there were a number of further Natufian innovations in mortuary practices, though establishing the exact sequence is hindered by the fact that experts – as so often – come to disagree on most points. Thus, while for a long time it was argued that the practice of secondary burial also started in Early Natufian, this has been postponed to the later period (Bocquentin 2003). Another innovation, at least in the region, include burials with decorations, or of men with dogs (Bar-Yosef 2002: 113; Bar-Yosef and Valla 1991: 6), which evidently were sacrificed. Natufian also marks the appearance of large cemeteries (Grosman 2013: 623).

In the Late Natufian buried corpses were no longer decorated, but another fundamentally new and clearly gory practice emerged: the removal of the skulls from some of the dead (Bar-Yosef 1998: 164; Byrd and Monahan 1995; Grosman 2013: 627). This practice would have a long future in the broader region, with equivalents to be found elsewhere (like skull shrinking, practised among others by certain tribes in Papua New Guinea and the Amazon region), but is hardly compatible with practices of treating the dead, going back at least to Neanderthal times.

With all these novelties as transgressions associated with the Natufian, one might wonder whether an ultimate transgression, the taking of human lives, could also be connected with the first settlements. For long, and for various modernist ideological reasons, Natufian was considered a particularly peaceful culture, in supposed contrast with its neighbours. However, recent discoveries refuted this presumption. According to a detailed study of Natufian mortuary practices, Fanny Bocquentin (2003: 456) claimed that especially the Early Natufian 'was not such a peaceful period as it was thought'. In particular, certain skeletons excavated in Kebara show that they were subjected to 'particularly violent and repeated aggressions' (456–7), including six young men who were all buried together (471). Several of the skeletons were found with projectiles inside their bones, another absolute and sad novelty, as only isolated and badly documented cases exist from elsewhere in the period (456–7). Similar evidence is present from the site of El Wadi, where a number of adults were buried more or less together, indicating probable simultaneity of death (457, 470). Still other studies indicate evidence of live decapitation (Orrelle 2014: 50).

House and domestication

Settlement and domestication, in the sense of reorienting and limiting life to a concrete, enclosed space, implied a radical shift in human existence, changing the perception of the world (Banning 2003; Watkins 1990). Following Peter Wilson, Banning talks about 'domesticating humans' (Banning 2003: 5).[8] Artificial, forced permanent settlement altered the normal movement and dynamics of life. Beyond the idea of limit as measure, rendering reciprocally meaningful life possible, the new walls inside and outside 'enhanced concepts of privacy, secrecy, envy and suspicion, ultimately allowing the replacement of egalitarian ethic by competition', while also leading to accusations of witchcraft and a game of hiding and displaying (5; see also Hodder 2006). This new game was not sanctioned and promoted by religion as awareness of divine love, but rather was marked by the emergence of a pervasive culture of death. The construction of houses, even according to recent ethnographic evidence, often started and ended with rituals of sacrifice (see in particular Eliade 1990). Such combining of celebration with a supposedly necessary, gruesome sacrificial ritual contributed to an excessive culture of orgiastic feasts, of which the enormous Natufian boulder mortars, which were used somewhat similarly to church bells, calling for the feasts, are important testimonies (Munro and Grosman 2010; Rosenberg and Nadel 2014). The difference between the two lies in the mechanical, pounding, pulsating movement necessary to keep sounding boulder mortars. As a result, feasting, sex and death became thoroughly conflated.

Interpreting the shift to Late Natufian

In our view, something quite sinister happened with this shift, inside the already sinister Natufian culture. The first crucial indication in this regard is that the peak point of Late Natufian explosion happened about a century earlier in the periphery, rather than the core areas, coinciding perfectly with the advance of the Younger Dryas. This indicates that a rather stagnant or dormant Natufian culture, riven with internal contradictions, was as if revitalised under the pressure of worsening climatic conditions and turned its internal void, a consequence of the parasitic, idle and closed existence generated by fixed settlement, towards geographic expansion, spreading its cultural features just at the moment when these features demonstrated an intensification of its already gory and morbid mortuary practices.

Archaeologists, experts in the field, tend to assume that there is something 'natural' in the Natufian expansion from core to periphery. Such an attitude is understandable, as human cultures spread in this way for hundreds of thousands of years. However, the difference is that Natufian was a sedentary culture, thus its expansion necessarily entailed something like an invasion or conquest; a permanent occupation. Walking people move around; they are at home in many places; for them, it indeed can be said that they are at home almost anywhere in the world. Settled people, however, are stuck to a fixed place where *others* cannot enter; they are exclusive, and others are excluded. This necessarily entails the setting up of artificial boundaries and their defence by violence.

Even more, violence – already endemic in Early Natufian, probably rooted in the insensitivity gained towards death, due to literally living among the dead – is already assumed by moving around for conquering land: a previously absurd idea, as land was there, in nature, free for everyone. This can make sense of the first documented evidence of warfare in history, which in our interpretation has been misconceived as intergroup violence, supposedly documenting the inherently violent nature of man. It was nothing of the sort, and can rather be understood as part of the Natufian reaction to the onset of Younger Dryas. The coincidence of timing is again perfect: the Jebel Sahaba war, or rather massacre, took place in 11,000 BC; the peak point of Late Natufian in the periphery was 10,900 BC, in the core 10,800 BC, while the Young Dryas dip in temperatures started around 11,000 BC. The fit is almost too perfect. It coincides with the presumed extension of Afro-Asiatic, and is in line with the dental traits of the victims (C. Turner 2008; Holliday 2015: 467–8). It also has evident parallels with the Late Natufian expansion towards the Harifian culture in the South, just as with the later, Lake Turkana massacre, where it was possible to identify obsidian projectiles.

Thus, we conjecture that the Jebel Sahaba massacre was produced by incursion of Natufian 'warriors', looking for food, but also areas of expansion. Given that Jebel Sahaba is only a few hundred kilometres South from Qurta, under the influence of Atlantic cave art, we can even hypothesise that this event was not only a first occasion of war in human history, but the first inter-civilisational conflict. We can hardly imagine today, after the 'wars of the 20th century and the 20th century as war' (Patočka 1976/7), what this could have meant 13,000 years ago, for our distant predecessors, who first faced people who wanted to chase them away and kill them – something probably they could not even understand. Two key aspects of the conflict indicate the momentous, hardly imaginable nature of the event. The first concerns the enormous degree of violence shown,[9] and the second the evident care taken by the survivors to bury the victims, turning the bodies facing the sun and the river, sources of life (Holliday 2015: 216).

The idea that Natufian extension from core to periphery may have been due to some kind of invasion and conquest, and that violence further in North-Eastern Africa can be interpreted along similar lines, is supported by some of the central findings of Fanny Bocquentin for which she could offer no full explanation. Thus, while Early Natufian showed some signs of social differentiation, these disappeared in the later period (Bocquentin 2003: 484–5). Similarly, while burials in the earlier period were eclectic and rarely collective, against previous interpretation, in Late Natufian burials became uniformised and collective (475–6). Finally, according to her, 'the most surprising findings are without doubt those that demonstrate an improvement of the conditions of life in Galilee in spite of the climatic deterioration in the Young Dryas' (478). She argues, along rather simplistic evolutionary Durkheimian reasonings, that all these were due to an increase of social cohesion.

However, social cohesion, as Girard argues, can be produced by violent means, through the sacrificial mechanism; and the conditions of settlement are strongly conducive towards producing the process of scapegoating, through escalating imitation, which is very unlikely to occur among hunter-gatherers. Even further, improved living conditions, especially when these cannot be attributed to natural factors, can be due to procuring goods through violent means, or exactly the kind of Natufian expansion we assumed. Sacrifice therefore was not the origin of culture, but rather a mechanism connected to the periodic breakdowns of settled existence, under conditions of recurrent violence, even warfare.

Making sense of Nietzsche, making sense through Nietzsche

The storyline presented so far has fundamental elective affinities with Nietzsche's *Genealogy of Morals*. This means that our discussion of prehistory sheds new light on Nietzsche's ideas, just as it can be further illuminated and supported by them, while helping to excise whatever is unacceptable among Nietzsche's always intriguing but often misfiring insights.

This is very much in the spirit of Nietzsche's inquiry, as while his book is a series of essays containing hypothetical ideas combined with conjectures about words and etymologies based on his philological background, it claims that these are related to real facts. The story Nietzsche is trying to reconstruct is concerned with concrete events: what *really* happened (*Genealogy of Morals*, II/22, Nietzsche 1967: 92), in history *before* 'world history' (III/9, 114), or evoking archaeology which hardly existed in Nietzsche's time. We can now corroborate or refute Nietzsche's conjectures, while using his work to develop ideas for ours. The fit between Nietzsche's conjectures and our archaeologically based storyline is striking, though there are fundamental problems with the story as told by Nietzsche. The ideas concerning the original, innocent violence and cruelty of man are untenable, just as is Nietzsche's understanding of Christianity as rooted in resentment.[10]

The book introduces a crucial figure for understanding human history, an ideal type in Max Weber's sense, the 'ascetic priest'. The term is not perfect, but serves the purpose. The central feature of the figure is distance from the self-evident and natural values of existence, corresponding to a happy, innocent, care-free living in contentment, due to physical infirmity (sickness and especially impotence; see I/7), combined with an excess of mental and spiritual capacities. Such combination resulted in negative feelings like envy, hatred, jealousy, rancour and vengefulness (I/14, II/ 11, III/14), culminating in *ressentiment* towards the more healthy, leading the ascetic priests to use their abilities for gaining control. The problem is that Nietzsche assumes as a starting point both a degree of self-consciousness that cannot be taken for granted, as part of a Hegelian mode of thinking; and on the other, that there *exists* a sphere of life connected to mental or spiritual concerns that is separate from normal human activities. In our interpretation this separation only took place with Chauvet, or the rise of representative art, as painting Chauvet – or at least its reproduction – required specific technical skills. The rise of representative art in 'prehistory' as a technique that can be altered in the direction of magic is the condition of possibility for the emergence of the 'ascetic priest'.

Nietzsche's second major conjecture concerns the mode of activity of ascetic priests: the taming of a people, all those who are healthy, happy and innocent in contentment. This is identified with civilisation as domestication, the glorious origin of civilisation as then understood was nothing else but the emergence of taming as a difference. From this perspective the '*meaning of all culture*' becomes to reduce man to a 'tame and civilised animal, a *domestic animal*' (Hausthier; emphases in original; I/11; 1967: 42); the enclosing of men behind and between walls (II/16, 1967: 84); or a process of *internalisation* (Verinnerlichung, emphasis in original, II/16, 1967: 84; as Foucault would explicitly claim, here is the main source of inspiration for *Discipline and Punish*). The term 'taming' or 'tame' is used recurrently at important places in each of the three essays (I/11, 16, II/6, 16, III/13, 15, 21), being a central term in Nietzsche's understanding of human history. While some of the uses are highly problematic, the overall point is spot on, as he comes to identify *settlement* as the crucial turning point of history, moment of the 'revaluation of values'. However, we still need to see how Nietzsche brings together the settlement and taming of man and the ascetic priest.

By doing so, far from imposing our reading on Nietzsche, we only follow his storyline from the inside. He defines his purpose, at Section 13 of the third essay, a crucial junction of the book, as explaining how the ascetic priest managed to find his 'herd'. This was only possible because man *became* a sick animal, ready for taming – and, indeed, while the first essay is devoted to presenting the ascetic priest, the second explains the development of a sense of guilt as the condition of possibility for taming. Here, however, we need again not only to complement but to correct Nietzsche, using archaeological and ethnographic evidence, as such a sense of guilt was not due to the ascetic priest, but rather derived from the problematisation of the act of killing, *especially* through the unfair, technological means of the spear, invented by *Homo sapiens*. In our view, this technological innovation, as Neanderthals immediately realised, threatened the balance of life on the planet, and eventually led to the immortalisation of a vision about the graceful beauty of the world, threatened and thus needing to be preserved, on cave walls. A sense of guilt, already due to hunting, and especially technically sophisticated hunting, giving no fair chance to the animals, was therefore indeed there, and was not a trick.[11]

The 'revaluation of values' effected by the ascetic priest was thus rendered possible by two factors: guilt felt due to technically efficient killing, and the technical skill of creating artistic representation. Thus, *pace* Latour (2013), technique, in particular action at a distance, *is* indeed a problem, even *the* problem, as it resulted not in empowering but enslavement, by enframing us into a standing reserve through settlement. The representations on the walls of Chauvet cave were created as ways of atonement for keeping the beauty of the world intact; however, eventually, starting with Pergouset cave, entering the cave was turned into a trickful and self-debasing ordeal, empowering those who passed pretending to be equivalent creators of the world through making artificial representations that first spiritually and eventually physically entrapped humans in-between walls. Eliade's (1989) shamanism has already been applied to Palaeolithic art; but this should be complemented with Nietzsche's 'ascetic priest'. The possible relationship between these two ideal types in the context of Palaeolithic culture is a theme this book cannot speculate upon.

While there is no sign of a Palaeolithic version of the 'ascetic priest' in Kebaran culture, some signs of art, as well as traces of 'shamanism' (Munro and Grosman 2010), do appear in the Natufian. A genuine encounter between settlement, rituals and art is visibly present in Çatalhöyük, while a peculiar sanctuary has been just recently unearthed in Göbekli Tepe. The next two chapters explore the findings of these two sites.

Notes

1 Kebara cave is close to the sea, south of Mount Carmel in Galilee.
2 See 'The Skeletons of Jebel Sahaba', *Archaeology*, 14 July 2014.
3 The etymology of this word, with its connection to strike and thrust, is intriguing, recalling the multiple use of mortars.
4 For an amusing contrast, see the 'domesticated' mice of Thoreau (1962: 272).
5 It is from this perspective that we can properly understand one of the most striking claims of the New Testament: 'Let the dead bury their dead' (Mt 8: 22).
6 Cosquer cave, discovered in 1991, is one of the most important Palaeolithic painted caves, with two series of visitations dated around 25,000 and 17,000 BC (Valladas *et al.* 2001).
7 This is visible even through the origins of comedy; see Szakolczai (2013a: 50–2).
8 This can again be supported through etymology, as 'domestication' is derived from Latin *domus* 'house'.
9 This type of violence, strikingly, was depicted in the 'first' engraving of Pollaiuolo, pioneer of a new, technological late renaissance innovation in art.
10 While Palaeolithic man was certainly not violent physically, he might have had a reaction to the ugly and strange that for us looks cruel, but which was a 'normal self-defensive reaction to the disconcerting discovery of gross deviations from the beauty and harmony of God's nature' (Rutherford 2000: xiii), borrowing an expression from an effort to understand *Don Quixote*.
11 On this, see also Calasso (2016: 13–72).

7

GÖBEKLI TEPE

Sanctuary as trickster bestiary,
or the revival of transgression

Natufian culture did not have a centre comparable to Chauvet or Lascaux, and could not have had, given the nature of this culture, even though Mount Carmel, with its caves and cupules, performed somewhat such a function, as it hosted both some of the earliest and most populous Natufian settlements. However, around the time when the Great Thaw at the end of the Ice Age happened, and Natufian culture terminally declined, a true ceremonial centre emerged just north of the Natufian areas, on a hilltop now called Göbekli Tepe. As this site was also discovered in 1994, just like Chauvet, 1994 was a genuine *annus mirabilis*, not only for archaeology, but for the self-understanding of man as well.

Both time and place have their importance. Concerning time, while its building cannot be dated with absolute certainty, it is most likely that this took place around 9600 BC, or just after the Great Thaw. Concerning place, Göbekli Tepe lies in-between and thus connecting the two major roads through which the gift-exchange of obsidian was conducted, from Cappadocia to the Southern Levant, and from the Lake Van area, especially Bingöl to the Zagros Mountains; roads which until that time were separate. Furthermore, Göbekli is about 15 kilometres North-East from the city of Sanliurfa, historically called Edessa (and having some significance for the rise of Christianity) and also Urfa. It is close to Aleppo and Harran, and only about 120 kilometres away from Malatya (ancient Meliddu), with the important archaeological site of Arslantepe, central for the transition to the Bronze Age. Even further, it is just about a day's walk (20 miles) East from the hilly flanks of Karacadağ Mountain, where the domestication of emmer and einkorn wheat were experimented with. Thus, the site has an evident centrality for the rise of religion, settlement, agriculture, the use of obsidian and exchange networks.

Göbekli is best known through the radical novelty of its enormous megalithic constructs, which predate not only the pyramids but even the stone temples of Malta by many millennia. Previously, it was considered impossible that hunter-gatherers could build such monuments. However, especially from the perspective of this book, just as important and interesting is the break it represents with Natufian culture and the relative return to the late Palaeolithic ways of distinction.

According to the judgement of Klaus Schmidt (1953–2014), discoverer and excavator of Göbekli Tepe (Schmidt 2000a, 2000b), the site was not inhabited and solely used as a cultic place. Evidently, it wasn't a cemetery either. The predomination of vulture-like birds in representation is usually considered a sign of practising excarnation (the exposition of dead bodies, practised for example in Tibet; see Schmidt 2011), but we rather connect it to the depersonalisation effect already seen in Pergouset cave (see Chapter 5). While the claim concerning the absence of settlement has recently come under attack,[1] it is on the one hand quite problematic to question the judgement of an excavator in such a matter from the outside, and on the other hand the failure to accept such a judgement was evidently due to an attempt to take the Natufian conflation of the living and the dead, continued in Çatalhöyük, as some kind of standard background horizon which, seen from the late Palaeolithic, the reference point of Schmidt, it clearly wasn't. Thus, while Schmidt of course admitted that it is impossible to formulate final judgements about a site of which only a small part is excavated, we take it as evidence that there is a radical break between the Natufian practice of mingling the dead and the living, and the effort at Göbekli to keep separate the areas of daily life, ceremonies and burial grounds; an attempt that corresponds to a return to Palaeolithic normality in respecting the order of basic prohibitions, following Bataille.

However, more than simply being located in-between the two main obsidian roads, the building of the cultic place at that particular moment and place was also rendered possible by the huge population movement that must have taken place due to the warming of temperatures and the rising of sea levels, even if we have little concrete knowledge about the details – due, among other things, to the fact that movements near the sea-side, a probable path, would have been soon erased by advancing sea levels. At any rate, the force beyond building the Göbekli megaliths clearly incorporates the experiences and feelings of the late European Palaeolithic.

At that moment, the middle of the tenth millennium BC, not only Natufian culture ended, but the cave-art culture was also abandoned, with the rise of Azilian culture, or the onset of the Mesolithic. This is a quite striking development, a sign of cultural decay, as the central feature of Azilian is a marked decrease in the standard and quality of stone tools, and the increasing importance of microliths. The site of Göbekli Tepe, with its connections to the Palaeolithic, seems to indicate that somehow again contact was found between the two regions.

Such contacts are not simply visible in certain aspects of the site, like the focus on rocks or the attention devoted to representative art, a radical contrast to Natufian, but permeate the entire undertaking. Building required an enormous effort, not simply concerning the physical work that had to be organised and performed in putting the megaliths into their place, but the novelty of such an idea – again recalling the novelty of Chauvet, the literal springing out of an amazing, transgressive idea without any precedent, out of sheer nothing. This is the sense in which 'it had been at Göbekli and not Jericho that the history of the world had turned' (Mithen 2003: 67). It could only have been formulated by people belonging to a culture of contentment which already had the idea of preparing something for eternity, a trust in reality – like painting the cave walls; but which for some reason came to the realisation that the walls of existing underground caves could no longer be used, perhaps because the dangers associated with such a close affiliation with the void became more prominent (as the underground imagination in dreams became polluted); thus, a similar work of art prepared for eternity now had to be made above the ground, assuming the gods have changed. However, now the logic of enactment was different. Instead of putting paints on the rock surfaces embedding themselves in the animal designs (horses, bison, mammoths, often with sweet human eyes), in Göbekli they built up human-shaped blocks for their own embodiment (the Round Head frescos at Tassili, to be discussed in Chapter 9, were a similar though not identical undertaking). Using the term of Mircea Eliade, Göbekli was a negative omphalos; however, it still evokes a certain continuity with the European late Palaeolithic experience.

A digression on the possibility of an Atlantic-Göbekli connection

While there is hardly any archaeological evidence about the direct connections between the late Palaeolithic in Europe and the Middle East, a recent discovery, or rather re-discovery, can be considered as a genuine missing link, and furthermore is exactly connected to rock-art. In 2004 Belgian archaeologists accidentally discovered rock-art along the Nile, which recalled similar representations found by Canadian researchers in 1962–3, but which then generated scarce echo (Huyge et al. 2007, 2009: 112; Smith 1976). In 2005 they managed to rediscover the site of Qurta, about 80 kilometres north of Aswan Dam, and judged that the depiction of animals, the majority being cattle, showed marked similarities with late Palaeolithic European art, while the weathering of the engravings indicated great antiquity, estimated at about 17–16,000 BC. Since then it was possible to measure the age of this rock-art with some precision, using both radiocarbon dating and the optically stimulated luminescence (OSL) dating method, which assesses the exposure of mineral grains to sun. According to such joint studies, the engravings were made about 15–12,000 BC (Huyge et al. 2011), thus contemporaneous with the engravings of the Magdalenian Teyjat cave, which most closely resemble the kind of representation discovered in Egypt, and which are dated 13,500–12,000 BC. The site is not unique, as several other sites with similar rock-art have been discovered in Egypt, though they have not yet allowed a similar dating.

Thus, in spite of the huge distance, direct connections between Göbekli and the Palaeolithic caves are walking possibilities. The character of the Göbekli site, however, while similarly aiming at eternity, had quite different characteristics from cave paintings. In terms of explanation, it is argued that these works were backward looking, and show evidence of ritual use. The first point, at a certain level, is obvious, but it is not at all clear what 'ritual' means in this setting. So far very little evidence has been found that would indicate some specific 'ritual' use, so it might well be the case that we are again misled by present-centric preconceptions. On the other hand, the site clearly exudes some kind of nostalgia, just as Tassili, to be discussed later – though, as it was built before the rise of agriculture, it is not imminently clear what is the reason for and the object of such feelings if not the same as in Palaeolithic settings: the search for sympathy with the enormous emotional charges of the void. However, neither its artistic qualities nor its character stand up to Palaeolithic standards.

Further clarity can be gained through a closer inspection of the facts. It can start from the most important aspect of the site, the enormous T-shaped pillars, the most visible, highly impressive and simply dominant elements of the complex. Apart from their sheer size – they are about 3.5–5 metres tall and weigh up to 50 tons, while a 7-metre-long slab remained in the quarry unfinished – they have two crucial features. They can be considered as highly stylised anthropomorphic figures – in some cases hands and a belt, and even a penis is clearly indicated;[2] and many have animals engraved on them. The character of these animals, arguably, offers a key for understanding the meaning of the site.

Göbekli animals as trickster bestiary

At a first level, such images establish a positive connection with Palaeolithic caves, and a negative connection with the Natufian. Just as in Palaeolithic cave art, the representation of animals is a central feature in Göbekli Tepe, and in contrast to the Natufian, where such representations are absent. However, the way animals are depicted is radically different. The graceful beauty dominating cave art is replaced by danger, apprehension and threat. In the words of Klaus Schmidt, in beholding them one feels 'danger, menace, fright, dread' (Schmidt 2011: 245); their presence exudes a 'supernatural and crashing force' (260).

Such emotional perceptions can be supported by the character of the images. They prominently contain dangerous animals: lions, wild boars, foxes, serpents and scorpions, which furthermore fully live up to their threatening character: the lions roar, showing their teeth; the wild boars similarly demonstrate their tusks; the fox is jumping; the serpents slowly but slyly and steadily advance; the scorpion's tail is pointed towards its victim. In descending to a Palaeolithic cave, one is overwhelmed by joy; in watching the images of Göbekli, one rather becomes apprehensive, if not frightened.

Such impressions are fully borne out by a quantitative study of the animals represented (Peters and Schmidt 2004). The starting point to notice is that, just as in most similar studies, whether in the Palaeolithic, Northern America or Southern Africa, there is no clear positive correlation between the animals depicted and those featuring in the local diet. The gazelle, main source of food, is hardly represented, just as there are few aurochs, goats or equids. The images are certainly not part of a hunting magic. However, apart from this negative result, the quantitative analysis offers surprisingly helpful clues to come up with a hypothetical explanation about the reason for the undertaking.

The animals most frequently represented on the megalithic pillars are the serpent (28.4%), the fox (14.8%) and the wild boar (8.7%) (185), while similarly frequent is the representation of insects, in particular spiders and scorpions (as the remains of these animals cannot be retrieved in the debris studied by archaeologists, no percentages were offered). This list is particularly instructive, as from our perspective one can immediately recognise in this list some of the most prominent and important trickster animals: the serpent (the par excellence trickster of the Old Testament, among others); the fox (the main trickster of the Middle Ages, captured even by Goethe, a point evoked by Schmidt 2011: 188–9); and the spider which, apart from its widespread folkloristic use, was rediscovered by the great novelists of the nineteenth century, Dickens and Dostoevsky, as a representation of 'absolute evil' (Citati 2000; see Szakolczai 2016a).[3] Thus, the great Neolithic sanctuary of Göbekli Tepe is nothing but a trickster bestiary; a cynical representation of the divine.

This is best visible in one of the most powerful images from Göbekli: a relief in enclosure D, filling most of a pillar, where a bull is looking upwards, with his horns pointed, ready to charge, confronting a snake which is sliding downwards, with his nose almost touching that of the bull (Peters and Schmidt 2004: 190).

The question now concerns the meaning of such an undertaking; the enormous exertion invested in arranging literally hundreds of stone pillars, each weighing many tons, on a hilltop complex, and engraving them with a trickster bestiary. Was it an attempt to warn; an effort to leave a warning comparable to the attempt at immortalising the vision of the awesome, graceful beauty of the world, and which is its exact twin: a warning against the forces that threaten this beauty; forces that represent the opposite of the joy of life, and that can only be a life-philosophy of death; a warning that could have been an allusion to the settled Natufian culture, which indeed *was* a culture of death?

If this was the effort, then it was truly heroic; yet, it evidently failed. The most impressive part of the complex belongs to the PPNA (Pre-Pottery Neolithic A, 9600–8800 BC). The buildings and artworks of the next PPNB period (8800–8000 BC) are smaller and of lower quality; and finally, at the end of this period, and certainly by about 8000 BC, the entire complex was filled up with soil, with another enormous expenditure of energy, and abandoned. This certainly was not, and could not have been, the original aim; the complex was created, just as the paintings in the caves, to last forever, as that, with its life span of about 25,000 years, evidently did. While the Göbekli project did not survive that long, it showed a certain resilience: it lasted for about two 800-year periods. The question of what it wanted to address and gain, however, is still unanswered; after this, the culture of death had the upper hand. We now need to explain how this happened, and why.

Answering the first question requires a review of the evidence. The second question, however, can be answered more quickly.

As it can be understood from the perspective of Plato's thinking, and practically only from there, even the representation of graceful beauty is a delicate and ultimately counterproductive enterprise. This is because such an undertaking might be sincere and full-hearted, but a representation is still only a representation, not the real thing, so it can only give rise to another representation, or a representation of the representation, and then of the representation of the representation of the representation, and so on, until wholesale trivialisation and decay. If one needs an example, one only has to consider what happened with the angels of Raphael, first through various modalities of artistic academism, then with devotional kitsch, and finally with the tourist industry.

However, if we consider the representing of the trickster, or 'evil', the stakes are even more problematic. No matter how much the original intention of invoking or warning might be genuine and deeply felt, it still only amounts to representing the fearful, the dangerous and the ugly, which then could be trivialised, losing all sense and – even worse – becoming desirable, a source of nostalgic afterthought, or outright the obscure object of desire. The effort to warn against the trickster and its bringing about a culture of death, as immortalising the threat represented by trickster figures thus inevitably ends up supporting and strengthening the very thing it was warning against. Such an effort, in contemporary terminology, such a 'critical theory', no matter how much it intends to serve the 'good', necessarily promotes the forces of 'evil'. However, perhaps Göbekli was not an effort of warning, but these figures genuinely represented their own 'gods'. At any rate, those in charge of the Göbekli Tepe project eventually, evidently managed to perceive this paradox, and thus gathered the force to nullify their own mission, hiding away the work that was created to last for eternity.

However, to understand the reasons for this strange, unexpected and unintended development, we need to discuss in some detail another crucial and much related process, the rise of agriculture, or – in a better terminology – the domestication of animals and plants, following the literal 'domestication' of man.

The origins of agriculture

Even concerning this topic, recent research has radically and dramatically revised the account that became established during most of the twentieth century. However, we need to be quite specific concerning the nature of this change: what is at stake is not to come up with a completely new and radical perspective that overcomes and renders obsolete everything we thought in the past and considered valid and meaningful, but rather it implies a thorough problematisation of the modernist, presentist, progressist, materialist, linear evolutionary narrative, keeping in mind that the Natufian, Göbekli Tepe, Çatalhöyük and Tassili show constant, recurrent efforts to gain sympathy with the void for the sake of certain secret self-interested undertakings.[4] Rather than taking another giant step forward, the central issue is to recognise how much most recent findings, radically improving archaeological understanding, are compatible with classical, well-weathered, pre-modern narratives.

The rise of agriculture was thought to have been a revolutionary change, indeed a 'first' revolution, comparable only to the industrial revolution in modernity (Wallerstein 1974), preceding settlement and the rise of religion, and caused by environmental factors, implying pressures like population growth 'forcing' human beings to adapt to a new behaviour. Such views took for granted that human behaviour was primarily concerned with procuring subsistence, and for this purpose 'rationally' 'maximising' food production. It was also thought that plant domestication significantly preceded the domestication of animals.[5] In contrast to this, recent discoveries made it evident that settlement, and even the building of megalithic stone sanctuaries, significantly preceded the rise of agriculture. Furthermore, even the expression 'rise of agriculture' is a misnomer, as it is now argued that one should rather talk about a process of domestication; a terminology that reflects and incorporates the primacy of settlement. Furthermore, this process was not a sudden and revolutionary change, but rather lasted for a long period, possibly up to several millennia. Even further, there was no gap between the domestication of plants and animals; and concerning plants, the primacy of cereal has been exaggerated (see again Zeder 2011; also Balter 2010a; Zeder 2015; Zeder and Smith 2009). In short, archaeologists increasingly find little evidence of a 'crisis' at the origin of agriculture (Balter 2010a: 406).

This was accompanied by a major shift in the location where these changes were primarily supposed to take place. In the past, for evident but also evidently wrong reasons, it was assumed that a central role was played by the Southern edge of the so-called 'Fertile Crescent', or Palestine, in particular Jericho. In contrast to this, by now it has been established that not only several areas of the Fertile Crescent were equally involved in the process, but the central role was played by Southern Turkey and Northern Syria, with Jericho and Palestine in general playing only a secondary role at best (Sagona and Zimansky 2009: 21–45; Schmidt 2011: 49–53). The pioneering ideas directing this research were formulated by Robert and Linda Braidwood, who first had the intuition that the rise of plant and animal domestication should be traced to the 'hilly flanks' of the Northern Fertile Crescent, and not the Palestinian desert; while the full consequences of this shift were first drawn by Jacques Cauvin (2000, French edition 1993), excavator of one of the most important sites now associated with the rise of agriculture, Mureybet, in Northern Syria.

Within the area of Southern Turkey, it is now believed that a series of settlements along the middle Euphrates were crucial. This is exactly where Göbekli Tepe was, presumed cultic centre of PPNA culture. Indeed, two of the most important recent findings trace the arguably most important aspects of this domestication process to the immediate surroundings of Göbekli. First, the origins of emmer and einkorn wheat, two of the central sources of modern cereals, can be traced to the hills of Karacadağ Mountain, just West of Göbekli, with the first signs of plant domestication appearing around the mid-ninth millennium BC (Balter 2010a; Heun *et al.* 1997); and second, the site where the transition from hunting to herding animals was completed was Nevali Çori (Zeder 2011), the settlement closest to Göbekli Tepe, and particularly close even in terms of its symbolism, including similar, though smaller, megalithic monuments.

Though there were some precedents in the last stages of the Ice Age, the process of domestication mostly took place and was certainly intensified only after 9700 BC, thus coincides with Göbekli Tepe and Tassili. We thus must try to understand what could have been the manner and reason in which the particular kind of mentality to be associated with Göbekli could have contributed to such a development.

As a start, we should recognise that the Neolithic as a process of domestication, in contrast to the purely technological-economic interpretation of an 'agricultural revolution', can only be successfully conducted as part of a culture promoting life, and not through a culture of death. The Natufians could not generate agriculture, only managed to organise a self-destructive culling of gazelles, the cold will of taking away from nature being evident even here. Maybe the point is that, beyond identifying the Natufian as a culture of death, we need to recognise that a culture that supposedly developed agriculture only to produce a 'rational' strategy of survival is also a culture of death – as any concern with mere survival automatically is. So animal domestication is a quite paradoxical matter for promoting life. The domestication of the cat or dog, to whom one can become emotionally attached, certainly required a degree of loving care, but interpreting the domestication of animals to be butchered – if that was the original aim and reason – as an instance of loving care is a more ambivalent argument.

To understand the possible – but in a way also necessary – connection between domestication and Göbekli, we need to review the evidence of such a domestication and compare it to the imagery of this complex. To begin with, the problematisation of killing animals did not appear with domestication, but was rather, evidently, a permanent feature of human culture. Hunters in many human communities, up to recent times, performed an elaborate ceremony – not a 'ritual' – around the killing of large mammals (identified with gods anyway), which was not a hypocritical attribution of the guilt for his death to the animal itself, but rather a way to reconcile the necessity of such killing with a self-image of decency (Bertolotti 1991; Frank 2008). Herding animals only to kill them was thus not a self-evident sign of human 'progress', except if you consider them low-class creatures, like your gods, as evidently Göbekli managed to persuade itself, with its trickster god-bestiary.

However, just as cave paintings hardly represented those animals that were most hunted for their meat and thus consumed, the animals domesticated around the ninth millennium BC were not the ones frequently depicted in Göbekli. The first domesticated animals were the sheep and the goat. Goat domestication originates in the hills of the Zagros Mountains, in Iran, in the ninth millennium BC, reaching Nevali Çori around 8200 BC, and the Jordan Valley, including Jericho, just after 8000 BC (Zeder 2011).[6] Sheep herding, however, originates in Turkey, with earliest evidence from Nevali Çori, around 8500 BC, and spreading from there to nearby sites. Evidently, in the areas where the sheep was first domesticated, the goat was introduced later. In Nevali Çori, this pioneer of animal domestication, the goat only appeared around 8200 BC, in Abu Hureyra even later, c.7600 BC, while in lower Palestine, where the goat was introduced early, from Iran (according to some, it was developed locally), the sheep appeared much later, around 7200 BC.

The domestication of cattle is a more controversial issue, as in 9–8000 BC it was still mostly wild. The heartland of this process was evidently the same mid-Euphrates area in South-Eastern Turkey. Pig was domesticated somewhat earlier than cattle, though certainly later than sheep and goat, in the later ninth millennium BC, in an area somewhat further to the North-East, in Cafer Höyük and Çayönü.

For an interpretation, we first of all need to realise that domestication became intensified in the PPNB, thus in the period when the quality and character of art in Göbekli already decayed. Thus, it probably was not a direct outcome of the kind of efforts that were immortalised in Göbekli. Furthermore, the kind of animals, and the manner in which they were depicted, also have a specific relationship to the way domestication and its consequences were possibly experienced, which can be perceived in the dual meaning of the term 'wild' in most languages. 'Wild' at one level means simply 'not domesticated' (a meaning that certainly made no sense before domestication); while at another level it means a behaviour that is threatening, dangerous, ferocious, out of control – though, interestingly, the same Latin root word *ferus* is behind the word 'fierce', which means 'proud' in the sense of 'noble', the 'other' sense of wildness.

Yet, while this 'domestication' effort was evidently successful, something went astray, within a few centuries, with Göbekli, as the sanctuary complex was filled up, and again with enormous effort. The meaning of this change can be reconstructed through the kind of cultic centres that emerged soon after, and which we read as representing a victory for the culture of death; a victory that lasted until the rise of the Halaf culture, in Northern Mesopotamia,[7] eventually culminating in the Sumerian culture, further on the South, and which – according to Schmidt (2011: 239) – can be directly connected to Göbekli Tepe.

The reassertion of a culture of death

The failure of Göbekli to counteract the Natufian death cult, and a certain cultic and religious shift back to the Southern Levant, is marked, most symbolically, by the building of the two most famous constructions of Jericho, the Tower and the Wall, both dated around 8000 BC (Bar-Yosef 1986). While the exact purpose of these buildings is still a subject of debate, it is unlikely that they were serving defensive purposes, and while the Tower was not used as tomb, and there is a strong case made for the wall serving flood control purposes (see also Mithen 2003: 54), their joint building suggests joint purposes, and their symbolic, ceremonial use is most likely. This is only more probable due to the quite close coincidence with the filling up of Göbekli Tepe.

The meaning of the shift can be first approached by the character of these two constructs, and their contrast to the Göbekli sanctuary. The stone Tower of Jericho, with its height of 8.2 m and total weight estimated at 1000 tons

(Bar-Yosef 1986: 157), is much higher than even the highest megaliths of Göbekli, and is considered the highest building of the ancient world, up to the construction of the Pyramids. This is all the more impressive, and intriguing concerning the original purpose, as – while Göbekli was built on a hill-side, overseeing the Northern part of the Mesopotamian plains – Jericho is situated in a deep depression, about 250 metres below sea level, thus locating the – for many years – highest building on the planet at one of its lowest dry-land places. The wall is similarly unique, the oldest 'city wall', with a most impressive size, a width of about 2 metres, a height of 3.5 to 5 metres, surrounded with a ditch cut into solid bedrock that is 8 metres wide, 2.7 metres deep and a circumference of about 600 metres. It was thus a most emphatic reassertion of the central value of settlement, a definite closing off; the marking of an inside and an outside; a binary division and schism within life; an at once material and symbolic way to end the culture of free walking.

The main problem of Natufian settlement, as discussed above, was that the limited, saturated and crowded mode of existence thus created also and in particular short-circuited the living and the dead, leading to a culture of the dead and of death. There are many and highly convincing indications that with Jericho, and its closest offshoot, 'Ain Ghazal, there was a heightened return to such a culture of death.

The three most important aspects of this culture are the plastered skulls, the stone masks and the life-size clay statues (Goring-Morris 2000: 106–7). While they have some precedents in Natufian settings, and there is one similar statue, the mysterious 'Urfa man', found not in Göbekli Tepe but actually the complex identified as 'The Pool of Abraham (Balikli Göl)', inside Sanliurfa, each of the three elements, but especially when taken together, are fundamentally unique and absolutely shocking. They can also be dated mostly to the period 7–6000 BC, with some aspects appearing as early as 8000 BC. The plastered skulls, first discovered in the 1950s by Kathleen Kenyon, are human skulls, severed from the bodies, plastered, often painted and decorated, with beads or precious stones fitted into the eye sockets, producing a terrifying impact. They are matched, however, by the stone masks, which – with their wide-open eye sockets and mouth – generate a similarly scary feeling. These masks can be and most probably were worn; they even have perforations on the side by which they could have been attached to the heads of performers (Hershman 2014: 4). While the skulls were discovered in Jericho proper, fragments of two stone masks were found in the Nahal Hemar cave, situated in a marginal area, on the boundary between the Judean and Negev deserts (Mithen 2003: 82–3); thus, a liminal place. These masks strongly evoke the later, Phoenician and Punic masks,[8] probably used by priests for the gory practice of child sacrifice, widespread in the tophets – an association all the more probable as the high frequency of young skeletons present in Jericho alludes to such sacrificial practices (Schmidt 2011: 41).

The life-size clay human statues, only found in 'Ain Ghazal, perfectly complement and complete the picture, as they are similarly terrifying and awesome, genuine golems, with their glaring gaze, armless body, and straight, linear, lifeless, rigid legs that come directly out of the upper body, without any indication of a waist or a bosom. This site came into prominence once Jericho started to decline, and acquired a significantly larger size. The burial ceremonies, performed using the life-size statues, were evidently quite shocking. Because of its size, however, 'Ain Ghazal also declined more quickly, and the exhaustion of the surrounding lands produced a quite remarkable collapse (Mithen 2003: 83–5).

A site offering a condensed presentation of all these wonders, or rather horrors, is Kfar HaHoresh, a Neolithic burial ground, used between 7200 and 6500 BC, situated about a 100 km North-West of Jericho, on the lower Galilee Nazareth hills, excavated by Nigel Goring-Morris (Mithen 2003: 83; Goring-Morris 2000: 107). Here the burial customs discussed previously were complemented with a number of even more exotic practices, which include mass slaughter of wild animals, the plastering of surfaces for burials and the combination of human burials with animal remains, which so far is unique for this site (Goring-Morris 2000: 109, 121; Horwitz and Goring-Morris 2004; Mithen 2003: 83). The site is also remarkable for its extensive use of lime plastering, which was the first pyro-technological device invented, indicating an early, and quite eerie, association between the technological promotion of speed and the cult of the dead (Goring-Morris 2000: 126), and explaining the rather curious title the excavator gave to his article, recalling the 'velociferic' speed in Goethe's *Faust* (see Müller 2011: 172; Szakolczai 2016a: 178).

Biblical allusions and traces

The Jericho-'Ain Ghazal-Kfar HaHoresh complex left its mark on the Bible as well, except that – following, among others, hints by Károly Kerényi and Thomas Mann – it must be read properly, paying attention to contexts and affinities with archaeological evidence, helped by anthropological theories, and not understood literally and in the light on ethnic-racial-nationalistic presumptions.

The destruction of the Walls of Jericho is one of the most famous stories in the Old Testament, and was supposed to have been confirmed once archaeologists found the Walls in the first decade of the twentieth century. However, as the Biblical events were supposed to take place in the Bronze Age, the eventual, much earlier dating of the Walls, confirming the early suspicions of experts, was incompatible with the Biblical narrative. However, such discord disappears once we realise, following the interpretation of the Abraham motive given by Thomas Mann in his *Joseph and his Brothers*, his little appreciated masterpiece, that the Biblical narrative, especially insofar as it focuses on exodus, conquest and foundations, is a condensed mythologem of many separate stories. The central elements of the Biblical 'Walls of Jericho' motif are the name of Jericho, the enormous wall and the decisive will to terminate it. The trumpets of Jericho also evoke other similar trumpets: those of the Book of Apocalypse, and perhaps even Kafka's likewise apocalyptic trumpets in the Hippodrome of Clayton.[9]

The case is analogous with the Tower of Jericho, except that here even the name was altered. The similarly famous Biblical story concerned a huge tower, having just as fundamental, foundational and even apocalyptic connotations as the

Tower of Babylon; a tower associated with an original discord between various people, leading to the split of languages. This event could well be associated with evident conflicts, signalled by the filling up of the Göbekli sanctuary, around 8000 BC; though we need to find a good reason why the name was altered, substituting here Jericho with Babylon. However, this is not so difficult. Concerning the Walls of Jericho, the Biblical story focused on their destruction, and by the time the Old Testament was written they were indeed long ago destroyed. However, concerning the Tower, it was supposed to still stand, serving as a memory for the hubris of human efforts – and indeed, the Tower of Babylon was standing, and just where the story was written down, repeatedly re-conquered, signalling the necessary demise of arrogant, hubristic human ambitions.

'Ain Ghazal and especially Jericho were mostly ceremonial sites, thus competing in kind with Göbekli; while Kfar HaHoresh was outright a burial ground. However, the elimination of any boundary between life and cult, between the living and the dead, so central for Natufian culture, was brought to a similarly striking culminating point in Çatalhöyük, one of the most important archaeological sites.

Çatalhöyük was the ultimate experiment of a culture that gave up walking as a way to live and understand itself and the world.

Notes

1 See Banning (2011), and the entire issue of *Current Anthropology*, devoted to the theme. The problem is methodological: Banning reads the earlier Göbekli Tepe through the prism of the later Çatalhöyük.

2 The same anthropomorphism is characteristic of the highly standardised Nevali Çori figurines (Morsch 2002), with the additional, quite significant feature that the women are sitting, some holding a baby, while the men are standing.

3 Strikingly, for Marx the spider was a main source for explaining 'rational action'.

4 Concerning the untenable character of such 'materialism', widely refuted by recent evidence, only two points will be made. First, physicists now have great difficulty in explaining what matter really is, given discoveries concerning subatomic particles. The bright optimism of progressive materialists is dissolved into the difficulties of conceiving the ways waves 'produce' something we perceive as matter. Thus, matter is something connected to our own mode of living reality. Second, etymologically 'matter' is derived from Latin 'mater', which simply means 'mother'; thus, not so different from the idea of 'mother earth', which is indeed fundamental for us humans, but in ways quite different from 'materialist evolutionism'.

5 For a review of the standard narrative, codified by V. Gordon Childe and recently reaffirmed by Ofer Bar-Yosef, see Zeder (2011).

6 While we extensively use the excellent work of Zeder, we do not accept the 'niche hypothesis' promoted by her, which is still too universalistic and rationalistic, and in contrast will follow the lines exposed by Ingold (2000), who here as well offers a series of convincing arguments to reverse the materialistic, at once neo-Darwinist, neo-Marxist and neo-liberal perspective, which he traces to Engels, who extended Marx's materialist dogmatism to early human prehistory.

7 This is discussed in Szakolczai (2016b).

8 The Archaeological Museum of Cagliari in particular contains several such masks.

9 For details, see Szakolczai (2017a: 97).

8

ÇATALHÖYÜK

The culmination of settlement

The first thing to notice about Çatalhöyük is its puzzling uniqueness. This uniqueness incorporates both the fact that the site is unique, in terms of its longevity and size for its period, and the manner of its uniqueness. Çatalhöyük consists of two mounds, of which the more important East Mound was inhabited 7400–6000 BC, continuously, after which it was abandoned and occupation shifted to the West Mound, a site of no particular significance. In this quite important period, lasting from the abandonment of Göbekli and the new assertion of Jericho as cultic centre up to the rise of the Halaf culture and its evident signs of social flourishing (Szakolczai 2016b), incorporating the shift from pre-ceramic to ceramic Neolithic, during the so-called 'crisis of the Neolithic' (Frangipane 1996), Çatalhöyük was consistently inhabited by several thousands of people, in its peak – during levels VII and VI, thus the middle of the 7th millennium BC – probably reaching as much as 8,000 (Hodder 2006: 7, 100–1). Because of its size, unparalleled in the period, Çatalhöyük was considered at its discovery as the first city; however, as it lacks all the main characteristics of cities, including public places, streets or buildings, it is now considered a large village, and can indeed be called the first 'global village'. The task, requiring the collaboration of all kinds of social scientists, is to understand what this could have signified at that particular place and time.

The use of the East Mound produced eighteen occupation layers (Hodder 2006: 7), though due to the continuity between most layers they cannot always be separated neatly. As the houses were built upon each other, the site was conserved exceptionally well, making it a genuine paradise for archaeologists. However, it is important to keep in mind that such preservation was not due to contingent factors intervening over the centuries and millennia, but rather was due to the nature of the site, its compactness and especially the manner in which houses were built, thus reinforcing its puzzling exceptionality. This is furthermore underlined by the quantity and character of its art, in stark contrast with

Jericho and 'Ain Ghazal, where art is all but absent, except for the bizarre, even terrifying objects associated with burial customs and rituals, and in some ways continuing the lineage of Göbekli Tepe and even the Palaeolithic caves in its transformative significance. Thus, the most exceptional aspect of the site was that every house was at the same time a cemetery (99), with the association reaching back to the Natufian, though in Anatolia by that time burial had become extramural, except for Çatalhöyük (123–4). Perhaps this is the root reason why ethnographic research discovered that the mound locally is still associated with the 'souls' of the past (14); a situation quite similar to Tassili.

Given the evident importance of the site, the first point is to understand why it was built at that particular place. Here we immediately encounter a major puzzle, as the site lacks clear characteristics to make it an evident centre. It was neither at the sea-side, nor along a main river, where most of the important sites in the previous and following periods were located; it was also much further to the North-West of the Fertile Crescent than any of the previous major sites – in fact, until its discovery it was considered evidence that there was simply no Neolithic in Turkey. Thus, suddenly, way further to the West than any of the previous Neolithic sites were located, thus at the margins, a new centre emerged, which even became the first large village. It was a clear case of transforming marginality into liminality.

However, even apart from its outlier status, it is not easy to explain why the site was built where it was. It was not in a particularly fertile agricultural area, and the fields were quite some distance from the site. A source of obsidian, Hasan Dag Mountain is somewhat close to the site; and obsidian was indeed central for Çatalhöyük. However, again quite strikingly, obsidian in Çatalhöyük was not derived from Hasan Dag, rather from two sites in Cappadocia, East Göllü Dag and Nenezi Dag (14), the first being the same quarry used in the Southern Levant already in Natufian times (Khalaily and Valla 2013: 197–9).

There is only one resource-related reason for the location of Çatalhöyük, and this – strange as it may sound – is the easy availability of *mud* (Hodder 2006: 79). Mud was central for the inhabitants due to two reasons: because the houses were built from mud bricks; and because it was a source of plaster, used abundantly both for house floors and walls, and having connection to burial practices, back to the Natufian – or perhaps there is something other, and more, in this fact? Given that – as we'll see in more detail – life in the site was singularly concentrated on the house, there being neither public places nor buildings, nothing but square houses, separated only by empty spaces that were mostly containing heaps of rubbish, while houses were accessed from the roofs, it should not be surprising that the village was located where the major ingredient for constructing such houses was readily available. All this leads to the striking conclusion that Çatalhöyük, this first mass-global village, was simply built on, by and through mud.

However, and further, mud is a similarly submissive and even transmitting, conveying, surrendering, passage substance as water, as it was analysed in the case of the Pergouset monsters, in Chapter 5. It transforms earth into a workable granular material by its mixture with water. As it has a combination of earth, silt and clay, it reacts well to heating and any other kind of treatment, through which it gains a different form than its original character. Bricks made from mud are resistant, hard, but forever losing the original, skin-healing and hydrating mud-character, curative features known over the ages (in fact, its manufacturing is exactly to take away its healing water component and transform soft mud into hard bricks). This is why mud and its capacity for fashioning have a strong spiritual component. The transformation from the muddy, dirty human body into a pure agent of perfection has the connotations expressed in Isaiah (64:8) as 'we are the clay, and thou art our potter; and we are the work of thy hand'. Mud is also closely similar to excrement; see again Hungarian *sár* 'mud', *szar* 'shit'. Finally, just as water, mud is also an excellent transmitting agent of electricity, though in its dried form it again becomes resistant to electricity. Its fugitive, unstable, Hermes-like character suddenly changed into a massive, impenetrable fortress after it was fired or heated – so its traditional association with the human body, soul and spirit is at hand.

However, the situation is even more particular, in both a negative and positive sense. Negatively, it confirms that the rise of agriculture did not play a major role in the rise of the Neolithic, thus – pace Childe – refuting, far from confirming, Marx's ideas about the role of the 'material base' throughout human history.[1] Positively, on the other hand, it supports not simply the crucial importance of settlement, but the existence of a particular transmitting (relaying or even 'broadcasting') complex around settlement, focusing on matter transformation. While in terms of agriculture, animal husbandry and plant cultivation was not yet fully integrated in Çatalhöyük, it can be considered as the culmination of the long process of settlement, the first fully settled society, aiming at transformation. Thus, given the uniqueness of the site, it can offer us some decisive insights about the puzzling question why human beings decided to settle (Hodder 2010: 2), and what consequences it entailed. A particularly intriguing puzzle concerns the exclusive focus in symbolism on wild animals, ignoring contemporary domestication (18).

We must again start with the basics.

The central novelty of Natufian culture, or of settlement, whether intended or not, was the coincidence of the dead and the living, and in particular the manner in which they merged with each other within the single place of the settled house. The centre of the house, concerning the daily life of the living, was the hearth, or fireplace, giving the name for the house in several languages (see Greek *Hestia* and Latin *Vesta*, also names for female divinities), fundamental both for cooking and as a source of heat and warmth. But fire was also central for mortuary practices, through the 'pyro-technology' (Goring-Morris 2000) it pioneered. It was this use of the fire that has been increasingly extended to the house as well, both as a plastering of the floor and the walls, or as a way to burn the brick muds. Thus, the world where the living and the dead became mixed increasingly concentrated around the manipulation of fire.

The centrality of this development can be understood if we bring in the significance of the mastery of fire for human history, combining the latest archaeological evidence with the oldest myths. The mastery of fire has been associated with civilisational progress in many cultures, of which the myth of Prometheus is only one of the best known examples. This myth is also intriguing as it considers such a feat as stealing, marking Prometheus as a trickster figure (Kerényi 1991), who offered a kind of enlightenment for humans that eventually made them much less content, as contained (meaning within proper mortal limits), than they were before. While this myth is considered Greek, and supposedly only goes back to about a thousand years BC, it arguably incorporates much older mythogems. This can be illuminated through recent evidence about the Neanderthal use of fire, while – in line with the Goethe-Weberian methodological device of 'elective affinities' – this evidence can shed new light on the myth as well.

The question of whether the use of fire was invented by Neanderthals preoccupied archaeologists for long decades. Some evidence was interpreted as use of fire extending back to half a million years or more, but others questioned the legitimacy of such an interference and considered that such burning was due to natural causes. Questions were also raised about the continuity of such practices. A recent article (Sandgathe *et al.* 2011) re-examined previous evidence through extensive research and the re-examination of previous findings in two major sites, Pech de l'Azé and Roc de Marsal in France, where the continuous use of the caves as refuge could be traced back about 100,000 years.

The research produced three main results. First, the use of fire by Neanderthals could be conclusively demonstrated, going back at least 100,000 years. However, surprisingly, such use was not continuous: in both sites fire was much more used in the earlier than in some of the later occupational phases. The authors at length and convincingly argue that this was not due to circumstances but actually documented decreasing use. Finally, third, there was a clear connection between the colder spells within the Ice Age and a decreasing use of fire in the studied Neanderthal sites. This led to the concluding idea that while the Neanderthals evidently mastered the use of the fire, they could not produce it. They had to keep whatever fire naturally occurred. The most frequent source of such fires is lighting, and such events are much more frequent in a warmer climate.

This evidence has clear elective affinities with the Greek story about Prometheus and the Olympian gods. The main Olympian deity, Zeus, was primarily a god of storms and lighting, thus a deity in charge of fire. It was thus primarily he that Prometheus deprived of his power, just as in the related story about the origins of sacrifice – the Greek term *thuos* specifically means 'burnt offering' – Prometheus tried to fool Zeus. Thus, the story corresponds to recent archaeological evidence about the origins of the human use of fire: as fire was probably produced by lighting, this could be attributed to Zeus, a mountain god of lighting; fire could thus be considered a 'gift of god'; and the trick of Prometheus, the great enlightener, was to invent a way to 'produce' fire artificially, not simply keep and rekindle a fire originally produced by lightning.[2]

This also helps us to understand the fundamentally anti-technological world vision of the ancient Greeks, preserved in some way, through whatever road of transmission, since the Palaeolithic.[3] According to this, animating the philosophy of Plato and rediscovered in the anthropology of Marcel Mauss, life is first of all a gift, the gift of being alive in this beautiful world entrusted to us, and thus must be lived through the receiving and transmitting of further gifts. A kind of knowledge that interferes with such an order of things alters the world, and so – while seemingly only beneficial – brings about various negative outcomes.

Interestingly enough, archaeologists interpret the case of Çatalhöyük from a very similar perspective. Mithen (2003: 93) contrasts Pech-Merle, where handprints on walls are read as signs of welcoming, greeting visitors, with Çatalhöyük, where handprints visible around the 'sharp, oppressive images' rather 'seem to be more of a warning or a plea of help – its people are trapped within a bestiary from which they cannot escape'. For Hodder (2006: 171) in contrast to 'societies structured around communal sharing and reciprocity', Çatalhöyük demonstrates '[w]hat happens when people start to keep and not give'. The question now concerns how exactly this development has come about. For this, we somehow need to reconstruct, genealogically, Çatalhöyük as a difference.

The horizon on which the rise of Çatalhöyük can be properly situated is offered by the two great events of c.8000 BC, the filling in of Göbekli Tepe (and the joint abandonment of Nevali Çori) and the return to prominence of Jericho. Of these, Çatalhöyük has clear affinities with the death cult 'spirituality' of Jericho, probably transmitted through Çayönü, the South-Eastern Anatolian site with the closest connections to the Levant, central for the domestication of pig, the first site showing the use of metals (cold hammering only, not yet smelting), and also the first as having a large, stone sanctuary with clear signs of the practice of animal and human sacrifice (Schirmer 1990). Göbekli was filled in at least five centuries before the mound of Çatalhöyük started to become populated. Yet, there is a return to the importance of art in Çatalhöyük that has no parallel in other sites. This poses the question of how such a legacy could have been transmitted, though this cannot be pursued here. We'll rather investigate the manner in which art became integrated into the Levantine death cult; a central part of the mystery of Çatalhöyük.

The 'mystery' of Çatalhöyük

The first step towards solving this mystery lies through realising that there is no real mystery behind Çatalhöyük, as the site does not offer genuine values. It is unique in terms of the quantity, variety and character of art objects found there, but their quality is poor, by no means comparable to the late Palaeolithic. Furthermore, while the site is also unique in size, giving place to several thousand people, it did not do so by providing high living standards, as inhabitants were not particularly healthy (Sagona and Zimansky 2009). Even further, living there was a frightening experience. This is rendered quite well through the otherwise often annoying time traveller that Steven Mithen inserted into his book, in order to render archaeological evidence more 'user friendly'. It was a place of entrapment, rather than a model of social flourishing, with people inside the houses trapped within a bestiary they cannot escape, offering a 'nightmare vision of the world that farming has brought to these particular members of humankind', with a pair of women's breasts sculpted on the wall, but with nipples split apart and in the company of 'skulls of vultures, foxes and weasels: motherhood itself violently defiled', thus offering a vision of 'Neolithic hell' (Mithen 2003: 93–4). Far from being a bright sun attracting people due to its splendour, it was rather a black hole, sucking people inside,[4] as a vacuum cleaner (which, as we know, collects dirt), who then became unable to leave it, as they are profoundly disempowered, evidently attracted by the gory, irresistible repulsiveness of the place.

If its size and longevity thus remain a perplexity, as it is not evident why people went there and stayed there,[5] this must have been due to some kind of enchantment. Hodder uses in this context the work of Alfred Gell (1998), in particular his ideas concerning the 'technologies of enchantment' and 'material entrapment'. Furthermore, just as Gell connected technology and magic, Hodder similarly argues that – while the distinction between magic and religion is of course quite difficult to make or prove – the character of symbolic practices in Çatalhöyük is more magical than religious in character. 'Magic is part of religion, but it also transgresses'; and thus the activities connected to depositions 'can be termed magical, in that they seem linked to particular practices that stand against the usual religious repertoire and can be seen as having a more direct instrumental character' (Hodder 2011: 115). This can again be best understood through Göbekli, through the effort it made and the vacuum left by its failure. The builders of Göbekli perhaps only desperately wanted to call attention to the threat of tricksters, symbolised there by particularly wild and especially cunning, rootless, parasitic animals, comparable to the way demons and monsters are depicted in medieval churches. However, capturing such threats in images has its own inevitable negative side effects, which might have led to the destruction of the site, due to the possible multiplication of such trickster operations through time in scale and power – as an evocation of demons and trickster in order to chase them away inevitably only attracts and proliferates them. Arguably, this is what has happened with Çatalhöyük, as the integration of the spirit of Jericho and the late Palaeolithic happened in a particular manner: by stealing the memory of the *late* Palaeolithic (here in both senses of the term), reanimated in Göbekli, perhaps as a past Golden Age, and re-integrating this stolen memory into the Natufian death culture.

The central instrument of doing so was the house, in particular the new kind of house system of Çatalhöyük, transformed into a ritual space in which every aspect of everyday life became ritualised, and where the memory of the distant past, before settlement and agriculture, became mingled with a suffocating, oppressive cult of ancestors, while this entire set-up managed to acquire the consent of everyone through a conflation of collective and individual memory by the privatisation of tradition, rituals and art into the space of separate houses. According to Hodder (2006: 18), this led to the emergence of the first mass individualised society, 'a prehistory of the mass', where – instead of a genuine community of concrete persons – a number of nondescript people were performing the same things, in parallel and at the same time, in their individual houses. A cave, as David Lewis-Williams argued, might have combined individual access to the paintings, through long and narrow corridors, with some kind of relaying of this experience in the larger halls near the entrance, but excluded the possibility of uniformisation through a hierarchised privatisation of ritual space. The cubes of Çatalhöyük, with their uniform arrangement and character, served exactly this purpose.

We could also refer here to the particular example of the unique underground cities in Cappadocia, in Derinkuyu and Kaymakli, about 150 miles East of Çatalhöyük, where going as far as 60–100 metres under the ground, there is an extended network of passages and tunnels, with hundreds of cells and an 80-m-deep ventilation shaft dug out of the soft tufa, including three-sink basin systems for a uniformly synchronised cult-service (Bixio *et al.* 2002). The complex is impossible to date, but evidently represents an extreme version of Çatalhöyük spirituality.

The dispositive of enchantment embodied in Çatalhöyük was composed of a number of tricks that together formed a coherent system.

Houses

The first of these enchantments was connected to the central institution of Çatalhöyük, the emblematic feature of settlement, the house. It was not simply the scene of many daily activities, just as the burial place of the dead, but also became the centre for the ritualised transmission of collective memory, integrating into the house the functions of sanctuaries, like the painted caves or the megalithic monuments, that previously were open, public and not closed, private spaces, thus integrating all three areas (everyday life, burials, sanctuaries) kept separate in Chauvet culture.[6] Thus, as Hodder (2006: 165) argues following Lévi-Strauss, Çatalhöyük could be rightfully considered as a 'house society', and it is in this sense that it represents the culmination of settlement as a process, with individual buildings to be associated with self-sufficient single families (7, 56–7). Such centrality of the house was rendered evident in the enormous care with which the floors and walls of the houses were continuously re-plastered;[7] a phenomenon that for Hodder illustrates the striking monotony and repetitiveness of daily life inside Çatalhöyük. This was done with all the more devotion as both floors and walls were sacred places, containing the main symbolic and sacred objects, like installations, paintings, skulls or obsidian (some hidden underground, or inside walls, or eventually filled in), just as burials: most skeletons and skulls were placed under the floors, but often in the walls as well. Skulls were sometimes removed from the skeleton, a practice evidently associated with prestige (179),[8] and that again leans back to the Natufian (Goring-Morris 2000: 107). Floors had clean and dirty parts, marking the difference *within* the house and *without* any separating walls between the profane and sacred spheres (Hodder 2006: 50–1, 110). The central difference, concerning houses, however, was between the inside, the house, and the outside, in-between the houses. The marked efforts to keep the houses clean can be contrasted with the utter lack of concern about these 'public' spaces, containing nothing but a heap of rubbish. They were not simply dirty, but also smelly and infectious.

Such care, however, fits ill with the scarce longevity of houses made out of mud-brick. Houses not only had to be continuously re-plastered, but also re-built; events that were highly ceremonial, just as the eventual demolitions, and which were most often done over the previous walls, at least at the level of foundations, thus keeping house structures stable for several generations, lasting up to a century or even more. The ceremonies accompanying the building or abandonment of houses were particularly enchanting, making use of two closely connected components (Carter *et al.* 2015). On the one hand, such events were probably marked by huge, even carnivalesque feasts, kept outside the village (Hodder 2006: 162). While inhabitants normally consumed sheep and goat, the preferred food of feasts was cattle (115), associated with collective memories of the past and not yet fully domesticated. Such links between carnivals and collective memory evoke the affinities between carnivals and the Golden Age, discussed extensively by Bakhtin (1984).

On the other hand, however, the foundation of houses was also associated with practices of human sacrifice; in particular, the sacrifice of neonates (Hodder 2006: 117; Carter *et al.* 2015: 100, 102), especially if the houses were built not over previous foundations, but middens (Hodder 2006: 148). Babies and children evidently carried little value for the inhabitants of Çatalhöyük as, while adults, whether male or female, were buried under the 'clean' floor of the houses, young children were buried close to the oven (123). However, skeletons of babies were also found under thresholds and inside walls, evoking the kind of sacrifice associated with the foundation of houses that survived in the folk traditions of many European countries, but especially in the Balkans (Eliade 1990), not surprising given longstanding connections with Anatolia. The similar practice of hiding obsidian under floors or in the walls, often in association with skeletons of infants, also intimates that obsidian was used as a sacrificial weapon. Combining these facts with the absence of any evidence for valorising motherhood led the new excavators to the conclusion that Çatalhöyük was far from being the site of a cult of the Great Goddess and motherhood. This reinforces the striking absence of female symbols, already noted in Göbekli: 'Imagery of a nurturing female is absent from Göbekli, and it is all but absent from Çatalhöyük' (Hodder and Meskell 2011: 250). This strongly contrasts with the Palaeolithic, where female symbols outnumber males by a ratio of six to one (ninety-six against sixteen) (Delluc and Delluc 2009: 658).

Animals

A further trick of enchantment can be recognised in the way animals were represented in the site. Houses contained wall paintings, sculpted reliefs and installations of animal parts into walls, representing a striking, bizarre combination of Palaeolithic wall paintings, Göbekli Tepe reliefs and Late Natufian installations.[9] However, beyond a comparison with Göbekli, here the 'monsters' of Pergouset and the *Shaft Scene* must be brought into the picture, due to the unique and combined focus on headless bodies (thus the practice of beheading and the cult of skulls), the cult of birds, in particular the replacement of human heads with birds, and the ithyphallic representations, culminating in the affinities between the proto-shamanic self-representations of the headless man of Pergouset and the lying man of the Shaft Scene. They all belong together, expressing, through shocking images and practices, a coherent vision of the world, behind which a professional class of trickster magicians or 'ascetic priests' must be present with their crucial aim for transformation, for merging characters into each other. The paintings contained mostly animals associated with the past, in particular red deer and especially leopards – a wild animal in all senses of the word. Reliefs also depicted leopards, but even more frequently cattle. Installations were dominated by cattle, while leopards were absent. Such installations almost exclusively contained dangerous parts of animals, like tusks, teeth or bucrania.

The literal obsession of Çatalhöyük inhabitants with the leopard, an animal whose bones are virtually absent from the site,[10] and which – though extant in Anatolia – was not present in abundance near the site, provides something like a master narrative for Hodder's basic book (Hodder 2006). However, here again, the mystery of the leopard can probably be best understood, together with the depiction of animals in general, as another master trick of enchantment, part of the stealing of (collective) memory by the 'guardians of memory' (161). At a moment when the domestication of animals was about to be concluded, the site did not celebrate this feat, depicting rather wild animals, evident testimony of times past, most certainly remembered as a Golden Age.[11] However, in depicting such memories, and in combining them with contemporary experiences, the artworks of the site subtly but clearly altered meaning. If in the late Palaeolithic emphasis was on the enormous emotion charges embodied in the figure of natural beauty and gracefulness of animals, even of the more threatening ones, and if in the 'trickster bestiary' of Göbekli dangerous animals were presented perhaps as a kind of warning about not so natural threats, in Çatalhöyük wildness as ferocity and savageness was applied – and implied – to all animals. A great paradox of such decoration, called in a chapter title 'The leopard's puzzle' by Hodder, is that in a site associated with domestication, the symbolic depictions all focus on wild animals, and in particular on their most dangerous parts, like tusks, teeth or bucrania, even showing a special interest in the excrements of small carnivores (24, 47–8). The message was that animals (or perhaps rather the divinities represented by animals) *are* savage, thus – instead of dreaming about the past Golden Age – one should rather be happy to live in this present when they are safely tamed, thus making more acceptable one's own similar 'taming', the reduction of living space to the grim reality of darkness, dirt and crowding. It is just in this sense that Nietzsche (1967) would identify the morality of civilisation as taming.

There is, however, another interpretation (and we somehow prefer this one): according to this, viewing the negative side of divine wildness, presenting it in a threatening way also stimulates punishing, and also catches the pulsation of emotions. At Çatalhöyük not only were the people caught and encircled, but their divinity also was trapped and imprisoned (and consequently the animals). This was because entrapping and enclosing was a precondition for gaining their vital forces.

Such hostility to animals and the divine, and thus to nature and the world as it is, amounts to a genuine nihilism, again in the strict sense of Nietzsche. It can be seen in several images, where animals – bulls and wild boar, but also stags and bear – are not simply hunted but teased and baited (Hodder 2011: 117), perhaps as part of initiation rituals (31); or which demonstrate the superiority of humans over animals, like the famous statue of a rather repulsive female figure domineering over two leopards. Even the strange pairing of animals, especially of leopards, can be understood in this sense, as leopards are solitary animals (91–2), thus a pair of them implies their supposed taming, always together of course with their coupling. Thus, the memories of the past, of the presumed Golden Age, were again stolen and transformed into a vehicle for justifying settlement as transformation.

A further, crucial trick, connected to the previous and instrumentalising them in a particularly effective manner, is the game of hiding and revealing, a central element of Hodder's analysis (169–84), which, together with game of restrictions and avoidances (57–9), was central for producing the 'spheres of entanglement' (59–64) in which everybody was entrapped; and which can be considered as a kind of hide and seek for 'adults', a kind of technique for infantilisation. It was by no means self-evident that such objects had to be 'hidden', instead of put into containers (174). Objects hidden under floors or inside walls were occasionally 'revealed', and in a quite pompous, ceremonial or ritualised way, legitimising the power and influence of those who were in possession of such knowledge (145–8, 175). It was this knowledge and not technical expertise or matters related to subsistence that defined the hierarchy of power in the site (183). Such games of hiding and revealing extended even to the art objects on the walls, as such walls, covered during the re-foundation and fill-in of houses, were occasionally dug up and 'revealed' by 'those in the know'.

This helps us revisit the old question concerning the difference between religion and magic. While recognising the difficulties in separating magic and religion, and that the central feature of magic is its transgressive aspect, Hodder still argues that '[i]n house based societies, houses are "religion"' (116, 120). We argue, in line with Hodder's persistent and recurrent focus on techniques of enchantment, that this 'religion' is rather a *transformative technology*. Furthermore, it is impossible to separate technology as a separate 'sphere' from the instrumentalisation of divine interference, which is always ready if the liminal void is at hand, as can be seen in the Palaeolithic paintings and the engravings in the liminal spaces of the cave, or in Göbekli Tepe and Tassili, by splitting man's character into human-shaped blocks and images, and in Çatalhöyük's mud-brick fortifications that imprisoned man and beasts as well. With this caveat, Hodder's recognition of the liminal role of religion *as* magic, in contrast to the question of causality or primacy, is well taken: 'religion and the symbolic were thoroughly engrained within the interstices of the new way of life' (121).

Çatalhöyük the incubator

One must beware of hasty generalisations. Çatalhöyük was not a completely iso-lated site. We have already mentioned the underground cities of Cappadocia in Central Anatolia, whose negative architecture was a kind of reverse mirror image of Çatalhöyük. Archaeology also revealed itself, over the past century and in par-ticular the past few decades, as the discipline of surprises, where new discoveries from one day to another can render accepted wisdom obsolete. Yet, Çatalhöyük is a quite unique site, discovered over half a century ago, excavated twice, with different methods, by major figures in the field and yielding complementary and quite consistent results. Furthermore, by now the broader area of Anatolia and the Fertile Crescent has been quite extensively excavated and mapped using survey techniques, thus it is not likely that a site of similar size and significance could have escaped attention. So the significance of the site seems beyond doubt, and one can properly attempt to offer an interpretation. The suggestion offered in this chapter is that Çatalhöyük was a kind of incubator.[12]

The question is what exactly was incubated there, and with what effect.

Closely following the facts unearthed, and the interpretation offered by archae-ologists, in particular the excavator of the site, Ian Hodder, it was argued so far that Çatalhöyük was a kind of ultimate embodiment and condensation of the con-sequences of settlement. Central to settlement was the entanglement of the living with the spirits of the dead, which resulted in a kind of culture of death. A certain echo of Palaeolithic legacy, evident in Göbekli Tepe, perhaps attempted to con-front this culture with a return to life-assertion and a possible warning about the rule of trickster logic. Such confrontation and warning was associated with the rise of the cultivation of plants and the domestication of animals, which at any rate was an extraordinary event, as the sudden appearances of new crops and their genetic modification are hardly explainable with ordinary logic, and surely could not have been brought about by a mere death culture – the Natufians, characteristically, only managed to undertake a certain 'culling' of animals, which proved counter-productive (Mithen 2003: 46–7). The significance of Çatalhöyük was that, through Jericho and Çayönü, among others, both agriculture and the Palaeolithic memo-ries were reintegrated into a revitalised, never completely forgotten death culture, through a transformation technology which was merging different characters: dead and living. In addition, this was helped, from one side, by a feeling of superiority over the divine (which is ferocious and wildly uncontrolled), and on the other, but connected with the first one, a similar superiority over the animals. Here we need to note the ambivalence of the very idea of domesticating animals to be butchered, as humans in this way substituted themselves to the animal's parents.

Domestication was thus a prolonged infantilisation of animals, with the parents being humans, who then eat their own children. From the perspective of the Palaeolithic profound respect for animals, even their association with the divine (something quite different from the evolutionist idea of 'animism'), this was a quite horrible practice. Çatalhöyük as an incubator functioned to break down any resistance to such practices; and central to this was the new practice of rituals of sacrifice, a kind of internalisation of violence, evidently first experimented, together with the use of metals, in Çayönü. Thus, in our view it was in Çatalhöyük that the 'ascetic priest' (or trickster-magician, Greek *goes* or Iranian *magus*) found its herd.

It was from this incubator that the spread of settled agricultural civilisation started its conquering march, transforming our world eventually into an 'ascetic planet' (Nietzsche 1967: 117).[13] The European Neolithic, both in Greece (in particular Thessaly) and the Balkans, was derived from Anatolia, even though the two trajectories were different, as the neolithisation of Greece happened not through the Balkans, as previously thought, but rather through the so-called 'island hopping' method (van Andel and Runnels 1995). Çatalhöyük also had an impact on Mesopotamia.

However, it is not the task of this book to explore in detail the causes, processes and consequences of the spread of agriculture and the rise of the connected mode of civilisation. The emphasis was only on bringing out the full impact of abandoning walking as a way of life, culminating in a particularly closed, suffocating world, where the freedom of horizons was replaced by the claustrophobic terror of everyday existence, evidently justified by a rising ideology of 'progress'.[14] It is to be noticed, however, that strangely enough, it was out of Çatalhöyük, the culmination of settlement, that a new kind of 'walking' practice emerged: new waves of migration by which groups of people carrying the spirit of *superiority* incubated in Çatalhöyük were spreading the 'benefits' of settled agriculture around the planet.

There is only one final point to be explored about Çatalhöyük, one puzzle to be resolved that so far hardly has even been recognised as such: the nature and character of the central 'guide' figures of Çatalhöyük, the 'guardians of memory' (Hodder 2006: 161), who were evidently 'persuasive leaders', whose mode of control over time seems to have gradually shifted 'from a more imagistic to a more doctrinal mode' (115), and who integrated in such a shrewd manner the so different spiritualities of the European late Palaeolithic and the Natufian, as embodied in and transmitted through Göbekli and Jericho, stealing and distorting the memory of the Golden Age. Given the association of the site with sacrifices, again through an evocation of divine interference through artificially incited liminality, they are bound to be members of some kind of sacrificial professional class; even more, the absence of temples and altars in the site seems to advocate such a possibility. This is why they are usually considered as elders, which is certainly part of the story, but cannot contain everything. Mere elders simply could not have managed such highly innovative combination, not to mention the striking reanimation of the practice of wall-painting.

We argue that the solution of this riddle lies through the similarly unique and even stranger site of Tassili, or the Tadrart Mountains, with its subversive techniques of identity formation.

Notes

1 The absurdity of Childe's position is best expressed in the hubristic title of his best known book, *Man Makes Himself*, originally published in 1936 (Childe 1951).

2 Even the famous story about Lemnos and the need to produce new fire every nine years must be connected to this story, thus reasserting the human power over the sheer forces of nature. Not surprisingly, the island of Lemnos is associated with Hephaistos, the smith god, and also with a cult of initiation, also connected to the nearby island of Samothrace, and linked to the Cabeiri.

3 We should recall that for Bataille the central reference point for Lascaux, as a similar 'miracle', was Greek culture.

4 This is further confirmed by the fact that a regional survey demonstrated that there were no contemporary nearby settlements Hodder (2006: 80, 82).

5 Hodder (2006: 74) explicitly names this as 'the "mysterious attraction" of Çatalhöyük'.

6 The distinction between public and private is a complex problem. We cannot transpose contemporary meanings to the past, but neither can we argue that such a distinction is purely modern.

7 There were buildings whose floors were seventy times re-plastered, without a structural change, while wall plastering could rich a thickness of 7.5 cm-s, containing as many as 450 layers (Hodder 2006: 127–8).

8 This applies in particular to the famous red skull of a male, held in the lap by a young woman in her tomb, discovered in 2004 and considered most exciting; see Hodder (2006: 23 and Plates 13–14); Carter *et al.* (2015: 100–2).

9 For a systematic comparison of Çatalhöyük and Göbekli Tepe, see Hodder and Meskell (2011). Centrally, they noted the lack of female symbolism in Göbekli, even marked in the general context of 'Neolithic Phallocentrism' (237–9), the presence of ithyphallic headless bodies and birds (240–2); and the focus on wild animals (241–3).

10 Until in 2004 a bone used for ceremonial purposes was discovered in the site, not a single leopard bone was found among the many thousand bone fragments analysed (Hodder 2006: 259–60).

11 This might explain the joint Latin etymology of *fera* 'wild' and *fiera* 'feast'.

12 About the original use of this term in alchemy, and for its application for social analysis, see Horvath (2013a) and Szakolczai (2013a).

13 Following the logic of schismogenesis, it also implies the promotion of its opposite twin, the spread of unbridled hedonism. Gnostic sects already in the Hellenistic period were famous for combining rigorous ascetic practices with rampant sexual orgies.

14 At least, one can interpret in this way the idea of Hodder about an increasing rate of 'change' becoming perceptible in Çatalhöyük (Hodder 2006: 164), together with the replacement of myth with history, and the rise of 'individualisation' and consciousness (141–68).

9

TASSILI

Incubating transformation, or a training ground for the magi

Tassili n'Ajjer and the surrounding areas of Tadrart, Abacus and Messak are a mountain range in the middle of the Sahara Desert, with heights reaching 1800 metres and located about 1500 kilometres from the Mediterranean Sea, maybe the closest place from where it can be reached. The sacred rocks of the region constitute one of the most extraordinary phenomena of figurative representations in human history, not least due to their extreme longevity and continuity of use, with the rocks and walls of Tassili engraved and painted for a period of about 10,000 years.

The starting date of these representations is the subject of heated debate. Most researchers, following the hints of Fabrizio Mori (2000) and Henry Lhote (1959, 1974), trace such activities to the Pleistocene or the Epipalaeolithic; thus, about 10–12,000 years ago. Others, in particular Le Quellec (2004, 2013) and Muzzolini (1996), argue for a later start, at about 5000 BC. The controversy and the entire issue of dating is not easy to follow, partly due to confusing terminology: first, between the 'BC' and 'BP' forms of dating; then, serious differences between the English, French and Italian use of words like 'Neolithic' and 'pastoral'; and finally, the not fully intelligible passion that constitutes an evident undercurrent.[1] It seems, however, that the later dating is based on objects that were found around the sites, and not directly related to the Tassili paintings; and it is also based on a degree of sustained ignorance concerning the phenomenon of the representation, characteristic of a secular Enlightenment mindset that tries at any cost to reduce all such manifestations to artistic concerns, considering them as products of sovereign artists, thus exporting the mentality of the twentieth or twenty-first century into prehistory. If we recognise as a fact that these works cannot be understood from this perspective, we become freed from anxiety about the world of 'artistic representation' and gain an enormously useful tool for understanding the nature of representation and its effects on character.

Furthermore, as such basic coordinates already make clear, to realise the importance of the site we need to incorporate the significance of its spatial and temporal liminality.

The multiple liminality of Tassili

In a geographical sense, Tassili presents a striking combination of marginality and liminality – thus, by this fact creating a certain affinity with Çatalhöyük. It is in the centre of the Sahara; but as the Sahara is a desert, the greatest desert on the planet, it means that this deeply scattered and fragmented rocky plateau is one of the most remote areas on Earth. In fact, Tassili was among the last places in the Sahara to have been discovered. However, not only the climatic conditions, but even the physical outlook of the site is extraordinary. The mountain range was produced by intense geological forces and – due to subsequent and often changing climatic conditions – it was particularly subject to the impact of the elements, especially water and winds, which sculpted incredible shapes into the rock.

These 'natural' shapes, certainly not formed by human activity, leave two sets of radically different impressions. First, they represent an awful, frightening and radical strangeness, giving the impression of emptiness; or, perhaps even better, capturing the kind of landscape that appears in nightmares when presence has left us. Second, however, and in a diametrically opposed manner, the landscape looks also strangely familiar, though not so much for us moderns, but from the perspective of the memory of humankind. This mountain range, and in particular those sites where the Round Head paintings are concentrated (especially Wadi Djerat, a river bed containing the highest density of images, widely considered the most important representation area, with their hollows cut deeply into the geological layers of rock and thus clearly revealed to the human eye), offer quite stunning similarities to three regions that each played a fundamental role over hundreds of thousands of years of human history. The first is the Rift Valley, but comprising the Rift Valley from Kenya up to the Levant and including the Western part of Arabia; the second the Dordogne, not only with its painted caves, but also with the manifold Neanderthal sites, in particular Roque Saint-Christophe, which among others gave the name to Mousterian culture; and finally Cappadocia, including the massive underground cities of Kaymakli and Derinkuyu, with air shafts and water tunnels, a kind of upside-down Çatalhöyük, using negative architecture, carved down in tuff, out of volcanic ash, instead of using mud bricks for building.

The main difference is that these other sites are not situated in an extreme desert area and thus look much more homely and familiar – but, then, in its heyday Tassili also may have looked somewhat similar to them. Thus, the physical features of Tassili epitomise alienness, while at the same resembling the oldest 'homes' of humankind. Yet, it has a third amazing feature, which furthermore only becomes visible from the present, meaning urban civilisation: that the centre of the plateau, which contains some of the most important paintings, looks like a city cut into stone, with its walls, corridors and hidden recesses. As the Tassili paintings were painted by non-settled walkers, they certainly could not have seen a place resembling a stoned and walled city. This is a coding of our modern eyes; still, anyhow, it is there.

Over the millennia, climatic conditions even in the Sahara differed. While during the last 10,000 years of the Ice Age the general climate of the Sahara was extremely dry, even drier than in our times, in the last millennia of this period there was abundant rain (or probably snow) in the mountains, creating quite a peculiar weather condition for any visitor to this zone. Evidence is very meagre, but this includes some pottery that was dated as early as 9500 BC (Huysecom *et al.* 2009), which offers, together with similar findings in Japan, the earliest dated pottery, long millennia before any sign of agriculture in the region, thus again reversing the standard temporal sequence of the Fertile Crescent, which argued for the primacy of agriculture before the invention of ceramics.

According to Mori, this is also the period where the earliest artistic manifestations, identified as the 'Wild Fauna' or 'Bubaline' art, can be dated. The definite shift to a more clement climate took place only about 8000 BC here. This is the time around which the second and most important artistic style, the so-called 'Round Head' period, can be connected. The two styles are completely different, greatly separated not only in time (most probably), but in space as well, each being extremely significant on its own. However, before analysing the content of these works, we must survey the reconstruction of their context.

Cultic activities continued in the region well into historical times. During the later Mesolithic and the Neolithic weather conditions were considerably different, especially in a warmer and much wetter period, lasting from about 8000 to 5500 BC. After the dry spell of the sixth millennium BC wetter conditions persisted up to about the middle of the third millennium, when desertification, persisting up to our own days, started. During these long millennia Tassili became a genuine 'liminal' centre of cultic activities, connecting the Mediterranean with Central and even Southern Africa, and arguably the Near East. Important areas to be connected to the Tassili's zone of influence include Egypt, the Spanish Levant, the island of Malta (ancient Melite), which in its temple period (4100–2500 BC) became a crucial cultic centre itself, and which had connections to Arslantepe (ancient Meliddu or Melitene), an important Bronze Age centre between Anatolia and Mesopotamia; the Dogon of Mali, whose famous masks show many similarities with the masks depicted in Tassili (Le Quellec 1993), a culture that has since long been recognised as exhibiting a series of particularly intriguing features (see the work of Marcel Griaule), and whose houses furthermore show close similarities with the houses of Çatalhöyük (Hodder 2006: 25–6); or the San/Khoisan of the South-African Drakensberg Mountains, whose rock-art has survived into the present, and whose culture again shows a number of particularly important and related features, concerning myths about the foundation of the world, the role of trickster deities and figures, and the importance of trance, a central aspect of shamanism (Guenther 1999; Lewis-Williams 2002).[2]

Spatial liminality is combined with temporal liminality. The position of Tassili seems to have shifted from extremely marginal into highly liminal in the Pleistocene-Holocene transition (c.9700–7500 BC), which in Tassili is related to the transition from the Bubaline to the Round Head periods. The key features of Bubaline representations include the exclusive use of engraving (no painting whatsoever); the dominance of animals; the high quality of art, in style recalling both Palaeolithic caves and rock-art in Egypt (Huyge *et al.* 2007). This suggests continuity between Bubaline and Palaeolithic art, indicating that the radiating influence of Palaeolithic art extended even here – though not passing into the Middle East.

The arrival of Round Head style marks a radical break. The most singular and significant features of Tassili images are associated with this style, so these have to be reviewed in greater detail in the next section. Here, concerning the general liminal coordinates, it should only be pointed out that this shift seems to coincide both with the end of the Pleistocene-Holocene transition and of the South-East Anatolian megalithic sanctuaries. The potential significance of such a coincidence can be understood through a third series of coincidences, between the start of re-desertification around Tassili, the start of pyramid building in Egypt (the first pyramid, Djoser's, was built around 2630 BC, and the three great pyramids of Giza in the 26th century BC); and the sudden abandonment of the Temples of Malta (this evidently took place before 2500 BC, around which time the island was complete abandoned, and a full century passed before it became populated again, though by a completely different culture, around 2400 BC). This leaves about five millennia (7500–2500 BC) when Tassili was a possible incubator – though a question remains concerning the exact sense in which it played this role.

All this is solely based, as it can only be, on circumstantial evidence. But in the absence of direct written or other testimonies, the very ambition of scientific research involves the need to ask questions and bring together problems and paradoxes. It is certainly of the greatest importance that the rise, persistence and eventual fading away of this extremely peculiar and remote place, Tassili, seems to have been closely correlated with some of the most crucial events in our prehistory, right up to the emergence of 'history', as we presume it to have happened.

It is within such broad coordinates that the singular significance of Round Head paintings can be properly assessed, as in them subversion instrumentalised the void in a unique way, never seen before or after Tassili.

Self-consciousness, memory, character

It seems to us that there are two main and fundamentally different approaches concerning the basic sources of the coherence and integrity of a character. By character we do not mean something very elaborate and complex, but a singularity and coherence at the same time – singularity in the sense of being different from everybody else; and coherence as having stability over time. According to one approach, character is defined by memory, or the record of accumulated experiences.[3] It is clear that without such a memory we simply stop behaving as persons possessing a character; the loss of memory is the gravest problem any human being can encounter, as without memory we lose any guidance we could have about our lives, becoming at the mercy of our own impulses or the guidance of others. In fact, memory is so fundamental that this became in most cultures the single most important identifying feature of human communities, at every level, from the self and the family up to cities and states.

On the other hand, however, there exists a radical counter-approach that puts the emphasis on self-consciousness, and explicitly considers its realisation as a break, even alienation; a view that can be traced in particular to Jean Paul and Hegel. To be 'rational' and 'mature', we must break away from our previous selves; we must repudiate everything in our character that was immature and not worthy of serious attention. Thus, it literally asserts that a rupture at the level of the character, or subversion, is a precondition of realising selfhood. This is demonstrated mainly by modern philosophical rationalism that forces its adherents to perform this break; thus to commit an irredeemable, destructive act, an atrocity towards oneself, and justifies it by the elusive quality of 'full maturity and rationality' (Argyrou 2013). On the one hand, it simply denigrates and devalues, even despises all those who fail to perform such an act of wanton self-destruction, while for those others who consent, it irrevocably alters their identity, thus twice making them conform to the assertions of these strange philosophical ideas: first, because it can actually shape and form the individuals who decided to give up themselves; and second, because – in the eventual situation that they come to regret their previous acts – they could only feel a vague and lingering nostalgia for their previous selves, but cannot actually mend the rupture, only replace their fanciful constructs with another. The only way is thus 'forward': towards ever new ideologies of progress, eventually formulated – as today – in the ever more ludicrous form of 'post' ideas, with the dream of industrialism, communism, secularism and modernism becoming 'post'-industrialism, 'post'-communism, 'post'-modernism or 'post'-secularism. The list can be continued practically without any limit; in fact, the phrase 'global' already alludes to such limitlessness.

The philosophical underpinnings of such wanton self-destruction are offered by theories of 'otherness', 'alterity' or 'altruism' (a schismogenic double of egoism), central for key modern and post-modern thinkers like Husserl, Derrida or Levinas, to be traced similarly to Hegel's obsession with mediation.

The question now concerns the manner in which it could be possible to capture and identify the emergence of subversion through representation, especially self-representation, following Plato, according to whom the deepest layers of memory are non-verbal and consist of 'forms' (eidos), a term closer to image than word, though containing both. Chapter 5 already discussed the problems Palaeolithic artists had with representing humans. The same apprehension about depicting the human face motivates the famous religious prohibition about 'graven images', probably due to the fear of becoming something else and losing one's character (Deleuze and Guattari 1987: 294);[4] a fear of establishing a relationship between what is given as real and the unknown beyond. However, here we must be careful, as such prohibitions logically can only come after previous efforts to make such images, while the evident absence of similar efforts is central to Palaeolithic cave art – except, of course, Pergouset and the Shaft Scene; exceptions perfectly reinforcing the rule. Thus, instead of the need to legislate such paintings, the real question concerns why becoming engaged in such a paradoxical and self-defeating activity as capturing the very person who is doing the painting arose. Pergouset and the 'Shaft Scene' are thus not simply exceptions, but strange kind of 'initiations' into representation *as* representation – a dangerous undertaking that must be hidden, demonstrated by the strange, secret locations.

Visitation of painted caves stopped around 9700 BC, and soon even their memory faded. This was an enormous cultural change, given that for about 25 millennia the painting and visiting of such caves played an enormous role in the lives of not simply the area where they were located, but for the entire cultural horizon in which they exerted their impact, which extended well into the area of Ukraine and the Middle East. For long centuries there are no signs of large-scale paintings in the broad region. The practice makes its reappearance in a sudden and striking manner in the most unlikely of places possible, in Çatalhöyük and the plateau of Tassili, an almost inaccessible high mountain range, in the middle of the Sahara desert.

Round Head paradoxes

It is widely agreed that the Round Head images represent the single most astonishing aspect of this already extraordinary site. Their novelty can be best understood by comparing it both to Palaeolithic cave art and the Bubaline period. While in Palaeolithic cave painting, a rudimentary human figure was only depicted once, in the Shaft Scene, and while Bubaline art only contains engravings, no paintings, in the Round Head period painting not only suddenly re-emerges but dominates engravings, and the majority of paintings depict humans.

The novelty of the site was immediately recognised (Hachid 1998: 173–4) – yet, at the same time its perplexing and troubling features also became evident, and this probably explains the fact that up to our times its significance still has not entered general understanding (Sansoni 1994: 101). Even a comprehensive review of the 'open female' or 'sacred display' image ignored Tassili (Dexter and Mair 2010). The Round Head style constitutes an 'extraordinary world' on its own (Mori 2000), which corresponds to nothing known (Hachid 1998: 195; see also Soukopova 2012). The pictures are enigmatic, intense and immense (191) and seem 'to appear suddenly, representing an enormous qualitative jump among the traces of human activity' (Mori 2000: 39). The sensibility of these artists, especially of the older periods, still simply escapes us, as their distant 'world' has a striking originality and strangeness (Hachid 1998: 217). It is in this context that we can make sense of the otherwise strange idea of Henri Lhote, one of the discoverers of Tassili and author of the first comprehensive book on it (Lhote 1959), which can easily be misunderstood, that some of the Round Head figures look like 'Martians'. The expression rightly conveys the experience of total alienness that the image evokes, so the utter uniqueness and estrangement of experiencing the Round Head images of Tassili can indeed be conveyed through the parable of watching Martians (Hachid 1998). Such an experience of distance from the normal and the familiar is so central to the Tassili images that the expression 'distancing from nature' was selected for the subtitle of Mori's basic work on Tassili (Mori 2000). However, the other part of the subtitle again brings us back from the greatest distance into the greatest proximity, as Mori argues that it was this experience of distancing that represented 'the birth of anthropomorphic religions', thus the kind of monotheism which established the most important current world religions. Most interestingly, this view of Mori closely recalls the manner in which another comparative archaeologist, Henri Frankfort, considered the emergence of Hebrew monotheism, in the crucial 'Epilogue' to his classic comparative work on Mesopotamian and Egyptian religion, similarly identifying the novelty with a radical break with nature (Frankfort 1948); and also brings in the work of Paul Radin, who wrote the classic book on the trickster (Radin 1972), but on this basis also ventured a hypothesis about the 'monotheism of primitive people' (Radin 1924).

Thus, proper appraisal requires the attention not only of experts, but also of social scientists, as these Round Head figures produce an effect: they were made to establish a relationship with the void, by absorbing the character of their makers into the void in a purposeful and conscious way – however, we dare to say, in a tired and cynical way.

The radical novelty of Round Head style stands in the paradoxical appearance of self-presentation, as here the self stands as an emptiness to be filled by emptiness, transposing man into a superior and foreign territory through inviting and getting the void to be involved in human shape and form. The result is astonishing: a kind of artificial communication was fabricated, as man is filling the void, while the void is filling the man, as best seen in the gigantic Great God of Sefar images. It suggests a peculiar communication that is senile, tired and infirm in its treacherous ways.

The laborious procedure that was involved in one of the strangest figures in the whole pantheon of Tassili images is emphatically documented. The most unusual

FIGURE 9.1 The Great God of Sefar. Source of image: Hachid (1998: 196, fig. 280)

is the 760 × 360 cm fresco of white-and-yellow pigmented outlines (Figure 9.1; see Hachid, 1998: 164, 192–6), which is lavishly decorated and comprises a dramaturgy of several figures. In the middle stands the God himself, his 3.25m high shape towering over the head of observers. On his left there are worshippers, female figures with outstretched arms, in a gesture of prayer, recalling the Pergouset Headless Man. A particularly decrepit figure is a woman-like creature with open, short and curved legs, but no feet; her arms are raised and she has a cylindrical body, as if pregnant; she is an open woman with swollen tummy. This female figure is lying on her back as if coming out of the figure of the Great God,[5] though her position and her swollen abdomen suggest that she is about to give birth and this birth is due to the Great God.

Two mouflons, one white and one black, accompany her, and she is just between the two, as if her presence were linked to them. The figures on the right are similarly feeble, with a mouflon stretched out and another having a fantastic, unreal shape.

Shifting from description to analysis, a possible interpretation of this curious dramaturgy is a newly found design for union with the void. The mimetic absorption of character in the projected figure of the Great God and the abundance following the act of union is told with surprising cynicism, or better through a deterioration of good sense. Here nothing stands for itself. The purpose of the birth motif, seemingly, is merging together unreal and real substances, and giving birth to new forms. But in this case, in Tassili, birth with divine assistance is just a crude joke. Assuring growth through pregnancy results in malformed creatures, or to gain benefit from the divine is a vain dream, and the depicters were quite conscious about this. While the Great God's testicles and his phallic form explicitly show desire, they are quite repulsive, and the desired outcome is also grotesque, shown by the manner in which the ugly forms lack self-confidence and cohesion. They rather accept the blame for their own malformed ridiculousness. The emitters, or the producers of these images, assign a sort of acknowledgement for the fault or error that they caused. Not that they feel guilty; rather, they express their equivalence with the malformations, without caring to see anything wrong with their action. Thus, a particular senility is revealed here, through the infantile images: a list of errors is presented through a mass of unshaped and ridiculous figures that divide and grow uncontrollably, invading every part of the whole with deprivation and eagerness, where understanding or comprehension becomes impossible, because those employed in these activities were without any responsibility, in complete deterioration. Their self-consciousness was childishly pure and clean.

A twisted animal figure in the background illustrates this point well. Its four legs are on the ground, but its stomach is turned up towards the sky, showing that a gruesome alienation is taking place that breaks entities into pieces and then turns them upside down. Such antagonistic bipolarisation is shown by the black-and-white-coloured mouflons that encircle the pregnant figure, symbolising descriptively what one has done, and showing a clear consciousness not to correct or master it. They have failed and they did not regret it: the world is now populated by mutants which do not provide any advantage whatsoever to anyone. The Great God unleashed unto world continues his wrongdoing, while the world is clapping its hands. They who have become what they now are and their conduct sometimes creates laughter and indeed merits ridicule – but rather it is appreciated. At least, this is what the images evoke.

What is really striking is the high artistic quality of the Tassili Round Head images, as they are very powerful. They use techniques that express an astonishing surrealism and – needless to mention again – we are in the Mesolithic, in-between 8000 and 5000 BC at a time with only sporadic settlements and no cities, at the start of the spread of agriculture and pastoralism, and in pre-metallurgy, just after the Natufian, as discussed before. This expressivity is especially true of the oldest, Round Head paintings, as they are more doubled, duplicitous, complicated and better executed overall than the schematic and mediocre more recent images from the Caballin or Camelin period, except for the Iheren paintings, recalling the similar situation in Göbekli Tepe, where – strikingly – the earliest works show the highest artistic qualities.

They are impressive and modern in their suggestive flight from reality. As we have seen, the Great God of Sefar even contains a unique pictorial narrative, with images around and through the body of the Great God. The open female figure lying on the horned animal is particularly unmeasured – asymmetrical, bizarre – in an already shocking painting. This image has a sad dramaturgy; it tells a story, but does not call for an action to take place; it is following the sequence of the ongoing drama in several layered dimensions without seeking any solution.

All in all these expanded, dreamy, swollen forms suggest 'illusionality', a badly formed, disjointed dream, where there is no space for memory, and where a morbid fantasy is given signs of life, representing the fertile, bodily depth of lustful impulsivity. Everything is pulsating, the praying figures especially, as their raised arms, showing even their fingers, communicate to us the visual appearance of the idea of 'conception': the etymological links between touching, keeping, biting and conceiving.[6] When we are bypassing reality, we are operating towards an alliance with the void. The second layer in the Great God of Sefar scene illustrates this, as it shows behind the deity the already mentioned deformed pregnancy, with open genitals and legs. The pregnant figure is somehow floating out of the body of the Great God, and if so, it will bring out his unquenchable urge for possession, well indicated by the numerous phalluses grown out of the Great God's body, coupled with a complete corporeal human representation.

If this is so, then we get an answer for our quest concerning self-reflection linked to the human body shape. Such a shape matters, as it can be occupied through possession, a central feature of masks as well (Pizzorno 2010), though not without a wilful agreement to this very action. You need to have a crystal-clear decision concerning what you would like to do to be conscious about the advantages that you would gain: you would have to be willing to undergo a self-transformation, a metamorphosis in the hope of gaining something for yourself. This awareness of the self, this knowledge of the existence of your unique, alert ego, this realisation of the human condition, this mindfulness about the exchangeability of advantages, this perception of differences between me and the others implies an apprehension about the self's attitudes concerning the infinite desire for acquisition.

Subversion

One way to reconnect the supposedly separate concerns of 'subversion' and 'representation' is through their common evocation of pulsating emotions or impulses. The images of Tassili, even at their most abstract or conceptual, in their sense of a distance from nature, were certainly poised to evoke impulses. Such impulses can be grouped into three categories. The first is astonishment at the bizarre. The bizarre and grotesque pairing of body members or of humans and animals immediately provokes repellent astonishment – of encountering designs that seem to represent something out of reality, and certainly do not correspond to any being we encounter in real life. The second, and closely related emotion is danger or threat, leading to fear, and being frightened. The unknown, for humans, always carries a degree of threat; but here the particular 'unknown' is a purposeful play with elements of real life in order to produce creatures that are superreal,[7] mixed and composite. A wild animal can be threatening; but such an animal with a human head, or a human with an animal head, a monster or a demon (hybrid beings by definition) is threatening on a second level, implying – beyond threats of death – destruction and annihilation. The third factor is the clearly rude, sexual connotation of the images: sexual members are freed from their concealment and exposed to generate an intensification of impulses of the brutal.

Yet, such emotions can be raised to a further level, and this is connected to the highly pornographic character of many such Tassili images. This again has three levels; and such levels represent a temporal succession of subversion, particularly clear in the important Wadi Djerat area. The first layer is the representation not simply of naked male and female bodies, or even genital organs (those were already present in the Palaeolithic), but ithyphallic men, and – most prominently – the so-called 'open women', or female bodies depicted with their legs spread and raised; a particularly humiliating (and vulgar) pose. Interestingly enough, such representations are also called in the literature the 'gynaecological position', where the direct, shocking rudeness of the image is hidden under a clearly inappropriate scientific terminology, or even a celebration of female eroticism (Le Quellec 1995). The second layer concerns explicit, numerous allusions to sexual acts. At a third level, such acts are simulated not simply between men and women, but humans and animals; in particular, between figures that combine human and animal features, culminating in shocking scenes of unbridled orgy between hybrid monsters.

It is simple to offer an interpretation of these images using a preconceived scheme. They could be considered as new or modern; they could be condemned as morally reprehensible, or defended as expressing a 'fertility cult' or even promoting a supposedly 'healthy' approach to sexual experience. Whether these interpretations are relevant or misleading, we now are offering a different one. What must be understood is the representation of transgression that was animating not simply some of these representations, but the entire liminal centre; and the effect which it exerted on its surroundings, including – without exaggeration – ourselves, our very mode of being, given the extremely long time period in which this centre exerted its impact. This concerns the reflection of oneself; a man that has knowledge about oneself and the results of his chosen actions. In other words, if Tassili was not simply, as it might look to us today, an exotic and remote location, but a crucial transformative centre of the world that exerted a formative impact on a number of major cultures and civilisations, then what was the force that animated these images? What was the character and combination of void concerns behind such activities? Of course, it is impossible to give a single response to such questions; but exactly for the same reasons nobody can claim singular access to or right for unveiling their truth. To understand the possible meaning of these representative activities, they must be placed in the broadest possible comparative framework, implying both other historical cases and recourse to the widest possible conceptual and theoretical frameworks in the social sciences.

This is all the more necessary as we need to understand why – apart from their subversive character – the images have an aura of crude senility.

Senility

The claim might seem strange, as the images look particularly modern. If Round Head imagery does not correspond to anything known from prehistory, including the preceding Bubaline period, it has strange, genuinely stunning affinities with modern, abstract and especially 'concept art', sharing a common submissiveness. The terms that recur in attempts to capture the character of this painting are 'abstract', 'bizarre', 'surrealistic' and 'conceptual'. They do not simply 'represent' human beings, but decompose the human body to its elements, to put them again alchemically together in new combinations. Thus, amazingly, it is in the plateaus of Tassili, in the middle of the Sahara, that the modern idea of *l'art pour l'art* was first born, but why?

Why is there this conscious desire to break and tear into pieces the wholeness of character, the images of the human, the frame of the body? Why is all this desired so much? Or, from another angle, given that Palaeolithic images lacked the representation of self, how could this be suddenly desirable now, in the Mesolithic? Why is this now the way to reach the void, to offer man for fulfilment? The last question is easier to answer; we only need to recall the special qualities of the void in algebra. The void in the form of zero has the special quality of being unbreakable (in the sense that it cannot be divided through fractioning into numbers smaller than itself), and is also closely connected to infinity (thus, for example, any number divided by nil yields infinity). And both nil and infinity have a special meaning in the occult. Given that the geometric equality between the divine and the human realms is held together by communion and friendship (Meier 2011), by orderliness, temperance and justice, a mentality of governing through qualities and ratio, as mentioned by Plato, and we assume as also being valid for Palaeolithic societies, the discovery of the breakability implies that the same result of infinity and 'unbreakability' can easily be obtained by physical and not mental equality (the latter is based on shared virtue). Mental equality could be seen in the beauty of Palaeolithic paintings. But, here at Tassili, we have a different result, and finally get a response to our question, as breakage is how the subversion of character offered benefits, through involvement with the void.

To influence and accommodate the void, a morbid constitution or design was anchored onto the rocks of Tassili, a wilful alienation from reality: subverting the character to the void, offering it up for fulfilment, though in the same way chang-ing the void itself. For this action no virtue is required, only sly submissiveness to the lustful forces that are always ready to gain life energy. The emitters of the Tassili paintings captured this new knowledge accurately: it is horrific, disgust-ing and disappointing: the loss of the paradise, as it no longer nurtures virtue and maintains order, as Milton described it. This is why we characterise such evidently infantile plays as senility, as it is the mark of a loss and a distance: the elimination of the self, but also a distance from the Palaeolithic world vision of beauty, the loss of the Golden Age.

These representations had a particular zeal for gaining this knowledge again and again, repeating a parasitic decomposition, consumption and artificial reconstruc-tion of characters. They worked and functioned quietly for thousands of years in the silence of these desert mountains. The central idea is quite similar to alchemy, as it stresses the assimilation of elements not only with each other but also with cosmic forces (Maxwell-Stuart 2012; Powers 2012), while the 'hieros gamos' was a very factual undertaking. To obtain creation, alchemy makes various abstractions: it emits images of fire, earth, water or air to capture the divine force by luring it into bodies, oscillating between the cosmic, incommensurable, unlimited sources and the fixed and limited bodily forms, stressing their mutual assimilation into each other. Whenever the void is present, either the operation itself loses its meaning, or numbers cannot be properly associated with the operation. The required unity or reconciliation of elements is not taking place even in multiplication, where as a result only the void is coming out, annihilating the number by itself. While the zero is unbreakable, it manages to dissolve, breaking and taking away the identity of any rational number, which is probably the key to the success of alchemical operations, as alchemy with various projections of limited and unlimited elements merges them together, where the unlimited nil is always used for dissolving the limited one.

This has two consequences. First, the limited form is less and less prominent; and second, the unlimited nil gains an ever-greater importance, or continues to grow. This idea can be illustrated through a characteristic of the zero: with this pseudo-number, by dividing any real number with zero, we obtain infinity. The result is the Bakhtinian cosmic grotesque, which is immeasurable and infinitely powerful, the frightening and terroristic fluxional of Callot and Newton (Horvath 2013a), a swallowing bacchanalia of projections, which uses doubles as receptacles for the erotic images of the jaws of Hell (an opening, like the mouth, extensively analysed by Bakhtin (1984)), as it is still visible in Tassili. The nil constructs and denominates (fractions) without losing its non-character; it is pure becoming without being, a passive receptor, but at the same time also the hunter that violates the borders (intactness, integrity) of others. The nil even has its own architecture, as seen in Tassili, being able to make a triangle or an arch out of nothing and a continuous filigree from its own motion; the nil is able to conjure up an emerging organism of universal hatred and apocalyptic destruction, where the aim is limited to transformation through contagion.

However, such transgression could not be completed without incorporating the most important force behind the senses: desire, or – as Newton called it – attraction, or taking it simply as pulsation. Only attraction, the pulsation of the arteries could propel the void into action. However, the void desires things about which we do not even have concepts. Needs grow out of the void itself, as the void is territorial expansion, the long-stated ambition for possession that ferociously attacks and annihilates when mixed with characters, exactly because of its growing deprivation from the fullness of reality. Here in Tassili, this desire became focused on human bodies, as always happens when strength and virtue deteriorate into senility.

Human bodies as objects of transformation in the Iheren murals

Not so far from the Round Head paintings there is another particular site, the Iheren murals (Hallier and Hallier 2012). Dated about 3000 BC (Camps 2011), they are over 3 metres wide and contain a series of minuscule compositions that present curious depictions of small-sized human and animal figures merging together, treated in an admirable and naturalistic way, from the Neolithic pastoral period (Muzzolini 1996). Here the projection series of the murals varies increasingly, in which absences are added to absences, whose end result is a transformation that functions as hybridisation. Its mental structure is destruction and unification that develops automatically, in an incommensurable way.

Here characters lose all their distinguishing features, becoming mere objects for transformation, converting pulsation into the engine of a generalised, amorphous growth. They are not just merging into each other, but are becoming part of a common body constructed out of a mutual dependence between the composite elements: stone, water, and the flesh and blood of humans and animals. This transformation even received a visual representation in the egg forms, depicted everywhere, and even exists in natural rock formations. This is why Tassili's Iheren does not echo anything other than itself: the pure possibility of endless transformation, the incubation of the scandal.

Notice two things about the empty sockets of the Iheren rocks: that they are filled by mural paintings like a pure shell of a womb, and are stamped by signs that are the sum of absent meanings. They are beyond and against time and space; the purpose and reason of their existence is unknown, being of uncertain origin and belonging to no known culture that survived; the only thing left to ascertain is that the surviving images are products of a transformative will. Their industry by contrast is very well and skilfully elaborated, as it is seen on the representations.

It is certainly easy to note that the manipulation of the void to input something into it requires one to combine knowledge about characters and the void. Characters have their motion, power and virtue within themselves, so understanding how to insert a change inside them, to entice them into regression, is a real problem. How did the Iheren people know about taking root in characters? The problem is that this exact method or technology is, in general, hard to come by. The idea of metamorphosis, proposed by Deleuze and Guattari (1987), is one of the best-known such methods, but if one does not think exactly about how one got that result, one will just recall the result – that individuals are taking each other's characters, bringing forth a result which has no resemblance to them – without remembering what conditions apply to the result. Conditions for metamorphosis do not simply occur; rather a heedful, calculative, human-made preparation is needed for catching the void to use it. Such a cautious preparation for metamorphosis and its very result are seen on the Iheren murals.

Yet, while the Iheren people located the true centre of their universe in nothingness, emptiness, void, maybe this was exactly because it fascinated the void itself, using Alfred Gell's (1998) theory about how art acts not only on the human

FIGURE 9.2 Artificial uterus or the egg motif of transformation. Source of image: http://encyclopedieberbere.revues.org/docannexe/image/1556/img-2.png, Encyclopédie berbère, 24 | Ida – Issamadanen [online], put online 1 June 2011, consulted 4 January 2017. We thank *Encyclopédie berbère* for permission to use

viewer but on the transcendental as well, with a living presence response, and eliciting love, hate, desire or fear (see van Eck 2010).

In this image (see Figure 9.2) men and goats all look in the same direction, towards the left of the image. There, in the top-left corner, there is a uterus-like form, out of which a woman is looking, leaning on her elbow. Beside her, there is a man, holding up a child in his hands. Three beings, with long fair hair and a beard, with ornaments that look like horns on their heads, dressed up in tight trousers and a frock-like coat, are lined up in front of the uterus form and the woman. In front of the man with the child there are two figures, one in a gilet and one in a suit. One of these is kissing the hand of the other above another strange, egg-like uterus shape. Further down on the left there are two or three women with broad, bell-formed skirts and covered with fur on their shoulders, dressed up in a way similar to the woman looking out of the womb-like form at the left top. The goats are looking at them. Strangely enough, the goats are more individual-ised, with different horns, patches and colours, than the humans. Furthermore, the forehead of several animals collides with the leg of the humans, while the horn of one goat touches the egg-like uterus form. One of these eggs is even offered to an unusually big, man-sized goat, at the top of the image, indicating a link or even a causal connection. The similarity between humans and goats is also emphasised by the pattern on the goats being similar to the dresses of the humans. But per-haps the most striking similarity is between the profiles of humans and goats. Such goat-men evoke the Cabeiri of Greek mythology (Kerényi 1980; Blakely 2006), inventors of metallurgy, as well as demons of winemaking, who are also associated with goats, being goat-like semi-divine men, and who were furthermore born out of eggs (see Figure 9.3).

The uterus (original source of birth, transformed into a place of production), the stone and the mother are linked to the arm of the stone (sic!) by a common knot, tying together the uterus, the goat on the stone and even the father figure. Those tied together by the knot have a power to transform everything around them into the making of a hybrid, the child (at the back of the image, in his father's arm). A goat is towering over the father's head, but they all (father, baby, audience) are in-between figures, sorcerers, *magi*. This is indicated by their animal-like profiles, with different degrees of bestiality – ears, muzzles, fur-like skin, caps, sometimes slanting foreheads. The child is a hybrid with a marked face; he was born with the same bestial skin features as all adults have, except the mother. The only 'normal' figure is the mother, an outsider to the group. However, she added the most significant instrument to a successful metamorphosis: her uterus. She is holding it outside her body, together with an arm erected from the slab of stone with a goat-head drawn on it. The mother lent her uterus for the fabricated transaction of producing the artefact, imagined as a baby in his sorcerer-father's hands. The baby itself is a hybrid, as indicated by the particular sign-mark on his face. Note the circlet form on the mother's arms, a kind of handcuff that resembles a wrist orna-ment, indicating that she is under a spell (under pressure or powerful influence), in a bewitched state. This circlet form is also visible on the father and the arm of

FIGURE 9.3 The successful metamorphosis. Source of image: http://www.rockart-sahara-hallier.de/media/2.jpg. We thank Ulrich W. Hallier for permission to use

the stone slab. Figure 9.3 is probably a later image than Figure 9.2, but the motifs are the same: the mother who is greeted by men, a father figure on her side with a baby in his arms, and goats around. Eggs are missing here, and the whole elegant, fussy, court-like atmosphere of Figure 9.2 was changed to a more didactic and simplified, pastoral scene of sorcerers in this Figure 9.3.

Circles and pressures for transformation

The idea of metamorphosis as proposed by Deleuze and Guattari, even if it does not incorporate the transcendental dimension, has significant explanatory power. For instance, we can apply it for these Iheren scenes, many of which strikingly recall fin-de-siècle Vienna, evoking splendid, classy, slow-paced appearances of phlegmatic consternation in a superbly decadent society waiting for transformation, a readiness best captured by Hofmannsthal (Broch 1984). The hypothesis, to be sure, is not falsifiable. The reason is that what we see (the visible Iheren murals) is only a fraction of what there was in pulsations, emotions, impulses. We have no evidence about the entire life-span of this liminal complex in the Sahara, this no-man's-land in existence and expansion for 10,000 years, producing such alert, artistic qualities, thus it is impossible to know about the functioning of its transformative power. We can only rely on the visible murals, these micro-documents of transformations of men, animals, demons and natural elements, in a world that is seemingly so far away both in reason and in time.

The question concerns the theoretical framework necessary to capture the nature of such transformation. The problem with Deleuze and Guattari is that transformation remains ill-defined if the transcendental dimension is neglected. Here their work can be complemented with some ideas from the political sociology of Max Weber, in particular the concept of charismatic power, taken from Protestant theology, but developed in a different direction, relevant for the analysis of transformative situations. Here Weber's analysis was also strongly influenced by the work of Nietzsche, especially in Weber's use of the language of 'out-of-ordinary' situations, and the need to overcome them. Given that Deleuze wrote a highly influential book on Nietzsche, the affinities between his work and Weber's are not surprising.

Applying contemporary theoretical frameworks for the remote time and place of Tassili also poses its problems. It is a question whether the method of transformation in these murals is stable over time. It might be true that such transformation started with manipulating transcendental power, but does it have fabricating potential now, so do we have men–god–goats here and now, around us? At any rate, can we say that the power of the void is a constant, only the conditions are variable for its application? And what are these conditions: liminality, emptiness, absurdity? Who are they, these representers who recognised this first and learned how to use it, and with what sort of practices?

At any rate, transformation was going on there, as in the Tassili images, in particular the Iheren murals men, animals and natural objects like stones continuously take up each other's positions, arms, shades, shapes, implying the transformation of one being into another. Here, absorption altered filiation, which is indicated by the huge eggs merging all these potentials laying around, carried by men dressed as courtiers (Figure 9.2). These productive eggs are without parents and thus without taking up a heredity, without the link of the correspondence between characters and intentions. The man-size eggs are the end-artefacts of a transformation, which perhaps begins anew every time, fabricating outcomes (the baby in the centre of both Figures 9.2 and 9.3) that increase exponentially over time, multiplying infinitely. Such unlimited growth is the result of a transgression, which can be captured through division or fracturing by zero. These eggs may just be containers, but as receptors what did they capture? What is the precious content offered to the giant goat king? If the picture is unreal, then every element of it is unreal, and so the content of the egg is unreality or the nothing (the void), as even its form demonstrates.

It is unknown whether this fabrication of a transformative device effectively worked. However, the representations are still there, showing the fusing, merging and blending of different entities into each other, by cloning or metamorphosis. Is this method different than the Darwinian, implying a human-made logic inserted into the world of nature, like a trickster jumping into another shape (see Chapter 5), taking its place and nesting inside it? Is this impossible in nature, or rather the road of parasites, which absorb and consume the being of others, until the sources dry out, and in that moment they die as well? While the trickster is a vengeance against nature, it punishes itself. If it is inseparable from self-destruction, being a harmful outlier in the free flow of nature, how is it that it survives? The trickster only survives through destruction, but this activity directly leads to self-destruction as well, as its void appearance neither generates nor produces nor creates, but rather its urge for elimination negates and liquefies any existence, including its own, unto death. It lives on in other beings, drawing benefits from the deprivation of their character. It cannot move itself except by destroying others. Its frenetic movements can only be stopped by the sudden emergence of a fixed form that sets insurmountable limits.

Conclusion: the connections between Tassili and Çatalhöyük, and beyond

The most striking confirmation of the Tassili-Göbekli-Çatalhöyük connection is a long shot, but a quite important and striking piece of evidence, discovered recently, which concerns the first written Chinese character (Mair 2012).

There is a modern Chinese character that is now pronounced as wū, but whose old Chinese pronunciation was *mʸag* (265–6; see also Mair 1990). Since ancient times, this was the sign of magicians. The word shows striking similarities with the Old Persian term *magush*, possible from *PIE *magh*, and while the character is now translated as 'shaman', this is not correct, as the duties of such figures were not like those of the shamans, but rather closely recalled the old Iranian *magus*. *Magu* or *Ma-ku*, furthermore, is an ancient Taoist mythical figure, associated with the elixir of life, a symbolic defender of females, in the earliest myths having birdlike fingernails and associated with mountain caves (Eberhard 1968: 123–6). The ancient sign is also all but identical to the cross potent sign (German *Krückenkreuz*),[8] which was found on the top of the head of a small Bronze Age figure (eighth century BC), cut out of mollusc shell, which had a European or Caucasian character. In autumn 2011, it was announced in a major Chinese newspaper that in two Banshan pots, now dated back to about 2700–2300 BC, the character was found, together with a woman in the so-called 'sacred display position' – an image which was known to exist in Machang vases (2300–2000 BC; 271–2). The inference of Mair is that 'we can be assured that the mages . . . were equally important in predynastic times' (273); so the first Chinese character stood for the 'sacred display' and was identified with the mage, of Persian origins. Concerning the possibility of such a connection, he argues that back to the third millennia BC the ancient Iranians exerted a great power over the settled people of Central Asia, just as later similar people did like the Scythians and the Huns, through their mobility, due to the power of their horses and herds.

The image is indeed central for Tassili, was found in Göbekli Tepe and even has similarity with Palaeolithic engravings, going back to Pergouset. It is also found in several different early cultures, each of which offers a quite striking addition to the storyline. Thus, such images exists in Ireland, the Sheela na gig carvings (these are medieval, but thought to be based on earlier motifs; we should also allude here to the striking connection suggested between Irish and Berber music by Bob Quinn, an Irish musician); in Tarxien in Malta, taking further the Tassili-Malta links; or in Lepenski Vir, the most important cultic centre in Balkan prehistory, going back at least to the period 7200–6000 BC, thus the exact contemporary of Çatalhöyük.[9] However, the perhaps most striking similarity is with images of the Hindu goddess Lajja Gauri (Bolon 1992), which is depicted in the exact same 'iguana' position as the Machang or Banshan ceramics, with her hands and feet raised, and which ties further the links between Indo-Iranian and Chinese 'magical' thought.

Such images, back to Gimbutas and informed by Bachofen, are often taken, even by Mair, as indicating a kind of female goddess cult, connecting to matriarchy and the power of women. However, they reveal nothing of the sort, as Hodder and others argue, based on the more recent evidence. They rather demonstrate a kind of 'magical' power through which an evidently closed, initiatic priesthood gained power over people, through by humiliating and subjugating women *as* women – and not even simply concrete women, but the very principle and source of divine love, best present in the combination of femininity, grace and mother-hood, which was the centre of Palaeolithic spirituality. This effort and conflict is visible in the tension between Chauvet and Pergouset; the Hall of Bulls and the Shaft Scene in Lascaux, and – with victory shifting to the mage – in Göbekli Tepe, Tassili and Çatalhöyük.

In our reading, it was this power of the *magi* that Nietzsche tried to capture through the not fully fortunate expression 'ascetic priest' in the *Genealogy of Morals*, which he then misapplied to Christianity, though understandably, due to the century-long infiltration of Christian structures by *magi*, signalled in particular by the popularity of the 'Adoration of Magi' theme in late Renaissance painting.

Çatalhöyük is a settled Neolithic site in South-Eastern Anatolia, while the Tassili Mountains are in the middle of the Sahara, showing no sign of settlement and agriculture, which at any rate would hardly be possible there. Their distance, even through the air, measures thousands of kilometres, so one cannot even imagine how somebody could have walked the distance and returned. However, while Tassili is immensely distant from practically anything inhabitable, some people eventually visited the site, and for quite a long time.

There are also striking affinities between Çatalhöyük and Tassili. Çatalhöyük for Ian Hodder represented a shift from myth to history, a kind of 'mass indi-vidualisation': a new emphasis on the private individuality of the self, not in the direction of personality, but rather as some kind of self-consciousness. For us the

Round Head images of Tassili, with their pioneering depiction of humans in wall paintings, indicate a very similar kind of process: a shift away from memory, its replacement by constructed images, and a corresponding altering of human character through self-consciousness. Thus, our hypothesis that Tassili was some kind of omphalos for 'training' the 'magi' of Çatalhöyük (perhaps among others) can be reasonably made.

Notes

1 See in particular the heated 2013 exchange around a recent publication of an article about such dating in the journal Quaternary Geochronology (Hachid 2013; Mercier *et al.* 2013).
2 See in particular the famous Linton Panel, selected for the title page of Calasso (2016), extremely close to Tassili imagery.
3 'Record', by the way, is rooted in Latin *recordari*, meaning remember, rooted in *cor* 'heart'; close to an etymology of *credere* 'belief', traced to *cuor dare* 'giving one's heart', popular in the Middle Ages, and perhaps not so far from the truth.
4 'Becoming' here is meant in the sense of Deleuze: establishing a relationship between humans and the supernatural, which is not real but sur-real, in the process of becoming real (see Deleuze and Guattari 1987, 'Memories of a Bergsonian'). It is also linked to Plato's *Timaeus*. Deleuze even claimed that '*Becoming is an antimemory*' (sic; 294).
5 For this observation we thank Diletta Tonatto.
6 The link between the activity of hands, teeth and conception is again best comprehensible through Hungarian, where the words for teeth, holding, grabbing and conception are the same (*fog, fog, meg fog, meg fogan*).
7 This term is introduced to the analogy of Marc Augé's *surmodernité*, translated as 'supermodernity', taking into account the affinities with the artistic movement 'surrealism'.
8 An earliest appearance of this sign can be traced to Pech-Merle cave, 3 km aerially from Pergouset cave, where a similar cross sign appears in-between two circles (see Lorblanchet 2010: 141–2). It is similiar to the Maltese cross.
9 For all these, see Dexter and Mair (2010), who strikingly do not refer to Tassili.

PART III
Returns to walking

10

WALKING IN PHILOSOPHY AND RELIGION

Çatalhöyük, as brought out so vividly by Steven Mithen (2003: 93–4), captures well the full parasitism of pure settled existence. Such destructivity is still present, in our days, in the slums and ghettoes of global cities, in the shanty towns of third-world metropolises, in ethnographic accounts about pre-modern village life (see Hodder 2006: 25–7) or in the experiences of hunter-gatherers recently forced to settle, like the Ik, a case presented so dramatically in Colin Turnbull's classic *Mountain People*, a follow-up and negative copy of his *Forest People* which captured, perhaps with a bit of 'Romantic' exaggeration but still in a fundamentally truthful manner, life among the Pygmies of the tropical rain-forest.

It was only through long centuries and millennia that settlement eventually came to be pacified, with Egypt and the city-states of Mesopotamia playing a fundamental, though also quite ambivalent role, until a full pacification, amounting to a kind of Golden Age, was reached with the Greek polis, immortalised in Plato's *Republic* and *Laws*, and also Aristotle's *Politics*, focusing on the fundamental question of *founding* a city – a question whose relevance was brought out and confirmed in the recent magisterial work of Jean-Claude Margueron (2013). However, as the central focus of this book is walking, and not the history of civilisation, it cannot go into further details concerning this storyline. It has to focus on the singular reassertion of the significance of walking, characteristic of the two most important sources of modern European culture, Plato's dialogues and the New Testament.

The ambivalence of walking among the settled

As a start, we must note that the dynamic between walking and settlement cannot be reduced to a simplistic dualism of good and evil. The pacification of settlement, almost inevitably, went parallel with the literal wildening, or degeneration, of walking. If people live a settled life, forming families and raising children in houses, then those who keep leading a wandering life among them are redefined as homeless nomads, or outright as tricksters. In the various anthropological accounts tricksters always come from the outside, stumbling upon the settled people, who at first are always and necessarily suspicious about such wondering outsiders, while the conflict between the settled and the nomadic is one of the oldest historical narratives, predominant in the historical part of the Old Testament. A version of this account, showing how a prehistoric divinity figure became the modern trickster, can be found in the European 'wild man' tradition, connected originally to the bear (Frank 2008), and being present in the carnival tradition, which preserves a certain, though highly distorted, memory of the 'golden age', and where the encounter with the divine, impersonated in the bear, shifts from a walk to the cave (still present in the folklore tradition; see Propp 1968) to the arrival of the bear as a host to the village — with the full ambivalence of the term 'host', ranging from the 'hospitality' due to the stranger as guest to the 'hostility' towards the stranger as a necessary enemy.

The origins of philosophy

The origins of philosophy are sought in a contrast sometimes with myth, sometimes with religion. In both cases, philosophy supposedly represented a sudden and glorious emphasis on human reasoning power, in contrast to previous forms of superstition. However, such an account applies better to the history of sophistic than philosophy. Plato, who coined the term, on the one hand extensively used myths, with a special emphasis on the myth of Atlantis, called a 'true myth'; and, in contrast to the Sophists, his philosophy was also a kind of theology, most visible in his contrasting the Sophist idea of 'man-as-measure' with the divine as measure. The central concerns for the *philo-sophos* are not simply reason and justice, and especially not 'rationality', but rather love, grace and beauty.

The exact difference represented by the rise of philosophy can be understood through a proper reading of two central elements in the tradition about the rise of philosophy: that the first philosopher was Thales; and that the word was invented by Plato. As it transpires from the anecdotes relayed by Diogenes Laertius, Thales was originally a kind of Chaldean astronomer and priest (no fragment survived from the writings), quite similarly to Anaximander, the second philosopher. The scarcity of evidence about their ideas can be understood by realising that both died in 546 BC, the date of the Battle of Thymbra, thus they evidently took part in the fight against the Persians. Philosophy, as an effort to understand 'nature' (the first philosophers were called physiologists, or those who had ideas about the 'nature of nature'), was thus a break away from the kind of sacred-priestly knowledge that can be connected to the rise of a settled priestly caste, offering the first, negative definition of philosophy as a distancing. Plato, however, gave a further, positive twist to it, by emphasising the element of *philia*, or loving care, thus returning, in particular in the *Timaeus*, to the kind of life-affirming world-vision dominated by the experience of overwhelming joy that was so central to late Palaeolithic 'Atlantic' Europe.

The connection between the philosophy of Socrates and a peripatetic or walking kind of teaching has been well known since Antiquity. The problem was that this was all too close to the activities of the Sophists, who were also walking around, from one city to another, selling their wisdom for money, leading careless modern analysts to ignore the difference between Socrates and the Sophists.[1] Even worse, this was evidently one of the reasons why Socrates was condemned as a Sophist. As a result, one of the central, though little understood concerns of Plato, whose turn to philosophising was sparked by his experience of the death of Socrates, was to find out how to avoid the conflation of a philosopher and a Sophist; and, even more, whether there were aspects of Socrates's philosophy that rendered him liable for such a confusion. The difference, of course, is clear and evident: Socrates had his home, Athens, his beloved city, which he would not leave for anything, not even to save his life; while the Sophists were wanderers from city to city, cosmopolitan in the sense of being nowhere at home, and – far from preserving the legacy and tradition of prehistoric walking – were rather parasites on the new and in a way unprecedented flowers of settlement, the Greek cities, doing everything to bring about its demise. Still, it was not simple to put the difference between Socrates and the Sophists in clear words.

Socrates was caught between the schismogenic doubles of ritualistic priests, officiating sacrifices, representatives of the settled world order;[2] and wandering teachers, who were not defenders of the purity of tradition, and rather developed an innovative parasitic style of life under the conditions of stabilised settlement.

The eventual answer to this dilemma is contained in a pair of dialogues about love, the *Symposium* and *Phaedrus*, which mark the passage in Plato's thinking away from the early dialogues, where Socrates was the main protagonist, culminating in the *Gorgias* and the *Republic*, to the late dialogues where Plato moved beyond the horizon of his master. These dialogues show Plato's awareness concerning limits in Socrates's understanding of the world, while also being connected to the valorisation of a new modality of walking. In *Phaedrus*, Socrates is made to perform an unprecedented step, marking the limit in Plato's thinking, as for the first time in the dialogues we see him outside the city limits of Athens, under the plane-tree (*Phaedrus*, 230B–C), defining himself as a lover of beauty (250E); and in a particularly striking passage describing those who gave up living as wanderers 9,000 years ago (256E–257A). This makes Socrates 'metamorphose' from a kind of pre-modern *flâneur*, strolling casually in the city – though not in any city, and especially not being simply attracted by the lights of a metropolis – into a genuine walker, which implies walking across long distances outside cities. It is certainly not accidental that Plato introduces the word *philosophos* for this new, his own and not simply 'Socratic' mode of thinking in this dialogue.

The *Symposium* complements this point by offering a positive counterpart to the problematisation of discourse, contained in the *Phaedrus*, in terms of an explicit philosophy of beauty. Still having a focus on love, Plato here contrasts the kind of education preoccupied with chasing after young student boys, characteristic of Sophist teachers, and evidently somewhat tempting to Socrates as well, to a kind of concern with love through recognising beauty and turning such recognition to the generation of children. To mark, most clearly and evidently, the decisive distance from his master, Plato makes Socrates not simply engage in dialogues, but deliver a myth, and furthermore attributes it to Diotima, a female prophetess, who thus replaces Socrates as a source of understanding.

It is this new mode of Platonic thinking that culminates in the three concluding dialogues: about the vision of the beauty of the world, exposed in detail in the *Timaeus*; about the 'myth' of Atlantis, already a motive in the *Timaeus*, but becoming a central theme in the *Critias* – a dialogue, unfortunately, mutilated by the Byzantine copyists, probably going back to Neoplatonist like Proclus, just as it happened with the *Parmenides* (Brombaugh 1982); and the walk in the *Laws*, occasion for the dialogue, conclusion to Plato's life-work, which leads from Knossos, centre of Minoan civilisation, to the Diktean cave, where Zeus was supposed to have been born. These dialogues connect the theme of beauty, the beauty of the world, that is most visible not in a city but in nature, proving – for Plato – that the world must have been created, and which – in contrast to the city and its politics – is more female than male; which can only be properly perceived and regenerated thanks to and due to women.

The origins of Christianity

If the conflict of Socrates, causing his eventual death, was with the wandering teachers, being presumably at home everywhere, at least in any city, though receiving his death sentence due to charges of impiety, thus from a position close to the officiating priests, some hundred years later the conflict of Jesus was directly with priestly intellectuals – the Sadducees, the Scribes and the Pharisees. This makes, at first sight, Jesus also just another wandering teacher, leading to the colossal misrecognition, paralleling Solnit's, of arguing that Jesus was a wondering Cynic.[3]

While Jesus often presented his mission as comparable to the prophets', a point central for Girard, his mode of action was quite different. He did not confront the political authorities and the moral corruption of the populace in the big cities, and neither did he set up his residence outside – both modes of activity closely following settled existence – rather, indeed, he *walked*. Such walking did not privilege the cities, or shun them, but rather extended to the entire area, even venturing into Samaria, an evidently highly unusual act. It not only included various areas, but the most famous episodes gave a particular and quite unusual attention to the landscape, or nature. Thus, his most famous preaching was a Sermon on the Mount, while one of the most renowned miracles was his walk on the Sea of Galilee.

Still, these walks and wonderings emphatically could not be conceived as a pilgrimage. A pilgrimage is a journey that starts from home, directed towards an aim, a sanctuary, and is completed usually by the same road back home (Dupront 1987). The mission of Jesus, however, did not start at home, but rather with the recognition by a prophet, St John the Baptist – not of his status as a true prophet, but rather of his being the Son of God, thus of the verification of an epiphany;

and a most particular one. This recognition, however, did not lead to an official sanctification, but rather a series of ordeals and temptations. Even after these were met and passed, the journey of Jesus did not lead to the main sanctuary, Jerusalem; rather, this was exactly the place he avoided, as he had to avoid it until the right time; thus, he was simply following his given road, though not directly to the centre. When his wanderings eventually ended, and he took aim at entering Jerusalem, he did so not on foot, but – quite unusually – on the back of a donkey; an animal associated with stupidity and stubbornness, not with a holy mission. His experience at the sanctuary was also different from those of pilgrims, as it was his passion; while at its end, he did not return home, in the sense of Nazareth, or where he started his mission, but rather to the Heavens – which, however, could indeed be considered his real home – and, through the Annunciation and the Nativity, one could then even say that his mission, in the sense of the epiphany, after all indeed had the character of a pilgrimage.

Reasserting the significance of walking

Plato's works are the foundations of not simply philosophy, but of European thought. Similarly, it goes without saying that the Gospels are the foundations of Christian spirituality. Yet, the amazing thing is that practically none of the works that followed, and tried to interpret, these foundational works have followed their character. Plato's works are dialogues, while the Gospels are stories told about the life and activities of Jesus, with his oral teaching mostly contained in parables. Philosophical works rarely contain dialogues and biographies, just as theological works similarly fail to give much emphasis to life stories and are not written as parables. They are theoretical treatises, usually written while sitting and not conceived while walking. In fact, the chair as a symbol belongs as much to a philosophy or theology professor as the throne is the symbol of a king, or the armchair of a corporate manager.

This means that, to a significant extent, even if it cannot be said that Plato and the Gospels were never properly understood, there are tremendous forces embodied in the organisations and institutions against which they formulated their ideas, and which are the official, priestly type of guardians of knowledge, and their schismogenic counterparts, the wandering homeless social critics. For some reason or another, which oscillates between some kind of inertia and law of entropy on the one hand, served by and serving the most trivial and mundane vested interests, and sheer will to destroy on the other, best captured by Milton in *Paradise Lost*, instances of intellectual and spiritual renewal have a tendency to become reintegrated into the very trivialised, worn-down, silly, meaningless, ossified framework they tried to escape. This, however, by no means implies the profound pointlessness of any efforts; rather, these instances of renewal can never be destroyed and dismissed, but can – and effectively are – always used by another movement of renewal – though these very movements must be aware, from the start, that they cannot bring about a full and decisive breakthrough either.

Concerning the activity of walking, while philosophy and theology as professions will inevitably be tied to people eventually acquiring a chair, sitting down on it and pontificating their wisdom to the world, the history of philosophy and Christianity is also the history of a series of movements of spiritual and emotional renewal. Strikingly, many of these movements, if not practically all, are also accompanied by a renewed emphasis on walking, and/or a return to 'nature', away from the suffocating character of settled, 'civilised' existence.

Movements of philosophical and religious renewal as revival of walking

Christianity as redemption from settlement

Apart from being a call to, and demonstration of, a return to walking, Christianity also represented a quite literal – geographically marked, and in the clearest possible way – effort to redeem from the evils unleashed unto the world by the hubris of settlement.[4] This starts with the place of origin, as Galilee was homeland of Natufian culture; and continued in a particularly striking manner in the first Christian centuries. Paul is from Tarsus, a port in Cilicia, about a 100 km from Çatalhöyük; he got his name and started his apostolate in Cyprus.[5] Even more importantly, for his first missionary trip, which of course he did walking, he went from Cyprus to Pisidia (Antioch) and Lycaonia (Iconium, now Konya), near Cappadocia. Even further, the first letter of Peter is addressed to the exiles, among others, in Cappadocia and Galatia; but Paul never went to Bithynia and Pontus, which became a single Roman province around that time, as the Holy Spirit explicitly prohibited him from going there (*Acts* 16:7). Such a symbolic convergence of the first journey of Paul and the first words of Peter on Cappadocia cannot fail to be symbolic. Thus, Cappadocia, which until then was a particularly remote place, with hardly any evidence available before 400 BC and lacking even rudimentary civic structures, being the only Province in the Roman Empire without any cities (Mitchell 1993, I: 63, 97–8), then came to play a central role in early Christianity, in particularly through the three key fourth-century figures of Trinitarian theology, Basil the Great, his brother Gregory of Nyssa and Gregory of Nazianzus, each from Cappadocia, a theology which is thus simply called Cappadocian Trinitarianism.[6] In his second journey Paul went to Galatia, an area named after the Celts who previous invaded Greece, sacking the Delphi sanctuary, and eventually settled there; the first document of Christianity in fact is Paul's Letter to the Galatians (Esler 1998; on the context, and its frequent ignoring, see Mitchell, 1993, II: 3). Urfa (Edessa) was also central for the rise of Christianity as – according to apocryphal legends – King Abgar of Edessa was the first ruler to convert to Christianity; a story also connected to the shroud of Christ, or the Veronica image (*vera icona*), allegedly found in the walls of Edessa.

The next point is metaphorical, but is closely connected to Cappadocia. The first Christian communities in Rome literally kept their meetings underground, in the catacombs; and for many centuries churches were built half underground, as if recalling the first Natufian stone houses, which were similarly half dug into the ground. It is from there that Christianity rose and emerged, into the ground, with Christian churches culminating in the spectacular arches of Gothic cathedrals, or the cupolas of the cathedrals of Florence or Rome. This metaphorically represents the redeeming mission of leading people out of the cave, and into the light – which is also identical to Plato's conversion and redemption message in the *Republic*.

Of course, given the 10,000-year-long history of settlement by the life and times of Christ, it was not possible to simply abandon cities. The central issue was to move back to a kind of 'good city', in contrast to global imperial cities and capitals. Here again the medieval experience is fundamental, and in three stages. The prelude is the conversion of imperial cities into the seats of religion, culminating first in the – much backfiring – efforts of Constantine to create, as if from scratch, a 'new Rome'. But eventually, Imperial Rome collapsed. When this happened, city life had to be maintained, after and against the Barbarian invasions, and this happened, in the 'Dark Ages', through the leadership of the bishops. A second stage, however, paralleled to the first, was represented by a genuine movement of leaving the cities. This was the reason for the appearance of Egyptian and Syrian hermits, a movement that started right after the conversion of Constantine, thus the transformation of Christianity into the religion of the Empire, as an effort to maintain 'purity'. However, European monasticism was also a genuine leaving of settlement, the nature-hostility of civilisation. This is most visible in the location of medieval monasteries, especially in Italy, selecting places that were not simply far from settlements but in the midst of the most beautiful natural landscape, thus genuinely recalling a Paradisiac state.

Still, this effort was always somewhat problematic, on the verge of hubris, as – taken to the extreme – eremitic asceticism is the end of human life on the planet. It also time and again led to the paradox of collecting hermits into monasteries, thus turning the escape from settlement into the most extreme form of settlement, a life closed into and behind the walls of a single building, the monastery. The original spirit was therefore always in danger of being lost amidst the routine of closed life, leading to new movements of monastic reforms.

These movements, in our reading, culminate in the rise of the mendicant orders, in particular the Franciscans, which played a central role in the rise of the most important European Renaissance, starting in Italy in the thirteenth century. The term 'mendicant' is problematic and misleading, as the central idea was not 'begging', something that generated immediate misunderstanding and excess, culminating in the 'spiritual Franciscans' and the need to re-found the order, accomplished by St. Bonaventure, but rather the return to a life of giving, receiving and returning gifts. And this assumed, fundamentally and centrally, walking.

The medieval return to walking did not start with the Franciscans, but with the rise, or rather the revitalisation, of the pilgrimage road to Santiago de Compostela in the ninth to tenth centuries. As a result, walking and pilgrimage remained also particularly central for Spanish (and Portuguese) Christianity. A main Franciscan saint, second only to St. Francis, was St. Anthony of Padua (1195–1231) – who, however, originally was not from Italy, but was born in Lisbon; while the second most important movement of Christian renewal, the Jesuits, was founded by St. Ignatius of Loyola, a great walker as St. Francis, and as much shaping the 'Spanish Golden Age' as St. Francis did with the Italian Renaissance.

Apart from Italy and Spain, pilgrimage roads were also fundamental to France, much involved in the Camino de Santiago since the start and also the main scene of the other central medieval road, the Via Francigena, starting from Canterbury, thus also bringing in England. Thus, walking pilgrimages played a major role in restoring the Atlantic as an omphalos, a position it kept from proto-Neanderthal (*Homo antecessor*) times until the end of the Ice Age, thus for almost a million years, but lost around 10,000 BC and never recovered.

Finally, we signal that it has been argued that the modern interest in narrative, eventually leading to the rise of the novel, can also be rooted in the renewed pilgrimage to Santiago (Gros 2014: 118–19, referring to Joseph Bédier), thus tying further together Plato, Bakhtin, the carnivalesque aspects of pilgrimage and the modern novel. It is not accidental that many of the best modern novelists (Dickens, Balzac, Tolstoy, among others) were passionate walkers.

Reformation paradoxes

As Luther was an Augustinian monk, the Reformation started as just another monastic reform movement. Its relationship to walking, and even the way of life characteristic of Palaeolithic walking culture, was highly ambivalent. From the beginning Protestantism was particularly hostile to pilgrimages, considering it the worst kind of 'Catholic' concession to popular, even pagan religiosity, only promoting idleness and promiscuity. On the other hand, however, it had a tendency to consider human life itself as nothing else but a pilgrimage, formulated paradigmatically in Bunyan's *Pilgrim's Progress*, the single most important Puritan devotional literature, considered as having the value of an ideal type by Max Weber (1992). The ultimate result of this tension became the purely metaphorical interpretation of walking in mainstream modernity, culminating in the culture of passenger cars in global cities or rather villages.

But Protestantism brought about similar paradoxes concerning mediation, especially the mediation of the divine. Central for its spirituality was the refusal of priestly mediation, basing faith on a direct personal contact with God, relying only on the Scripture. Such refusal is close to assuming quasi-universal personal charisma, and has strong affinities with Palaeolithic modes of religiosity, where awareness of divine presence did not require the activities of a specific priestly caste. The aim of returning to the spirituality of the Gospels thus had an element of a return to the Golden Age as well. However, this was countered by the Calvinist vision of the radical depravity of man, thus the impossibility of relying on one's inner forces, after the Fall and especially under the perceived Renaissance intensification of corruptness – a vision that, by interpreting Weber's ideas about the Protestant Ethic through the optic of the contemporary, could be considered a performative speech act. The resulting focus on textual mediation, originally only aiming at helping direct personal contact with the divine, eventually implied a dependency on technologically mediated representations. This culminated in Hegel's philosophy, an apotheosis of mediation, amounting to a radical denial of any unmediated experience, and eventually leading to a reassertion of unmediated personal experience in Kierkegaard and Nietzsche – together with a philosophy of walking as concrete practice, and not a mere metaphor.

A very similar, parallel move happened with the shift from Protestantism to Romanticism. The Romantic focus on interiority closely parallels the Protestant focus on personal religiosity, and can be considered as a reaction, particularly strong in Protestant countries, like England and Germany, against the eighteenth-century move towards mediation, with Rousseau being a crucial pioneer in every regard – though with evident and inevitable flaws, just as in Kierkegaard and especially Nietzsche. Romanticism in this sense was thus a source of 'modernity', just as ultimately Protestantism; but its anti-modern modernity also implied a return; a refusal to give assent to a corrupted mode of existence. In *this* sense, genuine modernity culminates in recognising that any important movement of renewal over not simply the last centuries but millennia was a return to a mode of living that was immortalised first in the walls of Chauvet cave, but that must have existed way before.

Philosophy beyond rationalism

Modern rationalist philosophy was founded by René Descartes and Immanuel Kant. Central figures of genealogy and reflexive historical sociology (Szakolczai 2000), starting with Nietzsche and continuing with Elias, Voegelin, Borkenau and Foucault did not tire in their critique of rationalism, of Kant and in particular of Descartes. Concerning the latter, founder of rationalism, Elias (2000) made him into the emblematic figure creating *homo clausus* (a particularly apt term, from the perspective of this book), misdirecting the European civilising process; the 'rotten apple' of a modernity that Elias still tried to salvage. Foucault similarly made him into a central target of *Discipline and Punish*, one offering a philosophical support for the project of disciplining, and in particular of the militarisation of human conduct, discussed concerning walking by Ingold (2004). Voegelin, in his correspondence with his life-long friend Alfred Schutz (see Szakolczai 2013c), repeatedly refused to identify European philosophy with the line of thought started by Descartes, which he rather considered an aberration; while Borkenau offered in his classic book, written for the early 'Frankfurt school', equivalent of a dissertation, a chapter-long discussion of the biographical background to Descartes's thinking. As far as Kant is concerned, Elias fought tooth and nail with his thesis advisor against accepting as unquestionable background Kant's philosophy for his dissertation; Foucault's *Order of Things* was fundamentally an attack on Kant, situating his thought inside the plane of the modern episteme, instead of considering it as the height of philosophising; while Voegelin devoted one of his first major writings, published in a *Festschrift* for Hans Kelsen, to a thorough attack on Kant. While later in their lives, given the enormous purchase of Kant in intellectual and academic life, they softened their earlier position, they still never questioned their earlier ideas in this sense and did not accept Kant's three 'critiques' as the height of philosophising.

It is difficult to dismiss such ideas due to presumed incompetence, as each of them had impeccable credentials in modern European rational thought. Foucault studied philosophy in Paris, at the Sorbonne, stronghold of Cartesian rationalism for centuries, among others under Merleau-Ponty. Elias similarly studied philosophy in Breslau, home-town of Copernicus, and under Richard Hönigswald, one of the most important neo-Kantian philosophers of that time. Voegelin and Borkenau finally studied in Vienna, at the time when it became the undisputed centre of modern rationalism, jointly through neo-classical economics, logical positivism and analytical philosophy, with Voegelin studying under Hans Kelsen, a major neo-Kantian legal philosopher. Yet, their critique did not have the desired effect.

We can thus safely resign ourselves to a similar fate, and yet we hopefully can be forgiven in offering a somewhat novel perspective, in the footsteps of Gros and Ingold (among others), on the perspective of walking. The problem is not that Descartes and Kant were not walking; rather, that they not only founded modern rationalist philosophy, but also epitomise two *bad* ways of walking.

Descartes is the par excellence *tourist*, before its time – somebody who goes everywhere, visits everything, to gain as many impressions as possible: single, isolated bits of information, which then can be put together into a coherent system – starting from his famous reflections in the 'stove-heated room'. He thus also embodies the kind of walking that is reduced to the 'eye', singled out for attention as a major problem by Ingold (2004: 317–19); it is not accidental that his famous *Meditations* were originally published as a Preface to his *Optics, Geometry, and Meteorology* – each a central concern for a traveller, especially if we consider his emphasis on 'natural geometry' and 'natural signs', pushing geometry closer – also following its etymological sense – to geography.

Kant, on the other hand, represents the archetype of the *recreational* walker, somebody who walks not to gain experience and knowledge, but rather to relax before and after writing, as work for Kant was exclusively related to sitting in front of his desk – no matter that Plato, founder of philosophy, emphasised and embodied peripatetic philosophy. Kant and Nietzsche were opposed to each other even concerning their attitudes to walking. Kant managed to re-found philosophy on principles opposite to Plato's – thus, he literally 'stole' the philosophical undertaking.

The tourist of Descartes and the recreational walker of Kant seem to have hardly anything in common. One roams the entire continent, while the other never leaves his native city. Yet, the two share fundamental common features: each embody a schismatic division of the interconnected aspects of human life into separate spheres: mind and body, work and leisure, self and other, object and subject, ignoring and thus destroying the unity of experiencing and placing such schismatic mode of living and being at the heart of modern 'rationalist' philosophy. Due to its elective affinities with the alchemic-technological vision of the world that underlies modern science, such re-founding 'worked', in the sense of managing to transform living in this planet into conformity with such a destructive world-vision.

Thus, it is not surprising that many of the great figures of renewal in modern philosophy, and even in modern culture in general, are also central figures in the return to walking. This starts with Rousseau, a highly problematic but important and genuine thinker, the only figure of the Enlightenment to whom Foucault turned with a degree of understanding, publishing an Introduction to a 1962 edition of Rousseau's *Dialogues* (Foucault 1994, I: 172–88, one of his first publications), considering Voltaire as the prototype of the wrong kind of intellectual (III: 156); while the same thing can be said about Voegelin, who considered Voltaire as a central figure in the 'apostatic revolt' (Voegelin 1998: 57–70), but showed more leniency with Rousseau. His call for a 'return to nature' can be criticised as idealistic and Romantic, but there is something fundamentally genuine about it; a cry in the wilderness against the oppressive rationalism of the *raison d'état* of the absolutist state – which would eventually be individualised and altered into the void and black hole of 'rational choice' theory. Significantly, Kant would be much impressed by Rousseau – not by his call for a return to nature, which left Kant cool, but rather his excessive educational ideas, based on calls for 'self-realisation' and 'autonomy'.

The list continues with Kierkegaard and Nietzsche, central opponents of Hegelian and Kantian 'idealism' in the nineteenth century, both passionate walkers, and also central for the highly related concern with the 'care of the self', thus central for both Pierre Hadot and Michel Foucault. However, these threads were already covered by Frédéric Gros, so this chapter can be brought to a close.

Notes

1 This culminated in Solnit's (2001: 14–15) absurd claim that therefore the Sophists were the real founders of philosophy.
2 This helps to shed new light on the origins of philosophy, showing that the focus was not on 'myth' or 'religion' 'as such', but rather on the closely connected pair of foundation myths and rituals of sacrifice, thus *the* enemies of philosophy.
3 See Szakolczai (2003: 223). This would support the relation between Jesus and the Cynics, argued in some recent publications (see Betz 1994).
4 Strikingly, here Nietzsche with his Zarathustra is at the same time very close to and farthest away from our claim. The point is very similar to the way Nietzsche thought that redemption from evil (which he associated with spiritual dualism) has to return to its source, which he identified with Zoroastrism. However, he came to consider that Christianity is just a part of this storyline, failing to realise that it was the opposite, its redemption, and exactly through mobilising Nietzsche's favourite activity, walking.

5 Cyprus was the first place 'colonised' by the Neolithic settlement-agriculture package, through a sustained and singular effort, when 'colonisers' brought with them not only domesticated cereals like einkorn and emmer, and animals such as sheep, goats, pigs and dog, but also fox and fallow deer, evidently attempting to transplant their entire world, around 8500 BC (Zeder 2011: 231).

6 It is not possible to enter here into details of this important matter. We can only signal that while Trinitarian theology, due to the strong anti-experiential, anti-historical and monotheistic character of Protestantism, and also because of the 'dogmatic' and 'mysterious' character of the Trinity, little present in the scriptures, was not much in vogue in modernity, the tide seems to be turning, much due to the revival of Trinitarian theology in the Orthodox East. A central figure of this revival, increasingly discussed by Western, especially Catholic theologians, is John Zizioulas, who advocates a return to the thinking of the Cappadocian fathers, argues that the mystery of the Trinity requires a historical understanding and situates a revitalised idea of the 'pilgrim Church' in this context. For details, see Clancy (2009).

11

WALKING IN MOUNTAINS

The vocation of losing oneself

> We know the existence of the infinite but are ignorant of its nature, as it has extension like us, but not limits like us.
>
> *Pascal,* Pensées *(1972: B233)*

The issue of representing the void is central for this book, for understanding the practice of walking, in particular walking into the cave, but it also requires us to enter the most difficult and tricky question of the void itself; the issue where, fortunately, Plato in the *Sophist* offers some guidance. The point is that in a way the question concerning the existence of the divine has a similar character concerning the existence of the void. In one sense, the void most obviously does not exist, as if anything exists inside the void, then it would not be void. And yet, the void, in the sense of pure empty space, is the absolute basis and starting point of Newtonian physics, just as of Kantian transcendental philosophy. So in the Newtonian-Kantian vision of the world, which is nothing other than the basis of our own 'scientific' world-vision, the void is not simply existing, but is the very condition of possibility of existence, so consequently changing existence as well, from reality into unreality.

However, quite paradoxically, it is exactly here, where the foundations of the scientific vision of the world are laid down, hoping to exorcise forever any concern with the divine and the transcendent, that the possibility of posing again the 'existence' of the divine reappears. This is because the existence of the divine, in a way, can be approached exactly like the existence of the void – even in the sense that the divine can be all but identified with the void (at least as an analogy). This implies, first, a recognition that something like god, or the divine, or supernatural beings indeed do not and cannot exist in the sense in which any being that has a body, or that can be directly identified with changes in a body, can be said to exist. But it does not mean that they are pure figments of the imagination – just as the void is not pure imagination; and just as – and here we enter the point of the *Sophist* – imagination itself, or any word or image, while not 'real' in the evident sense, can become real, and even alter reality, the moment in which we formulated or designed them.

However, the divine – let's use now this term in a somewhat technical sense, to capture what cannot be captured – has a further characteristic, more closely associating it with the void, and it is that it is not simply not of our own making, but somehow is 'out' there, outside us, without 'really' existing, in the sense of being part of our world. Such affinity between the void and the divine is indicated by the fact that appearances of the divine, epiphanies or hierophanies indeed often take place in a void, through a void, or due to the void. The most frequent places for epiphanies are mountain tops, deserts or – indeed – caves; occasions of death, illness or other liminal moments; occasions where stabilities are dissolved and thus replaced by emptiness or the void. Yet, it is exactly here that the radical difference of mere void and the divine appears, as the void is indeed empty, nothing but pure void, while the divine, for those who experience it, appears as plenitude. The void is thus necessary for the appearance of the divine, but only as a condition, where this same void and emptiness suddenly becomes filled with something that is not simply real but super-real, and which can appear as boundless, infinite divine love. But for this to appear, it seems that there is another condition that must be met: the human being who enters the void, metaphorically or literally, cannot be completely empty or void, cannot dissolve himself or herself into the liminal void, but must preserve something deeply stable and meaningful in his or her heart; must remain substantial, or even 'full': fully present. It is only if these two presences, the human and the divine, meet in the absence of the void, that something like a significant experience, or epiphany, can take place.

The experience of such an encounter with the void is vividly captured by the Italian mountain walker Franco Michieli (2015).[1] In a sense, the choice of this book is almost accidental; Michieli plainly states that he does not have any special pretence in writing this book; he received no revelatory experience, is no genius, just started to walk, kept walking and became a mountain walker. Thus the book offers a perfect way, in its mundane simplicity, to explain the more than philosophical depths of walking,[2] at once illustrating the central claim of this book: one just has to start walking, and an entire world opens up in front of our feet. This is almost the same thing that Kafka conveyed, though through the much more problematic, almost opposite way of sitting down at our desk; a way that only yields wisdom if it is combined with a wisdom procured with our feet, outside the crowded cities, which indeed came to Kafka outside Prague (or Berlin), in Zürau.[3]

The precondition for such an encounter with the void, at least in the modern world, is that we have to become lost; though in a particular way. How to do so, or rather how does it happen, or *should* happen, and what does it mean – this is what is captured first in the title of the book, then in its subtitle, then in more detail in its long first paragraph, and then in the entire book. *Perdersi* 'to lose one's way, to get lost', according to this title, is a *vocation*; a quite striking idea, certainly a title intended to raise some eyebrows; and particularly so for a sociologist, for any sociologist, but especially one having his first encounter with sociology through Max Weber's two famous lectures on science and politics as a vocation, and the crucial discussion in the *Protestant Ethic* about Luther's use of the word *Beruf* ('calling' or 'vocation') in his German translation of the Bible. It thus immediately enters the heart of the connection between the deepest essence of a human being and his evocation to the divine. The subtitle adds a crucial clarification: the theme of the book is how roads find the wayfarers, and not the other way around.

The first paragraph conveys the experiential basis beyond such hints. Its first word, beauty (*la bellezza*) (Michieli 2015: 11), makes it evident that this book about walking illustrates the core of Plato's philosophy, as exposed in the *Timaeus*, this tribute to beauty. Beauty is characterised by two words, 'visceral' and 'mysterious'. Seemingly, they cannot be further apart from each other: 'visceral' evokes the most material aspects of the body, the guts, connected to digestion, while 'mysterious' alludes to the most spiritual qualities of the human mind. Yet, they closely belong together, in the sense of capturing the two central poles mapping the range of human experience, instead of separating them following Cartesian and Kantian, dualist rationalism; keeping them together, and healing the rift through walking.[4]

The mysterious nature of such beauty, the beauty of nature when we encounter it in its pristine state, producing a visceral effect on us humans, is first of all due to its limitless infinity, where 'there is no clear boundary between the two extremes' (Michieli 2015: 11),[5] and also its being full with the unknown – which of course is another paradox, combining fullness and the void. As a result, such beauty might impose itself on us with increasing force 'until all reference points would seem to disappear and we find ourselves in infinity, waiting for another revelation' (12). And yet, such a confrontation does not crush us, but rather varies according to 'the intensity of our desire to encounter it'. Both the words used in this short sentence and its meaning are of extraordinary significance, capturing the heart of experiencing the void, the walking into the void. Far from liberating the void, the aim of modern scientific-alchemic experiments, or being reduced to it, the heart of Eastern spirituality, encountering infinity and the void is indeed a confrontation, a way of being personally tested, where the human side plays an equal, active, though not purposeful and conscious role; without this, there is simply no spiritual life (20). Together with granting spiritual well-being, such permanence also restores health in the most mundane sense, by granting easy sleep (54) – a not irrelevant concern in our age, where problems of sleep are disturbing ever increasing multitudes.

A central feature of this role is *intensity*, or the strength and force of concrete character; and, in particular, the intensity of *desire* – not in any trivial-modern sense, as the desire for possession, of some kind of objects or even of others, or even recognition, fame, success and certainly not in the infantile Freudian sense of reducing all desire to sexual fulfilment; rather, the desire to meet and stand up to the mysterious unknown. Bringing together the central elements in this willingness for encounter, we find – after the core of Plato's philosophy – the improved core of Aristotle's philosophy, the starting words of his *Metaphysics*, 'All man by nature desire to know'; except that this is not equal to a 'will to knowledge', to which Aristotelian ideas have been reduced in alchemic modernity, a search for decontextualised and fragmented pieces of information that can be used to subjugate nature and transform it into a means for satisfying our 'wishes' as consumers and voters, but rather – and most probably close to the Aristotelian intention – as a feature of our inner essence as human beings, a point that will be further clarified in Michieli's short and simple yet profound booklet. The last sentence of this first paragraph offers a condensed insight into the nature of the knowledge to be gained by such an encounter with infinity: it is something not belonging to human planning, rather 'coming from somewhere else: a glare (*bagliore*) of the philosophy of the universe' (12).

Here again, the short phrase requires a long commentary. 'Rational planning' and 'consciousness' are central terms for rationalist philosophy, neoclassical economic theory, communist administration and managerial ideology, among others, but irrelevant for the world-vision to be gained through walking: a way to liberate from such modernist modes of entrapment. This vision comes 'from elsewhere': and the booklet would repeatedly attempt to come close to capturing this 'elsewhere' that is somehow intimated behind the emptiness and infinity of the void. Finally, way beyond consciousness and planning, the encounter offers a genuine philosophy: the philosophy of the universe, or the cosmos; an order that underlies beauty, and which we can recognise if we are courageous enough to suspend our modern, rationalistic prejudices.

Before we can further try to present and capture the nature of the experiences and insights gained, we need to relay how the author came to reach them; or, how to find the proper way of losing oneself (60–2). They are important exactly because there is nothing particular in them. Michieli makes it clear that he neither had a revelation, nor a sense for magic or any special talents; indeed, one can only walk properly if one leaves behind any idea of being a 'protagonist' (56, 59, 72). He simply started to walk, and somehow kept walking – there was nothing more special than the gradual development of a certain elective affinity between the activity of walking and his own, increasing and ever more intensive fascination with such walking. While he already went for various walking and mountain climbing trips as a child, the first time he felt a particular attraction for walking was when at the age of nineteen he crossed the Alps from Ventimiglia to Duino (53); he then started to systematically experiment with walking into large uninhabited areas and staying as much in the open as possible, not bringing even a tent (55), and eventually, from his thirty-seventh year, travelling without maps or other artificial aids (7, 55), given that maps only mislead us, as they lack a proper vision of the whole (43); went for such trips either with his friends, or his wife; and finally, the direct motivation for writing his booklet was a particularly experimental walk in Lapponia, started on 1 March 2013, his fifty-first birthday (13, 52).

The contemplation of beauty, even when encountering the immensity of nature, risks becoming a mere spectacle, as it is evident in the particularly problematic fascination with the sublime in nature, a genuine obsession in eighteenth-century Britain, as a consequence of the Grand Tour and the visual impact of crossing the Alps, where the position of the spectator became idealised by travellers who of course progressed by coach (Nicolson 1959; on the sublime, see Szakolczai 2016a: 67–93). This is why Plato connected his appreciation of beauty in the *Symposium*, through Eros and in particular by Diotima replacing Socrates as main guide to a kind of conversion experience, beyond the more 'violent' conversion envisioned in the cave metaphor of the *Republic*.[6]

However, behind the 'visceral' and 'mysterious' aspects of beauty, there is something clearly not accessible to a pure spectator. This starts with an at first hardly perceivable, unfamiliar feeling (Michieli 2015: 53, 57). This feeling, perception, experience or sensation[7] has many aspects and elements, preconditions and ramifications, starting at first vaguely though already with a certain inner force, eventually becoming decisive, even overwhelming, which should not be surprising, as this experience was decisive for our becoming human, and still touches in a unique way the heart of being human, or human Being. Michieli takes a considerable effort in describing this 'feeling', certainly the core of the book, and giving it due value – a genuine way of showing up the most universal in the most personal and mundane.

He first encountered with this experience at the age of nineteen, and it proved decisive for his 'walking into the void'. It was a 'strange sensorial experience' (57) that hit him during a simple skiing excursion near Turin, when suddenly snowfall intensified and became persistent, and soon it was not possible to see beyond a few yards. The track became invisible; even the traces of skiers from the previous day were soon covered up with snow. At this moment, 'even if [he] took this route for the first time, he felt confident that he would not lose the track', thus started to lead the group (58). While the situation kept deteriorating, resulting in the weather condition called *whiteout* (59), and all external signs indicating the road disappeared, nevertheless 'the more time passed, the more in [his] eyes the trail appeared clearly, leading into the void (*nel nulla*) that was ahead' – so much so that he couldn't say whether it was really there or was just an optical illusion (59).

Michieli immediately adds two comments: that this experience was repeated several times, thus it cannot be attributed to mere coincidence (56–7);[8] and that there was nothing particular with it: it was neither due to magic, nor miracle, was simply a part of possible experiences (59). We can add that the description, in the terms used to capture its eventuality, uses most significant words, in particular the sudden feeling of inner confidence (*fiducia*) when one encounters, without dread, the void (*nulla*). We thus have to follow as closely as possible Michieli's efforts at capturing this experience and making sense of it.

To begin with, the first point to notice is that the experience starts randomly, as pure chance; even further, it has evident negative connotations, like bad weather. Michieli repeatedly uses two terms to characterise this starting point; both of exceptional significance. The first is 'error': we must expose ourselves to the possibility of error (13–14). It is only in this way that we can correct ourselves and have genuine experiences (14); making an error, or losing the road, is fundamental to our growth as human beings, and indeed the evolution of life, as nature itself is based on error (39). Here Michieli, as if unknowingly illustrating the point, accidentally hit upon the heart of Michel Foucault's philosophy, as exposed in Foucault's 'Introduction' to the English version of Georges Canguilhem's (1978) classic book *The Normal and the Pathological*, of which the French version, entitled 'Life: experience and science' (*La vie: l'expérience et la science*; see Foucault 1994, IV: 763–76), was the last article published with Foucault's *imprimatur*, thus has – among other works – the character of a last word or testament. The second term is rather a pair of words, danger and risk (see Michieli 2015: 39, 65, 70–1): exposing ourselves to the possibility of committing errors is dangerous and risky; yet, it is a risk we simply must take. Michieli is not espousing here the search for danger characteristic of modern extreme sports, which are only reckless titillations of the senses, often hardly involving any real danger, only a controlled, artificial inciting of emotions, producing 'adrenaline junkies'. Instead of a walking into the void, this can be captured by the term 'limivoid', developed by Bjørn Thomassen (2014: 167–90), in his study of bungee diving, in the analogy of Turner's 'liminoid'. The modern search for experience, already bemoaned by Max Weber, is only the schismogenic pair of the sterilised, effortless, prefabricated everyday 'reality' of the modern world, produced by technological means to reduce any danger and risk, thus to take away the possibility of inner growth.[9]

Walking means something else – and this is the experiential complex Michieli tries to capture. Walking into and in the wilderness offers us experiencing something genuine and authentic, as – strangely enough – the experience that overtakes us, the more we walk *away* from home, *away* from civilisation and *into* the unknown, the more we actually feel at home (Michieli 2015: 54),[10] once we manage to develop there a certain *permanence* (53), in authentic isolation (14). Thus, to walk properly, we need to expose ourselves to the possibility of getting lost; we need to get rid of our technological devices which do not help us but, on the contrary, imprison and impoverish us (24), prevent us from recognising our own inner force as human beings – and perhaps this is the exact goal of all those 'powers and principalities' around us, 'rulers of the darkness of this world' (Eph 6:12; see also Santayana 1951), directing our life by teaching us to 'realise' our best interests, who still reveal themselves through their false and corrupt life philosophy – true only for themselves – of man being uniquely concerned in maximising pleasure and money. Losing oneself in the proper way is not a reckless exposition to danger or its fake, but rather a way to recapture, and not let disappear, one of the most important, foundational human experiences (Michieli 2015: 65). Thus Michieli reached the point of going with a friend for the trip in Lapponia, where they had never been before, trusting nothing else but their own inner senses. The result was spectacular, as after skiing for days in an unknown and uninhabited land, they not only found the village, a unique possibility to get refreshment, but decided to set up their camp at exactly the spot where the sole refuge in the wilderness turned out to be – even if they did not need it (89–91).

To understand how such things are possible, we need to retrace the exact steps. Exposing oneself to the risk and danger of getting lost is only a first step; the central point concerns how then to find the way, without relying on external instruments and help. Here again, we only need to evoke the way nature works. While the first step in nature is pure error, from genetic mutation up to the chance encounter of cells resulting in conception, 'as soon as an individual or a community has come into existence, chance no longer rules sovereign' (40). In the wilderness or the void, deprived of any external direction and certainties, one starts to perceive, and be guided, by two different forces, which work in complete unison, recalling *harmonia mundi* (see Szakolczai 2017a: 154–65). One is the inner power of any living being; a reliance on one's own force and energy; a confidence in oneself. To realise this inner force we in the modern world, and going back a very long time, need to become lost, thus gain an 'acute desire' for retrieving the way.[11] Second, under such conditions a 'strange feeling' starts to appear, 'inside [oneself] (*dentro di me*)', that 'the road opens itself up in front of our steps (*che la via si aprisse da sola davanti ai nostri passi*)' (Michieli 2015: 56).[12]

We are now in a better position to capture the exact nature of this experience or feeling – the core of Michieli's book, and also of ours. To begin with, there is nothing particular about it – it is available for everyone; indeed, it is one of the most elementary and basic experiences of humankind. However, while it can happen to anybody, it does not happen to anyone under any condition – it is not a 'right', it requires a proper attitude, or rather a certain, again basic and simple, but not empty and universal predisposition. These are captured in two pairs of concepts.

The first pair, amounting to a genuine 'philosophy of nature' (in contrast to 'natural philosophy'), is 'participation' and 'patience' (59). Participation is the most basic of life experiences: it simply means that we are *part* of the world – part of the planet, having our habitat *on* the ground (not above or under it, or in water, as it happens with many other beings), belonging to nature, part of various communities, our family and so on; but it still cannot be taken for granted, as technological and sacrificial worldviews, of which modernity has become a part, as a deviation and betrayal of its roots, in Plato and Christianity, in Europe, trying their best to suspend such participation by enclosing us into boxes and cages, blocking one's open horizon, and replacing it with the chimera of progress. One of the central experiences of modern global cities is to deprive us of any horizon: we do not see anything but buildings and walls, thus cannot possibly have a vision of open, infinite horizons (80). This is indeed the main difference between modern and archaic experiences: while participation could be taken for granted in archaic times, in modern times it has to be acquired by leaving the city (this, as Michieli again repeatedly and rightly evokes, is the core of the Abraham experience, the leaving of Ur or Urfa) and then getting lost, being deprived of all modern 'amenities'. The second crucial term of the first pair is patience. Nature only reveals itself, its wonders and beauty, to a patient interlocutor; one who participates and thus starts to listen (59). Such combination of participation and patience again reaches the utmost philosophical heights, as they literally capture the two key modalities of experience: participation simply *is* the most basic experience, even meta-experience, as precondition of any other, concrete experience; while patience is etymologically rooted in the Greek word for experience, *pathein*, which furthermore incorporates its archaic, 'passive' component. Needless to say, such passivity does not imply the modern experience of helpless subjection, as – we have seen – it is rather the precondition for gaining awareness of our full inner force. Impatience, from this perspective, is the hubristic assertion of the actual self, which has become integrated into a life- and nature-denying machinery, whether modern or not; the atomised individual of 'rational' choice theory, which is not concrete at all, only a pawn in the game, recalling the 'court society' of Elias. Here Michieli again unknowingly stumbles upon one of the heights of modern thinking, the *Zürau Notebooks* of Kafka, where Kafka would strikingly identify impatience as the greatest of sins and reason for the expulsion of the Paradise – written when Kafka, this eternal prisoner of cities and his desk was spending, uniquely in his life, half a year in a mountain village, having his happiest period and developing his best ideas, focusing on the key word 'indestructible' – though never bringing himself, back in the city, to publish them.

The second pair, closely related to the first, is humility and curiosity (73–6). Humility is the other side of patience, not mere resignation and self-annihilation, but rather making one ready and accessible for experiencing the world and nature as it is, which 'allows us to leave space to events that don't depend on us' (74). It is only if we patiently and humbly participate that we gain confidence in the road which we don't know in advance.[13] Furthermore, we also need the active force of curiosity (11, 19), the desire of knowing, or again a predisposition that, as Aristotle already recognised, at the heart of classical philosophy, it belongs to all of us, being at the centre of human nature.

Regaining our inner force by exiting the 'city', leaving behind 'technology' and retrieving the experience of participation through daring to enter the void is not to pursue something new and unprecedented, but rather is a true return not simply to our 'origins', but the road that we abandoned. In the most simple and basic sense, it is a return to normality (16, 65) – to our own normality, which is just the same, though in several ways also different, as the normality of everyone, exactly in the sense of the 'normal' theorised by Canguilhem (1978), or in the Heraclitean sense of *panta einai* ('All is one', or 'All things are one', Fragment 50). To find this normality, to recuperate its memory, the central purpose of Michieli's book, the 'vocation' mentioned in the title, we might need to go back tens of thousands of years, before the 'so-called civilisation' was set on, with settlement and agriculture (Michieli 2015: 16–17); thus, back to the 'Golden Age' or the 'Garden of Eden'. Yet, such experience at the same time implies a different kind of return, a return to the times when we were children, to the experiences of children – we need to become children again (89).[14] While the 'wise men' of our days, who actually do not know anything, only regurgitate what they appropriated from their teachers, and most of all the greatest trickster and Sophist of modern times, the media, consider this mere Romanticism, foolish trifles, it rhymes with profound evangelical wisdom: 'Let the little children come to me, and do not hinder them, for the kingdom of heaven belongs to such as these' (Mt 19:14; see also Lk 18:16, Mk 10:14); or, 'unless you change and become like little children, you will never enter the kingdom of heaven' (Mt 18:3; see also Mk 10:15). This same wisdom was central for the single greatest figure of medieval Christianity, fountainhead of the Italian Renaissance, St. Francis of Assisi (Michieli 2015: 74); not simply a great walker, but sharing a similar, archaic philosophy of nature, attuned to 'Brother Sun' and 'Sister Moon', much in the footsteps of another central evangelic wisdom: 'Take therefore no thought for the morrow: for the morrow shall take thought for the things of itself. Sufficient unto the day is the evil thereof' (Mt 6:34).

Even further, we deeply long for such origins, whether historical or personal, as we all feel that we need to regain access to something we all miss (Michieli 2015: 84). It is this same yearning that motivates such desperate and self-invalidating searches for authentic, genuine, ultimate experiences as extreme sports, stimulants like drugs and alcohol, or obsessive sex, and so while such means are hopeless, the yearning and striving are genuine; or, as Bruce Chatwin (1997: 106) put it, 'Drugs are vehicles for people who have forgotten how to walk'. The same can be said about new age spirituality, or various searches for self-realisation that – paradoxically – push us further and further away from what they try to reach, due to the modality of the search: hubristic, dogged, reckless, relentless, purposeful.

The road, and the access to our authentic inner force, is actually much simpler; it is really simple, though also in a sense much more difficult than going to New Zealand or Nepal for bungee jumping. We only need to get lost and listen; though we have to carefully prepare to acquire the right attitude. And then, if we start walking, and keep walking, the world would indeed come to us; the road will open itself, though something else would also encounter us, *in the void*. This is the ultimate and deepest part of any experience, and Michieli – a mountain trekker, not a pilgrim – does not shy away from capturing and naming it, though he keeps his utmost care and cool. When we really let ourselves get lost in the void, we not only recapture our own forces, by we also encounter something else, another dimension of reality (or what we call a super-reality), which is 'more profound and less explicable', coming not from things but 'a spirit hidden behind them', belonging to 'another realm in reality', an experience well accessible to archaic men (Michieli 2015: 24–7). This is identical to the archaic experience about the 'animated' nature of the world, which is very different from the trivialising terminology of 'animism', a label used by evolutionary anthropologists; this is why nature is at once poetic and spiritual (87–8). Here at the heart of darkness and in the middle of the void we touch upon the super-reality of the divine: recognising the cosmos, following Plato, as a 'magnificent work of God'; and recognising our task in recognising this profound truth, and thus in our *confronting* nature (69) – not by destroying or subjugating it, but rather, in the proper sense of 'confronting', characteristic of Max Weber, and also Plato,[15] in order to work together with the forces of nature, rather than against them (36, paraphrasing Fridtjof Nansen).

Whether trying to recapture the true experience behind the creation of Palaeolithic cave art or the phenomenon of pilgrimage, central for most religions, the rise of (Platonic) philosophy and (Christian) religion, or the Renaissance, sparked by the Franciscans, we encounter the same combination of walking and the void; a unique access to true philosophy, about the mysterious beauty of nature, and thus also of culture, guided by an unquenchable desire and curiosity (74), an 'innate stimulus for exploration' (19). It is this search and experience that is conveyed in the last sentence of Michieli's book: 'I recognise in myself the desire to encounter the mystery that walked next to us' (91).

Notes

1 The same experience is captured by Thomas Mann, both in *Death in Venice*, as a strolling at the sea, and in the *Magic Mountain*, as the encounter with a snow-storm, both being presented as encounters with infinity. It is also theorised by Freud, as an oceanic feeling.

2 Given the previous linguistic excursion, it might be worth noting that 'explain' in Hungarian is *magyaráz*, rooted in the word used for Hungarian language or people (*magyar*), relevant because of the connection of the *magy-megy* root of *magyar/megyeri* with going on feet (*megy*), recalling the Batek identity between 'walking' and 'talking'.

3 For details, see Szakolczai (2017a).

4 The same idea is expressed by Harvie Ferguson, connecting the deepest human feelings with 'guts', close to the 'language of the heart' (2000: 76).

5 It is something to be pondered about by rationalist philosophers, social-constructionist sociologists and the institutional engineers of the EU alike that no limit is so clear and absolute as the boundary between sea and continent, earth and sky, or snow and the sky-line in the mountains, separating the three basic states of the elements, solid, liquid and gas; yet, in none of these cases is it possible to draw a clear, fixed, stable, borderline.

6 On this, see the Special Section on Plato's *Symposium*, entitled 'Plato and Eros', in the December 2013 issue of *History of the Human Sciences*, in particular Horvath (2013b), Horvath and Szakolczai (2013), and Szakolczai (2013b).

7 It can be uniquely conveyed in Hungarian, as *érzés*, given that this word, through the root *ér*, connects 'sense', 'sensation', 'maturation', 'reaching', 'reason' and many other related or similar terms.

8 'Coincidence' as joint presence is part of the very structure of the world in which we live, and its mystery, and cannot be reduced to rationalistic explanations based on probability theory, as Pascal, inventor of probability theory, was well aware.

9 Labbucci (2011: 63) makes the same connection between danger, walking and freedom: 'Walking is freedom. Freedom is autonomy. Autonomy is risk. Walking is risky'.

10 This is captured in the Hungarian twin words for home, *itthon/otthon*, as discussed in Chapter 2.

11 About desire, see also the book entitled *The Spirit of Feet* by Andrea Bellavite, which closes with a discussion of the link between walking and desire, and ends – slightly pathetically, but to the point – with the following words: 'Desire is walking and walking is desire, in the long road that leads, beyond the oceans and the high mountains into the depth of the human heart, up to marvellous springs of Love' (Bellavite 2016: 86–8).

12 This experience can again be relayed through a particularly disturbing Biblical parable, contained in Matthew and Luke: 'You don't have enough faith,' Jesus told them. 'I tell you the truth, if you had faith even as small as a mustard seed, you could say to this mountain, "Move from here to there," and it would move.' (Mt 17: 20); or 'If you had faith even as small as a mustard seed, you could say to this mulberry tree, "May you be uprooted and thrown into the sea," and it would obey you' (Lk 17: 6).

13 Humbleness is also linked to two central values of Eastern Christianity, *kenosis* and *hesychasm*, both closely connected to walking and the figure of the 'holy fool' (see Labbucci 2011: 44; Gros 2014: 214; Bakhtin 1984).

14 This theme was also central to the book of Gros (2014), and singled out for particular attention by Roman (2014).

15 Here I rely upon the PhD thesis just completed by Julian Davis (2017).

12

EXPERIENCING WALKING

It is evident that a social-scientific writing must be more than a personal account, without belittling the significance of such an account. However, in this case, our book was indeed much sparked by our own experiences, and – though the book so far has conformed, at least to a large extent, to the exigencies of social science – we felt the need to incorporate directly the personal, experiential dimension, as another sign of the truly special character of this most simple and 'pedestrian' of activities, walking.

To a person accustomed to looking at walking from the point of view of utility, the increasing prevalence of long-distance walking and the spontaneous and sudden appearance of walkers could seem, at first glance, a most singular and problematic phenomenon. Does it not far exceed the measure of the necessary or the useful? What can possibly be the significance of walking, without interruption, for several hundred miles? The revival of the Camino de Santiago de Compostela and other pilgrim routes since the mid-1980s is receiving increasing attention, both by books that, in various languages, describe the experiences of the participants, and by studies that attempt to offer an explanation for this move. Walking is about how to return to becoming who we are, but under very particular circumstances.

Does this take place with the precision of a clockwork, where the boundaries of your self are ritualistically erased and you are transformed into a form prepared by the official conversion stamping ceremony, or is there something else also present? Such issues pose a fundamental question from the perspective of political anthropology: whether one should interpret the practice of walking using the standard, mainstream vision of modernity, dominated by the exchangeability of everything on the one hand, and on the other caught between the rigid fixity of the rational self and the possibility to 'educate' everyone to everything; or whether we should take seriously the possibility that walking represents an ensemble of experiences that challenge the modern vision of an at once positivistic and voluntaristic worldly order.

Our book relies on the four pilgrimages we have completed, together: to Santiago de Compostela (from Saint-Jean-Pied-de-Port, 800 km, 2011), to Rome (Via Francigena, from Altopascio, 340 km, 2012), to Máriagyűd (Hungarian Pilgrimage Road, from Esztergom, 380 km, 2013, continued to Belgrade) and to Brindisi (Via Francigena Sud, from Rome, 650 km, 2014, including a walk to Monte Sant'Angelo), just as a series of shorter mountain treks in the Transylvanian Carpathians and the Tuscan-Emilian Apennines; walks covering nearly 3000 km where we found something unexpected, the void (fortification of strength and power in flux). This implies, first, the rectitude of movements, when all bonds have been suspended, and second, how the *res* (the word for 'real' in Latin, etymologically meaning 'goods' and 'wealth', and according to Mauss gift) component builds up through the contentment of the walkers this quality – as everyone really wants the good, this is the centre of Plato's philosophy, so one should not be specifically *taught* what is good, but rather should be given the possibility of expressing it freely; but for this the active misdirection implied in modern settled civilisation must be suspended, and this is what walking truly accomplishes. Third, how in this way the condition of soundness and sobriety, necessary for a right judgement, can become fortified as an indispensable condition.

Without this, it is impossible to regularly cover 25km daily, one cannot be under the influence of any drugs or alcohol, as one continuously has to be attentive, be present, as one must concentrate his consciousness on the task, reading the signs, finding the roads, controlling the conditions (food, water, clothes, shoes). This requires constant sharpness and an acuteness of the mind, while in the flux. Walking is a dangerous state; it is a liminal, in-between condition, implying a contact with the void. Finally, the aim is to reach satisfaction, something that was lost with the boredom of settlement, thus the central aim is to regain what was lost, when one lived dangerously though at the same time lightly, with ease and without care, free from rigid attachments, where the only burden was the giving of gifts, the wonder and delight that you could give, according to the etymological origin of grace (charis) in **gher* 'pleasure', without immediately anticipating counter-gifts.

So why did we walk?

It is quite difficult now to give an exact account of why we decided to go on the Camino de Santiago in 2011. We certainly did not expect what we found; and had no idea that a few years – and several other long-distance walking pilgrimages – later, we'd be writing a book on walking. In reality, we cannot give any good reason for starting to walk. It just came, through the coexistence of multiple components, like this was the first time when we could afford to go for a long time away from our family of five children, as even our youngest son grew up, and – especially on the back of the previous summer, when instead of the beach we took them into quite a few Palaeolithic caves – were quite unwilling to spend the summer with us. We also needed a long and complete break away from our mundane world, and were quite happy to walk as part of a pilgrimage, regularly receiving benedictions and listening to services, even if we were not doing this as part of a specific religious vow. Still, we had our evident apprehensions, concerning whether we'd be able to walk 800km in five weeks, spending the nights regularly with several other – occasionally many dozen – unknown people in the same room; and so on. We were also not well prepared at all – one of us started with a cheap tennis shoe, trusting his feet as a former football player; we hardly brought with us warm clothes or covers against rain; and we shouldn't even mention our backpack, as it was really an old school bag of one of our sons; we only bought a decent rucksack next year in Kolozsvár (Cluj), in Transylvania.

As anybody who has ever done a walking trip or pilgrimage knows well, even though such moves in a way are the same for everyone undertaking them, every trip, and in fact every day, is also fundamentally different. Our Camino certainly started in a very particular way at 7 am on 13 July 2011, from Saint-Jean-Pied-de-Port, the most classical of departure points, at 200 metres above sea level, as shortly after we started our ascent through the Pyrenees, it started to drizzle, which turned into a steady rain, and we walked up to a height of 1430 metres and down again another 500, for about eight hours, in pouring rain, to Roncesvalles – the last hour or so of our descent in fact not walking, but rather running. Even though it was the middle of summer, our fingers became all but frozen, so that we could hardly open our pockets to take out a tissue to blow our noses, not to mention further inconveniences. We thus had, as it is only proper for students of liminality, a true 'baptism of fire', or rather of water, arriving completely soaked, with our provisions being saved only because at the last minute, literally the moment when the specialised shop was closing in Saint-Jean-Pied-de-Port, we bought a plastic bag covering the old schoolbag.

In a sense, one could hardly have imagined a worse way to start a five-week walking trip. However, the opposite is just as true, or even more proper, as – faithful to the eternal ambivalence of liminality – perhaps indeed this was the best way to start the road, as after 'suffering' this experience, in the true Greek sense of *pathein*, every other tribulation of the road seemed a mere trifle.

This was, however, not the way we felt on the evening of 13 July (a Wednesday, not a Friday), or the next morning, though of course we tried to show our best faces under the conditions. This was much helped by the dinner organised for pilgrims, where we could meet our fellow 'sufferers', some of whom we would indeed meet again and again on the road – in the case of one, such meetings culminated in a chance encounter at about 6am on 12 August in a bar on the outskirts of Santiago de Compostela. A truly chance encounter it was, as we had to start our last leg unexpectedly, in the middle of the night, as in the sport palace where we got accommodation, literally on the floor of a basketball court (furthermore, on our wedding anniversary, which again was not calculated to happen in this way, but all other places in O Pedrouzo were full once we got there – too late, as we were turned away from the place we intended to stay for the night, Santa Irene, where the forty beds were booked up by about midday), we were woken up every 15 minutes by various alarm clocks which some well-meaning people placed at every conceivable place in the complex, part of a plot against the papal visit on World Youth Day in Madrid, so could not get sleep. At any rate, returning to our first evening, we were particularly sad, feeling almost cheated, as in the summer before, when visiting various caves, we also had some passage in the Pyrenees, and thought that crossing the mountains would be the highlight of our entire walking trip. Well, we hardly could see the trees in the forest, due to the rain and mist, not to mention the beauties of the landscape.

The weather changed radically the next day, and soon the landscape as well. The beauties of the Pyrenees were soon traded for some particularly ugly landscape, starting with something that looked like an abandoned quarry, in-between Zubiri and Larrasoaña, and which for us recalled the sight of Mordor in Tolkien's *Lord of the Rings*: a devastated, grey land with acidic air, full of poisonous gases, without drinking water or birds that sing, and no source of refurbishment. We could have called it the Zone, from Tarkovsky's *Stalker*, but for some reason we didn't. This experience time and again repeated itself, when suddenly the beauties of nature or culture were replaced by this or another sign of modern civilisation: an industrial plant, a highway intersection or high-rise estates of a town. When this happened, we time and again looked at each other and stated the inevitable: we again arrived at Mordor, or Trickster Land.

The more we walked in Europe, after Spain in Italy, then in Hungary, Croatia or Romania, the more we realised that this is not an unfortunate accident; rather, ugliness is one of the most profound and permanent features of our modern Europe. Day after day, week after week, our vision and understanding of the modern world became modified and deepened. We were never – at least, not since we really grew up – staunch believers in modern progress, but we accepted the reality of the modern world. This became untenable due to our walking experiences. It was the result not of a sudden conversion experience, but rather the sheer fact of walking through the territory of a modern country; a kind of knowledge gained, as Herzog (2014: 5) stated, by our 'soles'. If one keeps walking, steadily, for dozens and dozens, even hundreds and hundreds of kilometres, one gains a particularly intense, profound, continuous – as uninterrupted – knowledge about the repulsiveness and disgust, or the *real* 'unreality' of the modern world. Businessmen, politicians and academic 'stars' who fly from one global city to another (and seeing only very particular parts of these as well), preaching about 'progress' and 'globalisation', don't really know, or rather *really* don't know what they are talking about. Walkers do know, anybody who just starts walking and keeps doing so can know, as they literally see the whole, *as it is*, from 'a' to 'z', from the heaps of garbage produced by modern 'civilisation' to modernity as a heap of garbage. It does not take much to look at any product of the modern world and envision it, instantaneously, having walked some hundred kilometres, as the heap of dangerous and polluting garbage it would become in the not-too-distant future. Thus, we social scientists *as* walkers started to see things differently, with our noses, ears and eyes. This led us to the conclusion that the modern world is indeed Trickster Land: a disgusting, parasitic, invasive mode of living that literally pounces on the planet, wherever it pleases, in the name of 'progress' and 'development', sucking the vital energies of life, exploiting carelessly whatever was there as a given, thus literally as a gift, and replacing characters with hybrid creatures, lifeless and characterless survivors that would soon be collapsing and decaying, thus leaving the debris and the desert, and searching for further areas to be developed, meaning to destroy and consume, two words that are practically synonyms, thus making money and gaining votes, through the combined trickster techniques of parasitism, euphemistically called 'market economy', 'mass democracy' and 'scientific technology', but in reality just a way of cheating us out of our eyes, feet and mind.

Mordor, of course, has many modalities, and it is difficult to rate which is worse than the other. The heaps of garbage surrounding settlements, especially the larger ones, are of course bad, due to their massive, ugly sight and odour, but they can be rather quickly passed through. The industrial plants and quarries are much worse, and though pilgrimage roads try to avoid them, they often cannot do so. We walk from city to city, as pilgrimage is much about visiting churches and shrines. In the pilgrim's eyes highways are also dreadful, especially the highway intersections which, surrounding the bigger cities, are again impossible to avoid. They also offer a telling tale, as the progress of walkers is particularly hindered by such roads, supposedly made to facilitate communication and movement – a paradox similar to the way railroads, built to connect towns, systematically separate the parts of towns they traverse. This point cannot be dismissed by the usual incantation concerning the 'price' to be paid for 'progress'; it rather reveals the intolerable, unacceptable, trickster character of the 'progress' we were told and sold. Eventually, generations after us will realise, as they must, how much 'we' moderns were being misled, at once infantilised and senilised, induced to live in deterioration, though it is difficult to specify who are the culprits and the victims, as culprits can suddenly transmogrify themselves into victims and vice versa, being all part of the same infallible and also eternally failing machine, already identified by Jean Cocteau or James Joyce – although there *are* some concrete people who started the spiral and occasionally give further boosts, though it is very difficult to identify them. One would need at least another Dante, Milton or Goethe, combined with Plato, Nietzsche, Weber and Foucault.

Still, the worst parts of any walking pilgrimage arguably are the outskirts of large cities. Walking miles and miles through the asphalt of Burgos and Leon, Rome and Brindisi, or Budapest and Belgrade, through the traffic, is simply inhuman. This poses an interesting question about 'cheating' and the problem of 'rigid legalism'. A pilgrim is not supposed to take a means of transport; and yet, the rules of pilgrimage were made unaware of the 'realities' of a modern city. Walking in this asphalt jungle is not the kind of trial pilgrims were supposed to meet – not to mention the evident and manifold health hazards of such an undertaking. Beyond the dilemma of whether it is right to 'cheat' in such an occasion – our answer is a resounding 'yes' – this example brings out again, with particular clarity, the profound cruelty of modern trickster life: cities are supposedly there to 'help' men live together the 'good life', and yet nothing is so profoundly inhuman as living in a modern metropolis – and we are only talking about Burgos or Rome, and not the 'global cities' of the third world, like São Paulo, with its 30 million people covering an area extending to 50–80 kilometres, where some people have to commute four hours daily, in one direction only, in order to work. The principle, however, is the same: living in big cities is a cheat. The fact that they exist is the consequence of parasitic trickster life. If one starts to walk in the modern world, one is forced to realise that this is the case.

A less intrusive but still annoying aspect of this cruel mode of living is constituted by the large monocultural agricultural fields, demonstrating the clear connections between 'industrial Mordor' and 'agricultural Mordor'. On the one hand, these fields have the same boring character, repeating infinitely an identical landscape, wherever the eye looks, whether it is a Spanish sunflower field, a Hungarian cornfield, a tomato field in Apulia or a wheat field in Croatia. Such boredom must be even more intolerable for those who do not simply pass by, but live and work there. Thus, activity is transformed into work, work into boring mechanical robots (overlooking the important etymological difference between 'labour' and 'work', a difference already ignored by Marx and his followers in their unreserved glorification of mere 'labour'), leading to mechanisation, which adds to the boredom felt by the eye the even more intrusive noise perceived by the ear. This is another recurrent experience of walkers, another encounter with Trickster Land, when the eternal, calm stillness of the landscape is suddenly interrupted by an at first barely audible droning, which soon can be clearly attributed to a harvesting machine, working on the fields. The noise becomes a steady part of the walk until we reach the place where the machine is working, so that after well over an hour, we would finally be liberated from it – unless in the meantime another machine started work some kilometres ahead. Here again, such noise must be even worse for those working on the machines – except that now they plug their ears with an iPhone or similar devices; thus, eliminating noise through an even more intrusive radiation. Modern progress truly knows no limits; it has a solution for everything, managing to make the bad always worse. And the worst is that we do not even realise the trick, due to the enchantment it produces.

One of the central effects of walking is to recognise that we are living in a poisoned land, where not only the fruits are poisoned but the tomatoes as well, and even in Apulia, one of the sunniest parts in Europe, where grapes are now forced to grow prematurely by irrigation, plastic cover and the use of tons of fertilisers. The results do not lag behind: the price of producing 10% or 20% more is that *all* the grapes now taste, in these fields in Apulia, directly from the vine, as if one bought them in a supermarket in London. A true feat of 'democracy' and the 'market'! However, such recognition at the same time is a first step to become liberated from the hold of the enchanter-exploiter.

One has to be careful here not to become entrapped in wishful thinking; however, the point, rightly understood, is crucial, as it can actually make us see aspects of the modern world that are different from those of Mordor. We clearly cannot walk out of modernity; such a radical denial of the present would entail the kind of escapism into which many of the better-meaning movements of the modern world became shipwrecked. But one can indeed walk out of the taken-for-granted hold exerted by modern conveniences and gadgets. To give only one example, we perceived at the start of our trip that one can only keep walking if one turns off completely the mobile phone, and not only during walking, but for long days; and similarly, if one does not control e-mails regularly. Indeed, we noticed in the Camino that of the people we kept running into, those who kept their mobile phone on and were regularly stopping to take calls eventually – and rather sooner than later – gave up the journey. Some of them had a 'reason', while others simply disappeared. They never really walked, only imitated walking, putting a leg after the other, without catching the rhythm. Their mind (and soul) always remained imprisoned.

Similarly imprisoned in the 'iron cage' of modernity were those who were regularly cheating, taking the Camino as a mode of cheap tourism. It was a recurrent experience, and certainly not only for us, that in the larger cities, be it Burgos, Leon or Astorga, with many touristic attractions, pilgrim hostels with hundreds of places were filling up quickly, whereas in the intermediate legs it was much easier to find accommodation in considerably smaller places. In such large hostels we also encountered scores of new people whom we would never see again – of course, as they regularly took the bus, covering 50, 100 or even 200 kilometres per day. Many, if not most of them were also from certain parts of Europe that we knew only too well. Apart from the not negligible inconvenience caused by the sudden crowding of hostels, rendering every new leg a source of worry, whether we could find a place to sleep, it makes the entire undertaking meaningless; a way to secure entrapment in Trickster Land, far from escaping it; recalling and promptly reproducing the experience of communism. While these people, or others ready for their defence, would argue that they do not have the money to do otherwise, this is simply not true, as walking is trivially cheaper than taking a bus. The issue rather is that communism was truly efficient in making the escape from the genuine spider web of modernity (of which communism was only a grotesque imitation) all but impossible mentally.

This was brought home to us with particular clarity when we offered to share some of our food with those brought together at the same table. Pilgrims of course often divide their food, as the entire experience is based on participation, presence, sharing and giving, but when in Leon we offered some of our watermelon to our fellow 'pilgrims' – something clearly not to be carried in the backpack anyway – they almost choked on their own food by the very idea, as if we humiliated them by the need to reciprocate it eventually – which they knew would never happen anyway, so immediately revealing themselves as cheap tourists. Sharing is not part of trickster 'rationality', as one can never be sure that one would receive the equivalent of what was given – so it is better not to take chances.

It was also in Leon that a senior nun, superior of the Benedictine monastery (Carbajalas) where we were staying, resumed the central features of a pilgrim, again transforming events happening to us into a Biblical parable. A pilgrim should not desire anything in particular, but accept where the road takes him, as the road knows better what he needs than himself; and the true pilgrim is recognised not only by accepting everything the road offers him, but by being always playful, though not silly. We took up the advice even before it was formulated, and accepted everything where the road took us – until we encountered cheating.

So where is the character that deserves our attention?

The friendly one. The central feature of contentment substance is its reality. Walking only condenses the experience of contentment. Walking requires and renders possible an effort, lasting for hundreds of kilometres, during which tiredness and contentment fill the in-betweenness, where even the possibility of encountering the void is not ruled out as an experiential basis for goodness. In all this, walking secures a balance literally in-between extended time and unlimited space, and so the walker is the one who retains. Walkers do not change or convert; rather, their inconvertibility gains or regains good power after the successful accomplishment of the walk. As the cause of our reason is in us, we are not the consequence or the product of a certain process, but we ourselves are the process itself, to become real again.

Do not all of us wish a simple procedure for securing such results? However, the exchangeability or usefulness of any convertibility that guarantees the successful 'transformation' paradoxically lies not in this but in inconvertibility itself, in the quality of not being exchangeable. We do not change by walking; or, paraphrasing the title of Latour's famous book, *We Have Never Been Modern*, 'we have never been different'. So a man, having got a task, will keep moving it forward, elevating it into the best levels – at any rate, until he learns that all his self proceeds from the whole – and then with this knowledge he retains himself. These conditions never changed – we have power inside! This was searched and has been found, as walking survived settlement and domestication in the form of pilgrimage. Though marginalised or incorporated into dominant forms of priestly rituals, by its very features pilgrimage kept alive authentic traditions and an independent, even personal, in-depth form of spirituality inside a given structure. The investigation of walking, this particular void situation – where walkers lose their time, their past and identity and confront the void, becoming an object 'in the stream of immemorial life' (Gros 2014: 7) – offers a uniquely promising path to capture the opposite condition that is increasingly marking our time of wants, and thus can contribute to the character of the walker.

Such a character is different both from nomadic wandering, which does not have an aim, and also from visiting shrines, where the emphasis is on what one does at the shrine, irrespective of the way of reaching it. Thus, much of what today is called 'pilgrimage' in reality is shrine visitation. If we ask the traditional questions: Does the completion of such a walking have a lasting effect on the individual undertaking the trip, to the extent of even altering his or her identity? Is this an explicit aim, guiding the walker to undertake the journey? How many of those who engage in long-distance walking want to change their habits and ways of doing things? For whom and to what extent does the walking process accomplish the desired change? – the answer is always the same: the walk, the liminality itself does not create anything that was not there before, but makes one correspond with the contentment substance of reality. In this sense, it is effective in producing this desired 'change'.

Inconvertibility

Walking, as understood in this book, has four major characteristic features. To begin with, it has to be a long-term and long-distance activity. It means long weeks, occasionally even months spent on the road, covering hundreds of kilometres. Second, it must have an aim. Walking is radically different from aimless wandering – a major misunderstanding in Bauman (1996) and Chatwin (1997), who identified (even pilgrimage) with wandering and nomadism, where one is continuously on the road, having neither a home – from where one started and where one intends eventually to return; nor a target – which one wants to reach in order to visit, before returning. Third, as basically implied in the previous, and in analogy to Mauss's gift relations, this aim cannot be 'utilitarian' in any sense: walking does not have an economic, military or political aim; it has no interest, no profit, no surplus; it involves no exchangeability or convertibility. Even health as an aim is not utilitarian, as by definition it implies 'wholeness' and so the fullness of *res*, just being real, far away from any conceptualistic pragmatism. Finally, in spite of having an aim (in fact, even two aims: first, to reach the goal, to arrive; and second, to return home, or *really* arrive), the travel, the road, the time spent walking matters: it is not merely a 'means' to reach the end, but is very much part of the entire endeavour. Furthermore, as it neither fits pragmatism, nor positivism, nor any automatic understanding, offering invariant yet exchangeable principles that guarantee success, the irreducible popularity of walking argues against symmetrical convertibility. Exchangeability can be misleading in two aspects: in its emphasis on an external framework of controlled changes, when convertibility is in question; and concerning the basic conditions of reality. It would be a mistake to suppose that the usefulness of something, qualified as its worth and exchangeability, measured in terms of its value, gets a definite currency in reality. It is simply impossible to overturn or refurbish reality; it is here around us in friendship and good feeling, and evidently only friendliness and contentment find it.

Who walks?

Is there one wallet for storing all our investments? an economist once asked, analysing exchangeability theory. The answer is definitely not. Is there any usefulness in defining the walker, qualified by his worth, measured in terms of his character? What is his currency? His currency value is that he is without any, having a quality that is not exchangeable. He is self-same and complete in this condition, there is no validity of the mythical medium or intermediaries that emerge from the dissolution of tradition, or the outcome of the liminal interval in the rites of passage, or any other breakdowns. Only in this way can we understand why it is that, in walking, we never lose the feeling of 'I', though it is true that our primarily coordinates gradually sink away and we start to reckon contentment.

If we can define reality through *res*, then we are also able to catch the gratification and gladness related to reality. This idea finds a resonance with Mauss's ideas in his classic essay on *Gift*. According to Mauss, in Latin *familia* and *res* were closely connected, especially in ancient times; even further, '*familia* equals *res* and *substantia*' (Mauss 1966: 48–50; 119, fn. 10). Through the term *res*, 'the idea of a power inherent in a thing was always present' in Roman law (49). Even further, Mauss conjectures that the legal meaning of *res* is only derivative; etymologically *res* is 'a gift or a pleasant thing', and originally meant 'that which gives a person pleasure' (49–51). If there are concrete, real entities, and not just particles and masses filling pre-existing space and time, then the walker becomes a participant in this cooperative, essential character of reality, freed from exchangeability, from this odd feeling of wanting, from involvement in undertakings that bring advantages to us, or affect us through earning – one cannot earn something which is not surplus, but an essential ingredient, contentment. Examples include good air, peaceful breathing, odours of the spring or the silent joy of living. Indeed, the whole reality around of us received a concrete shape in contentment. With the help of such charismatic dimensions we can get an apprehension of reality.

Let us say then that, whether one is existent or not, in appearance or does not even appear in anything at all, it seems that the walker is in relation to contentment, and so in relation to all (existent and non-existent). We should be able to decide which of them, the existent or the non-existent, suits us better to solve the problem of what reality is, as they both participate in it effecting contentment. This was the question Plato asked, and following him also Aristotle, but the definite answer came from Goethe, through his ideas on nature and contentment.

Plato addressed the problem at a general level, through his idea of the existent non-existent. In *Cratylus* Plato questioned the Heraclitean doctrine of infinite movement in a state of void, saying through Socrates that if everything is in movement, then we can have no knowledge about it, and so only the finite can move:

> How, then, can that which is never in the same state be anything? For if it is ever in the same state, then obviously at that time it is not changing; and if it is always in the same state and is always the same, how can it ever change or move without relinquishing its own form.
>
> *(Plato,* Cratylus, *439E)*

Having a finite form with distinct borders and characters is the prime condition of any knowledge:

> But we cannot even say that there is any knowledge, if all things are changing and nothing remains fixed; for if knowledge itself does not change and cease to be knowledge, then knowledge would remain, and there would be knowledge; but if the very essence of knowledge changes ... there would be no knowledge.
>
> *(440A)*

This paradoxical situation concerning void, the state where one is not, that could appear both the same and as different in form, changes immediately with contentment.

Friendship gives reality both for existent and non-existent, forming any character into a perfect likeness of itself. We can perceive both kinds of motion on Earth, the existent (finite) and the non-existent (infinite), but our knowledge always remains dubious about the second one, as Plato presumed. Finiteness is limited in duration, it runs its course and comes to its natural end, while the infinite is in eternal flux, without destination. Seemingly there is a huge contrast between them, but in fact there is no disparity, they easily mix and merge with each other; in this way all our forms have a likeness to divine form (Plato, *Phaedrus*, 249E–251B).

Before considering the philosophical consequences of this doctrine, we must look in detail at Plato's analyses of this exchangeability, where any order is equally likely. First, he considered the reality of divine perception as an infinite force pushing the finite into a moulded, incomprehensible frame. Second, this force was related to the resistance opposing this motion, which he formulated like this: man becomes real, if he rises up to divine perception, and is able to retain himself (Plato, *Phaedrus*, 256A–257B). Finally, in summary, to be real is to hasten towards your goal of self-sameness, fulfilling the divine law to be the same with yourself, and find the same good in others. At the very foundation of archaic thinking is this view, which gained diffusion in a later mimetic version as the idea that infiniteness could not exist in nature in pure form, only if it merged in existence with the finite. This is how from Parmenides to Aristotle reality is treated as a balance between the finite and infiniteness in the effect of contentment. This line later was taken over by Goethe, when he concluded that reality is a living being, a substance whose master is the idea of contentment, which must correspond with everything in nature, in forming substance into a perfect likeness to itself.

As we now know, when friendship is lost, then we are left alone in a weak and humble state of liminality, first theorised by the Neoplatonists. It is no accident that in the period between the Neoplatonists and Kant discussion on reality kept returning to these problems. For Neoplatonists man is unable to relate by his senses what is happening around of him, so a transformation is needed in all senses (man should convert to an idea, to a system, to a generality; nature should be controlled; the divine should be bound). But why was an argument rooted so firmly in conversion, in transformation, if it leads as the sole conclusion to generalities and various artificialities, which basically cover the process when man becomes inoperable for himself and for the society he lives in? We can see this in the transformation of archaic contentment into a modern, artificial state of happiness, from mental self-possession into manufactured exaltation. For the former man does not change, man is complete in his good composition and in bettering oneself. But for the latter the individual is not complete, finished in his composition, but a mere interval, the middle term between lower and higher impulses, especially the seductive ones, with a further interval opening up towards new stamping images projected by the transcendental. This kind of prosaic, cold transcendentalism imitated itself in

Kant's fake metaphysics, which is a confiscation of the classic tradition. Artificiality produces an impact, as a result of the systematic completion of a given sequence of acts, modelled on metallurgy, alchemy and rituals of sacrifice, by exchanging man with a mechanical creature, including the reasons for and the manner in which such changes take place.

Since the world does not consist of mysteries that by their inter-action produce creatures, conversion is not independent from the concrete intentions of walkers, in particular whether the road was taken for partly or entirely by religious reasons. The adoption of various thoughts to reality have their own accord that are in their own turn spontaneously reproduced by thought. This is the way an organised, generalised stamp can take place through conversion, as if by an alchemical trans-formation, but also as a smuggled contradiction into the system of ratio that does not accept that something can be anything than its own character.

For Neoplatonists man is an intermediate race of seductive trickster-daimons, in radical contrast to the firmness and friendly stability that Plato emphasised. For the first, man hovers in-between the transcendental and reality, his natural condition being in void, in total or complete subordination to the elements, 'in-between', pulled and pushed by good and evil, moving continuously through transformations, while for the second man is a character, with determine qualities standing in constant reference to their meaning.

Therefore the theme of contentment, as something real, revealed in long-distance walking offers a rival explanation to modern understanding, caught between a rigid fixity of the self, central for rationalism and the transformative development of the self, dominating social theory. Since Neoplatonism European thinking has been leaning towards exchangeability, denying inconvertibility. The essential thing is not the denial that future specimens behave like earlier specimens, and so any changes can be controlled, but that one is not exchangeable, and this should be tied in with other ideas about society and the world around us, how it all works in our given universe. What sort of 'novel concepts' are needed? One can at least talk about contentment without embarrassment. Similar points concerning the *res* as part of each of us were made by Voegelin, and even by Weber on charisma.

Walking with an aim

The walker demands and receives back his lost as stolen reality through walking, an atonement for what he was deprived by settlement. Walking as metaxy, as limi-nality, takes him up and leads him into the lost world of reality, where everything was still in its place. This is the real aim of walking, beyond reaching a destination, whether a sanctuary or back home.

Through walking, by walking, the fooled one demands the restitution of reality.

CONCLUSION

Whatever is to be good must come at once; for 'at once' is the divinest of all categories and deserves to be honoured ... because it is the starting point for all that is divine in life, and so much so that what is not done at once is of evil.

Kierkegaard, Stages on Life's Way, *'In vino veritas' (1988)*

We live in an extremely complex world, so we are told. There are no easy solutions. Every change, even the minutest alteration in the standard practices of our interconnected global world, brings about consequences that only further complicate matters, necessitating further tinkering with our already incredibly intricate legal machinery. If one follows in a minimal way matters related to food health regulation, one knows that one cannot get a proper understanding of the issues concerned without working through literally hundreds and thousands of pages of legal documents, written in a language that is hardly understandable even to those with a legal degree.

Yet, food is what we eat; health concerns our lives; and these are matters quite simple and fundamental enough. After all, 'we', at least many of us in the 'advanced' countries, supposedly live in free and democratic societies that exist for the health, well-being and happiness of their 'citizens' (a deeply problematic word that in itself tells us much about the lies of modernity). So it is quite understandable that, as a result of this impossibility of following and understanding what is going on, people revolt against the establishment, the experts, in particular the politicians, anybody they see regularly in the media. Thus, as the – so far – ultimate paradox of our global media age, where there is no such thing as bad publicity, people as voters look for new faces; at least, faces in new places.

What then happens, of course, is that the more things change, the more they remain the same. To be sure, the populist quasi-politicians that are now being elected everywhere will not bring any improvement in practically anything – which will allow our fellow intellectuals, reared on the media, *the* source of knowledge and influence for 'intellectuals' since the eighteenth century, to reassert that as they have told us already many times before, there are no easy solutions, so *they* finally have to be listened to, so they can take matters into their expert hands – which are universalistic, rationalistic, legalistic, standardised, lifeless, dead.

But this is not so. Maybe the entire modern metaphor, to gain control by taking things finally in our hands, is wrong. We should indeed 'vote' rather with our *feet* – but not simply by not voting, or by leaving the modern asphalt jungle in a metaphorical sense, but to do so in a very real way – though of course not completely, with a leap into the void, as other 'intellectuals' have enticed us for a similarly long time. We should rather start, gradually, slowly, to walk again: walking into the world, into nature as it was given to us, as a gift; walk without any 'utilitarian' aim, thus in a sense walk into the unknown, even the void. This can slowly start reversing trends, forgetting about 'progress', the single greatest lie of modernity, root and origin of all the others, and return to decent, normal existence on this planet. Who walks well sleeps well and eats well, and eats what he finds where he walks, instead of taking the car to where food is: accumulated, stored, prepared in advance, ready-made for quick consumption – and mostly abominable and disgusting, in ways we do not know and do not even want to know about, a situation which merely legal tinkering, without some proper idea about the good life, cannot resolve, can only render systematically worse.

Walking *is* really simple. You just have to start putting one of your legs after the other, as you learned around age one, the single most important sign for any newborn of 'growing up'; and continue it. For quite a long time. It will help us all grow up again, after the debilitating infantilism of modernity, culminating in sitting, for hours and hours and hours, every day, increasingly sleepless, in front of flashing screens, pullulating with images of bodies, preferably naked or dying, and pushing buttons.

Try to walk again.

Just do it.

BIBLIOGRAPHY

Agamben, Giorgio (1998) *Homo Sacer*, Stanford, CA: Stanford University Press.

Agnew, Jean-Christophe (1986) *Worlds Apart: The market and the theater in Anglo-American thought, 1550–1750*, Cambridge: Cambridge University Press.

Alinei, Mario (2009) *L'origine delle parole*, Rome: Aracne.

Antoine, Daniel M., Antoine Zazzo and Renee Freidman (2013) 'Revisiting Jebel Sahaba: New apatite radiocarbon dates for one of the Nile Valley's earliest cemeteries', *American Journal of Physical Anthropology* Supplement 56:68.

Argyrou, Vassos (2013) *The Gift of European Thought and the Cost of Living*, New York: Berghahn.

Aristotle (1955) *On Coming-to-be and Passing-Away*, London: Heinemann.

—— (1957) *Physics*, London: Heinemann.

Arsuaga, Juan L. *et al.* (1997a) 'Preface', *Journal of Human Evolution* 33, 2–3:105–8.

—— (1997b) 'Sima de los Huesos (Sierra de Atapuerca, Spain): The site', *Journal of Human Evolution* 33, 2–3:109–27.

—— (2014) 'Neandertal roots: Cranial and chronological evidence from Sima de los Huesos', *Science* 344, 6190:1358–62.

Aujoulat, Norbert (2005) *The Splendour of Lascaux*, London: Thames & Hudson.

Azéma, Marc (2011) *La préhistoire du cinéma: origines paléolithiques de la narration graphique et du cinéma*, Paris: Errance.

Bakhtin. Mikhail (1984) *Rabelais and His World*, Bloomington, IN: Indiana University Press.

—— (1986) *Speech Genres and Other Late Essays*, Austin, TX: University of Texas Press.

Balter, Michael (2010a) 'The tangled roots of agriculture', *Science* 327, 5964:404–6.

—— (2010b) 'The first feast', in *Science Magazine*, accessed at http://www.sciencemag.org/news/2010/08/first-feast, 20 January 2017.

Banning, Edward B. (2003) 'Housing Neolithic farmers', *Near Eastern Archaeology* 66, 1/2:4–21.

—— (2011) 'So fair a house: Göbekli Tepe and the identification of temples in the Pre-Pottery Neolithic of the Near East', *Current Anthropology* 52, 5:619–40.

Bar-Yosef, Ofer (1986) 'The Walls of Jericho: An alternative interpretation', *Current Anthropology* 27, 2:157–62.

—— (1998) 'The Natufian culture in the Levant', *Evolutionary Anthropology* 6, 5:159–77.

—— (2002) 'Natufian: A complex society of foragers', in B. Fitzhugh and J. Habu (eds) *Beyond Foraging and Collecting: Evolutionary change in hunter-gatherer settlement systems*, New York: Kluwer, 91–149.

—— and François R. Valla (eds) (1991) *The Natufian Culture in the Levant*, Ann Arbor, MI: International Monographs in Prehistory.

Bataille, Georges (1970) 'Lascaux ou la naissance de l'art', in *Oeuvres complètes*, vol. IX, Paris: Gallimard.

Bateson, Gregory (1958) *Naven*, Stanford, CA: Stanford University Press.

Bauman, Zygmunt (1996) 'From pilgrim to tourist, or a short history of identity', in S. Hall and P. du Gay (eds) *Questions of Cultural Identity*, London: Sage, 18–36.

Bednarik, Robert G. (1995) 'The Côa petroglyphs: An obituary to the stylistic dating of Palaeolithic rock-art', *Antiquity* 69, 266:877–83.

—— (2014) 'Data and interpretation in the Côa valley, Portugal', *Rock Art Research* 31, 1:107–10.

—— (2015) 'Kinetic energy metamorphosis of rocks', in B. Veress and J. Szigethy (eds) *Horizons in Earth Science Research 13*, New York: NOVA Science Publishers, 119–34.

Beekes, Robert (2010) *Etymological Dictionary of Greek*, Leiden: Brill.

Belfer-Cohen, Anna and Nigel Goring-Morris (2014) 'On the Rebound: A Levantine View of Upper Palaeolithic Dynamics', in M. Otte (ed.) *Modes de contacts et de déplacements au Paléolithique eurasiatique*, ERAUL 140: Université de Liège.

Bellavite, Andrea (2016) *Lo spirito dei piedi*, Portogruaro: Ediciclo.

Beltrán, Antonio (ed.) (1999) *The Cave of Altamira*, New York: Harry Abrams.

Benkő, Lóránd (ed.) (1970) *A magyar nyelv történeti-etimológiai szótára*, Budapest: Akadémiai.

Bernheimer, Richard (1956) 'Theatrum Mundi', *Art Bulletin* 38, 4:225–47.

Bertolotti, Maurizio (1991) *Carnevale di massa*, Turin: Einaudi.

Betz, Hans Dieter (1994) 'Jesus and the cynics: Survey and analysis of a hypothesis', *The Journal of Religion* 74, 4:453–75.

Bixio, Roberto, Vittorio Castellani and Claudio Succhiarelli (2002) *Cappadocia: le città sotterranee*, Rome: Libreria dello Stato.

Blakely, Sandra (2006) *Myth, Ritual, and Metallurgy in Ancient Greece and Recent Africa*, Cambridge: Cambridge University Press.

Blanchot, Maurice (2002) 'La bête de Lascaux', in *Une voix venue d'ailleurs*, Paris: Gallimard.

Blažek, Vaclav (2015) 'Levant and North Africa: Afroasiatic linguistic history', in P. Bellwood (ed.) *The Global Prehistory of Human Migration*, Oxford: Wiley-Blackwell, 125–32.

Bocquentin, Fanny (2003) 'Pratiques funéraires, paramètres biologiques et identités culturelles au natoufien: une analyse archéo-anthropologique', PhD, University of Bordeaux.

Boland, Tom (2013) *Critique as a Modern Social Phenomenon*, Lewiston, NY: Edwin Mellen Press.

Bolon, Carol Radcliffe (1992) *Forms of the Goddess Lajja Gauri in Indian Art*, University Park, PA: Pennsylvania State University Press.

Bolzoni, Lina (1984) *Il teatro della memoria: studi su Giulio Camillo*, Padova: Liviana.

—— (1995) *La stanza della memoria*, Turin: Einaudi.

Broch, Hermann (1984) *Hugo von Hoffmansthal and His Time: The European Imagination, 1860–1920*, Chicago, IL: University of Chicago Press.

Brombaugh, Robert S. (1982) 'The history and interpretation of the text of Plato's *Parmenides*', *Philosophy Research Archives* 8, 1–56.

Brown, Peter (1982) *Society and the Holy in Late Antiquity*, London: Faber.

Byrd, Brian F. and Christopher M. Monahan (1995) 'Death, mortuary ritual, and Natufian social structure', *Journal of Anthropological Archaeology* 14, 3:251–87.

Calasso, Roberto (2002) *Literature and the Gods*, New York: Vintage.
—— (2008) *La Folie Baudelaire*, Milan: Adelphi.
—— (2010) *L'ardore*, Milan: Adelphi.
—— (2016) *Il cacciatore celeste*, Milan: Adelphi.
Camillo, Giulio Delminio (1990) *L'idea del teatro e altri scritti di retorica*, Milan: Res.
Camps, Gabriel (2011) 'Iheren', in *Encyclopédie berbère*, vol. 24, accessed at http://encyclo pedieberbere.revues.org/1556, 4 January 2017.
Canguilhem, Georges (1978) *On the Normal and the Pathological*, Dordrecht: Reidel.
Carbonell, Eudald and Marina Mosquera (2006) 'The emergence of a symbolic behaviour: The sepulchral pit of Sima de los Huesos, Sierra de Atapuerca, Burgos, Spain', *Comptes Rendus Palevol* 5, 1–2:155–60.
Carvalho, António Faustino de, João Zilhão and Thierry Aubry (1996) *Côa Valley: Rock art and prehistory*, Lisbon: Ministério da Cultura.
Carter, Tristan *et al.* (2015) 'Laying the foundations', in I. Hodder and A. Marciniak (eds) *Assembling Çatalhöyük*, Leeds: Maney, 97–110.
Cauvin, Jacques (2000) *The Birth of the Gods and the Origins of Agriculture*, Cambridge: Cambridge University Press.
Cervantes, Miguel de (2000) *Don Quixote*, London: Penguin.
Chatwin, Bruce (1997) *Anatomy of Restlessness*, London: Picador.
Chauvet, Jean-Marie, Eliette Brunel Deschamps and Christian Hillaire (1996) *Chauvet Cave: The discovery of the world's oldest paintings*, London: Thames and Hudson.
Cherpillod, André (1998) *Dictionnaire étymologique des noms d'hommes et dieux*, Paris: Masson.
Childe, V. Gordon (1951) *Man Makes Himself*, New York: Mentor Books.
Citati, Pietro (2000) *Il male assoluto nel cuore del romanzo dell'Ottocento*, Milan: Mondadori.
Clancy, Finbarr (2009) 'Trinity and Ecclesiology: The need for a patristic *ressourcement*', in D. Marmion and G. Thiessen (eds) *Trinity and Salvation*, Oxford: Peter Lang.
Clottes, Jean (2002) 'Review of *La grotte orneée de Pergouset (Saint-Géry, Lot): un sanctuaire secret paléolithique* by M. Lorblanchet', *Bulletin de la Société Préhistorique Française* 99, 1:163–5.
—— (2003) *Return to Chauvet Cave: Excavating the Birthplace of Art*, London: Thames and Hudson.
—— and David Lewis-Williams (1996) *Les chamanes de la préhistoire*, Paris: Seuil.
—— and Jean-Michel Geneste (2007) 'La grotte Chauvet dix ans après', *Les dossiers d'archéologie* 324, 10–9.
Coverley, Merlin (2012) *The Art of Wandering: The writer as walker*, Harpenden: Oldcastle.
Davis, Julian (2017) 'The problem of the individual and the synthetic in Max Weber, Harold Cherniss, and Michel Foucault', PhD, University College Cork.
Deleuze, Gilles and Félix Guattari (1987) *A Thousand Plateaus: Capitalism and schizophrenia*, Minneapolis, MN: University of Minnesota Press.
Delluc, Brigitte and Gilles Delluc (2009) 'Art paléolithique en Périgord: Les représentations humaines pariétales', *L'anthropologie* 113: 629–61.
Détienne, Marc and Jean-Pierre Vernant (1989) *The Cuisine of Sacrifice among the Greeks*, Chicago, IL: University of Chicago Press.
de Vaan, Michiel (2008) *Etymological Dictionary of Latin and the Other Italic Languages*, Leiden: Brill.
Dexter, Miriam R. and Victor H. Mair (2010) *Sacred Display: Divine and magical female figures of Eurasia*, Amherst, NY: Cambria Press.

Dickens, Charles (2001) *Dombey and Son*, Oxford: Oxford University Press.

Dietrich, Oliver *et al.* (2012) 'The role of cult and feasting in the emergence of Neolithic communities: New evidence from Göbekli Tepe, south-eastern Turkey', *Antiquity* 86, 333:674–95.

Doi, Kiyomi (2011) 'Onto emerging ground: Anticlimactic movement on the Camino de Santiago de Compostela', *Tourism* 9, 3:271–85.

Douglas, Mary (1970) *Purity and Danger*, Harmondsworth: Penguin.

Dupront, Alphonse (1987) *Du Sacré: Croisades et pèlerinages*, Paris: Gallimard.

Eberhard, Wolfram (1968) *The Local Cultures of South and East China*, Leiden: Brill.

Eliade, Mircea (1989) *Shamanism: Archaic techniques of ecstasy*, London: Penguin.

—— (1990) *I riti del costruire: Commenti alla leggenda di Mastro Manole*, Milan: Jaca Book.

Elias, Norbert (1987) *Involvement and Detachment*, Oxford: Blackwell.

—— (2000) *The Civilizing Process*, Oxford: Blackwell.

Ernout, Alfred and Antoine Meillet (1959) *Dictionnaire étymologique de la langue latine: histoire des mots*. Paris: Klincksieck.

Esler, Philip (1998) *Galatians*, London: Routledge.

Ferguson, Harvie (2000) *Modernity and Subjectivity: Body, soul, spirit*, Charlottesville, VA: University Press of Virginia.

Fitch, W. T. (2009) 'Fossil cues to the evolution of speech', in R. Botha and C. Knight (eds) *The Cradle of Language*, Oxford: Oxford University Press, 112–34.

Florio, John (2013) *A Worlde of Wordes*, Toronto: University of Toronto Press.

Foucault, Michel (1966) *Les mots et les choses*, Paris: Gallimard.

—— (1970) *The Order of Things*, New York: Vintage.

—— (1977) 'A preface to transgression', in D. F. Bouchard (ed.) *Language, Counter-memory, Practice: Selected essays and interviews*, Ithaca, NY: Cornell University Press, 29–52.

—— (1979) *Discipline and Punish*, New York: Vintage.

—— (1984) 'Nietzsche, genealogy, history', in P. Rabinow (ed.) *The Foucault Reader*, New York: Pantheon, 76–100.

—— (1994) *Dits et écrits, 4 vols*, D. Defert and F. Ewald (eds.), Paris: Gallimard.

Frangipane, Marcella (1996) *La nascita dello Stato nel Vicino Oriente: dai lingaggi alla burocrazia nella grande Mesopotamia*, Rome: Laterza.

Frank, Roslyn M. (2008) 'Recovering European ritual bear hunts: A comparative study of Basque and Sardinian ursine carnival performances', *Insula* 3, 41–97.

Frankfort, Henri (1948) *Kingship and the Gods*, Chicago, IL: University of Chicago Press.

Frey, Nancy L. (2004) 'Pilgrimage and its aftermath', in E. Badone and S. R. Roseman (eds) *Intersecting Journeys: The anthropology of pilgrimage and tourism*, Chicago, IL: University of Illinois Press.

Gell, Alfred (1998) *Art and Agency: An anthropological theory*, Oxford: Clarendon Press.

Gernet, Louis (2001) *Recherches sur le développement de la pensée juridique et morale en Grèce*, Paris: Albin Michel.

Giesen, Bernhard (2006) 'Performing the sacred', in J. Alexander, B. Giesen and J. Mast (eds) *Social Performance: Symbolic action, cultural pragmatics and ritual change*, Cambridge: Cambridge University Press.

Gilbert, Gregory P. (2015) 'Levant and North Africa: Archaeology', in P. Bellwood (ed.) *The Global Prehistory of Human Migration*, Oxford: Wiley-Blackwell, 133–38.

Girard, René (1977) *Violence and the Sacred*, Baltimore, MD: Johns Hopkins University Press.

—— (1989) *The Scapegoat*, Baltimore, MD: Johns Hopkins University Press.

Godfrey-Smith, D.I. *et al.* (2003) 'Direct luminescence chronology of the Epipaleolithic Kebaran site of Nahal Hadera V, Israel', *Geoarchaeology: An International Journal* 18, 4:461–75.

Goring-Morris, Nigel (2000) 'The quick and the dead: The social context of Aceramic Neolithic mortuary practices as seen from Kfar HaHoresh', in I. Kuijt (ed.) *Social Configurations of the Near Eastern Neolithic*, New York: Plenum Press.

—— and Anna Belfer-Cohen (2006) 'A hard look at the "Levantine Aurignacian": How real is the taxon?', in O. Bar-Yosef and J. Zilhão, *Towards a Definition of the Aurignacian*, Lisbon: Trabalhos de Arqueologia.

Grandsaignes d'Hauterive, Robert (1948) *Dictionnaire des racines des langues européennes*, Paris: Larousse.

Graziosi, Paolo (1987) *L'arte dell'antica età della pietra*, Firenze: Le lettere.

Green, Judith (2009) '"Walk this way": Public health and the social organization of walking', *Social Theory & Health* 7, 20–38.

Gros, Frédéric (2011) *Marcher: une philosophie*, Paris: Flammarion.

—— (2014) *A Philosophy of Walking*, London: Verso.

Grosman, Leore (2013) 'The Natufian chronological scheme: New insights and their implications', in O. Bar-Yosef and F.R. Valla (eds) *Natufian Foragers in the Levant*, Ann Arbor, MI: International Monographs in Prehistory.

Guenther, Mathias (1999) *Tricksters and Trancers: Bushman religion and society*, Bloomington, IN: Indiana University Press.

Guilaine, Jean (2015) *Les hypogées protohistoriques de la Méditerranée: Arles et Fontvieille*, Arles: Errance.

Hachid, Malika (1998) *Le Tassili des Ajjer: aux sources de l'Afrique, 50 siècles avant les pyramides*, Paris: Paris-Méditerranée.

—— (2013) 'Comment on Mercier, N., Le Quellec, J.-L., Hachid, M., Agsous, S., Grenet, M., 2012. OSL dating of quaternary deposits associated with the parietal art of the Tassili-nAjjer plateau (Central Sahara), *Quaternary Geochronology* 10, 367–73', *Quaternary Geochronology* 15:36.

Hadot, Pierre (1993) *Exercices spirituels et philosophie antique*, Paris: Institut d'études Augustiniennes.

Hallier, Ulrich W. and Brigitte C. Hallier (2012) *The People of Iheren and Tahilahi*, accessed at www.wissen-online.com, 19 June 2015.

Heidegger, Martin (1977) *Basic Writings*, London: Harper and Row.

Hershman, Debby (2014) *Face to Face: The oldest masks in the world*, Jerusalem: The Israel Museum.

Herzog, Werner (2014) *Of Walking in Ice*, London: Vintage.

Heun, Manfred *et al.* (1997) 'Site of einkorn wheat domestication identified by DNA printing', *Science* 278, 5341:1312–14.

Hodder, Ian (2006) *Çatalhöyük: The leopard's tale*, London: Thames & Hudson.

—— (ed.) (2010) *Religion in the Emergence of Civilization: Çatalhöyük as a case study*, Cambridge: Cambridge University Press.

—— (2011) 'The role of religion in the Neolithic of the Middle East and Anatolia with particular reference to Çatalhöyük', *Paléorient* 37, 1:111–22.

—— and Lynn Meskell (2011) 'A "curious and sometimes a trifle macabre artistry": Some aspects of symbolism in Neolithic Turkey', *Current Anthropology* 52, 2:235–63.

Hofmannsthal, Hugo von (2008) 'Book of friends', in H. von Hofmannsthal (ed.) *The Whole Difference: Selected writings of Hugo von Hofmannsthal*, J. D. McClatchy (ed.), Princeton, NJ: Princeton University Press.

Holliday, Trenton W. (2015) 'Population affinities of the Jebel Sahaba skeletal sample: Limb proportion evidence', *International Journal of Osteoarchaeology* 25:466–76.

Horvath, Agnes (2008) 'Mythology and the trickster: Interpreting communism', in A. Wöll and H. Wydra (eds) *Democracy and Myth in Russia and Eastern Europe*, London: Routledge, 29–44.

—— (2010) 'Pulcinella, or the metaphysics of the nulla: In between politics and theatre', *History of the Human Sciences* 23, 2:47–67.

—— (2013a) *Modernism and Charisma*, London: Palgrave.

—— (2013b) 'The fascination with Eros: The role of passionate interests under Communism', *History of the Human Sciences* 26, 5:79–97.

—— (2015) 'The genealogy of political alchemy: The technological invention of identity change', in A. Horvath, B. Thomassen and H. Wydra (eds) *Breaking Boundaries: Varieties of liminality*, Oxford: Berghahn.

—— (forthcoming) 'Charisma/trickster: On the twofold nature of power', in B. Thomassen and H. Wydra (eds) *Handbook of Political Anthropology*, Cheltenham: Edward Elgar.

—— and Arpad Szakolczai (2013) 'The gravity of Eros in the contemporary: Introduction to the Special Section', *History of the Human Sciences* 26, 5:69–78.

—— and Bjørn Thomassen (2008) 'Mimetic errors in liminal schismogenesis: On the political anthropology of the trickster', *International Political Anthropology* 1, 1:3–24.

Horwitz, Liora K. and Nigel Goring-Morris (2004) 'Animals and ritual during the Levantine PPNB: A case study from the site of Kfar Hahoresh, Israel', *Anthropozoologica* 39, 1:165–78.

Huizinga, Johan (1970) *Homo Ludens*, Boston, MA: Beacon Press.

Huyge, Dirk (2009) 'Late Palaeolithic and Epipalaeolithic rock art in Egypt: Qurta and El-Hosh', *Archéo-Nil*, 19:108–20.

Huyge, Dirk *et al.* (2000) 'Arab el Sahaba, an Epipalaeolithic Site', in P.M. Vermeersch (ed.) *Palaeolithic Living Sites in Upper and Middle Egypt*, Leuven University Press.

—— (2007) 'Lascaux along the Nile': Late Pleistocene rock art in Egypt', *Antiquity* 81, 313:1–4.

—— (2011) 'First evidence of Pleistocene rock art in North Africa: Securing the age of the Qurta petroglyphs (Egypt) through OSL Dating of their sediment cover', *Antiquity* 85, 330:1184–93.

Huysecom, E. *et al.* (2009) 'The emergence of pottery in Africa during the tenth millennium cal BC: new evidence from Ounjougou (Mali)', *Antiquity* 83, 322:905–17.

Hyde, Lewis (1999) *Trickster Makes this World*, New York: North Point.

Ingold, Tim (2000) 'Making things, growing plants, raising animals and bringing up children', in T. Ingold *The Perception of the Environment: Essays on livelihood, dwelling and skill*, London: Routledge, 77–88.

—— (2004) 'Culture on the ground: The world perceived through the feet', *Journal of Material Culture* 9, 3:315–40.

—— (2007) *Lines: A brief history*, London: Routledge.

—— (2013) *Making: Anthropology, archaeology, art and architecture*, London: Routledge.

—— and Jo Lee Vergunst (eds) (2008) *Ways of Walking: Ethnography and practice on foot*, Farnham: Ashgate.

Jarvis, Robin (1997) *Romantic Writing and Pedestrian Travel*, Basingstoke: Macmillan.

Johansson, Sverker (2013) 'The talking Neanderthals: What do fossils, genetics, and archeology say?', *Biolinguistics* 7:35–74.

Kafka, Franz (2006) *The Zürau Aphorisms*, R. Calasso (ed.), London: Harvill Secker.

Kerényi, Károly (1980) 'I misteri dei Kabiri', in *Miti e misteri*, Torino: Boringhieri.

—— (1991) *Prometheus: Archetypal image of human existence*, Princeton, NJ: Princeton University Press.

Khalaily, Hamoudi and François R. Valla (2013) 'Obsidian in Natufian context: The case of Eynan (Ain Mallaha), Israel', in O. Bar-Yosef and F. R. Valla (eds) *Natufian Foragers in the Levant*, Ann Arbor, MI: International Monographs in Prehistory.

Kierkegaard, Søren (1988) *Stages on Life's Way*, Princeton, NJ: Princeton University Press.

Koselleck, Reinhart (1988) *Critique and Crisis*, Oxford: Berg.

Labbucci, Adriano (2011) *Camminare, una rivoluzione*, Rome: Donzelli.

Lahr, M. Mirazón *et al.* (2016) 'Inter-group violence among early Holocene hunter-gatherers of West Turkana, Kenya', *Nature* 529, 7586:394–8.

Latour, Bruno (2013) *An Inquiry into Modes of Existence: An anthropology of the moderns*, Cambridge, MA: Harvard University Press.

Le Bon, Gustave (2009) *Psychology of Crowds*, Southampton: Sparkling Books.

Le Quellec, Jean-Loïc (1993) *Symbolisme et art rupestre au Sahara*, Paris: L'Harmattan.

—— (1995) 'Aires culturelles et art rupestre: théranthropes et femmes ouvertes du Messak (Lybie)', *L'Anthropologie*, 99, 2/3:405–43.

—— (2004) *Rock Art in Africa*, Paris: Flammarion.

—— (2013) 'A new chronology for Saharan rock art', in B. L. Malla (ed.) *The World of Rock Art: An overview of the five continents*, New Delhi: Indira Gandhi National Center for the Arts.

Leroi-Gourhan, André (1986) *Le Fil du temps: ethnologie et préhistoire*, Paris: Seuil.

Lewis-Williams, David (2002) *The Mind in the Cave: Consciousness and the origins of art*, London: Thames & Hudson.

Lhote, Henri (1959) *The Search for the Tassili Frescoes*, London: Hutchinson.

—— (1974) *Il Sahara*, Milan: Fabbri.

Liddell, Henry G. and Robert Scott (1951) *A Greek-English Lexicon*, Oxford: Clarendon Press.

Lorblanchet, Michel (2001) *La grotte ornée de Pergouset (Saint-Géry, Lot): un sanctuaire secret paléolithique*, Paris: Éditions de la Maison des sciences de l'homme.

—— (2010) *Art pariétal: grottes ornées du Quercy*, Paris: Rouergue.

—— and Ann Sieveking (1997) 'The Monsters of Pergouset', *Cambridge Archaeological Journal* 7, 1:37–56.

Lund, Katrin (2008) 'Listen to the sound of time: Walking with saints in an Andalusian village', in T. Ingold and J. L. Vergunst (eds) *Ways of Walking: Ethnography and practice on foot*, Farnham: Ashgate, 1–19.

McNamee, Eugene (2012) 'I walk the line', *International Political Anthropology* 5, 1:95–7.

Mair, Victor H. (1990) 'Old Sinitic *M^rag, Old Persian Maguš and English Magician', *Early China* 15, 27–47.

—— (2012) 'The earliest identifiable written Chinese character', in M. E. Huld, K. Jones-Bley and D. Miller (eds) *Archaeology and Language: Indo-European studies presented to James P. Mallory*, Washington, DC: Institute for the Study of Man, 265–79.

Margueron, Jean-Claude (2013) *Cités invisibles: la naissance de l'urbanisme au Proche-Orient ancien*, Paris: Geuthner.

Martínez, Ignacio *et al.* (2008a) 'Human hyoid bones from the middle Pleistocene site of the Sima de los Huesos (Sierra de Atapuerca, Spain)', *Journal of Human Evolution* 54:118–24.

—— (2008b) 'Auditory capacities human fossils: A new approach to the origin of speech', *The Journal of the Acoustical Society of America* 123, 5:4177–82.

—— (2013) 'Communicative capacities in Middle Pleistocene humans from the Sierra de Atapuerca in Spain', *Quaternary International* 295:94–101.

Mauss, Marcel (1966) *The Gift*, London: Cohen & West.

—— (1973) 'Techniques of the body', *Economy and Society* 2, 1:70–88.

Maxwell-Stuart, P. G. (2012) *The Chemical Choir: A history of alchemy*, London: Continuum.

Meier, Christian (2011) *A Culture of Freedom: Ancient Greece and the origins of Europe*, Oxford: Oxford University Press.

Mercier, Norbert *et al.* (2013) 'Reply to M. Hachid comment on Mercier *et al.* 2012', in *Quaternary Geochronology* 15:37.

Meschiari, Alberto (2014) *Filosofia del camminare: strategie del reincanto*, Florence: Tassinari.

Michieli, Franco (2015) *La vocazione di perdersi: piccolo saggio su come le vie trovano i viandanti*, Portogruaro: Ediciclo.

Mitchell, Stephen (1993) *Anatolia: Land, men, and gods in Asia Minor*, Oxford: Clarendon.

Mithen, Steven (2003) *After the Ice: A global human history, 20,000–5000 BC*, London: Weidenfeld & Nicolson.

Montelle, Yann-Pierre (2009) *Paleoperformance: The emergence of theatricality as social practice*, London: Seagull.

Mori, Fabrizio (2000) *Le grandi civiltà del Sahara antico: il distacco dell'uomo dalla natura e la nascita delle religioni antropomorfe*, Torino: Boringhieri.

Morsch, Michael G. F. (2002) 'Magic figurines? Some remarks about the clay objects of Nevali Çori', in H. G. K. Gebel, B. Dahl Hermansen and C. Hoffmann Jensen (eds) *Magic Practices and Ritual in the Near Eastern Neolithic: Studies in early Near Eastern production, subsistence, and environment 8*, Berlin: ex oriente.

Müller, Hans-Peter (2011) 'Goethe: The ambivalence of modernity and the Faustian ethos of personality', in C. Edling and J. Rydgren (eds) *Sociological Insights of Great Thinkers*, Oxford: Praeger.

Munro, Natalie D. and Leore Grosman (2010) 'Early evidence (ca.12,000 B.P.) for feasting at a burial cave in Israel', *Proceedings of the National Academy of Sciences* 107, 35:15362–6.

Muzzolini, Alfred (1996) 'New data in Saharan rock art 1995–1996', in P. G. Bahn and A. Fossati (eds) *News of the World I, Rock Art Studies*, Oxford: Oxbow Books.

Nicolson, Marjorie H. (1959) *Mountain Gloom and Mountain Glory: The development of the aesthetics of the infinite*, Ithaca, NY: Cornell University Press.

Nietzsche, Friedrich (1967) *On the Genealogy of Morals*, New York: Vintage.

Olsen, Daniel H. (2013) 'A scalar comparison of motivations and expectations of experience', *International Journal of Religious Tourism and Pilgrimage* 1, 1:41–61.

Onions, C. T. (ed.) (1966) *The Oxford Dictionary of English Etymology*, Oxford: Clarendon Press.

Orrelle, Estelle (2014) *Material Images of Humans from the Natufian to Pottery Neolithic Periods in the Levant*, Oxford: Archaeopress.

Palacio-Pérez, Eduardo and Aitor Ruiz Redondo (2014) 'Imaginary creatures in Palaeolithic art: Prehistoric dreams or prehistorians' dreams?', *Antiquity* 88, 345:259–66.

Pascal, Blaise (1972) *Pensées*, Paris: Librairie Générale Française.

Peters, Julie Stone (2004) 'Theater and book in the history of memory: Materializing Mnemosyne in the age of print', *Modern Philology* 102, 2:179–206.

Peters, Joris and Klaus Schmidt (2004) 'Animals in the symbolic world of Pre-Pottery Neolithic Göbekli Tepe, South-Eastern Turkey: A preliminary assessment', *Anthropozoologica* 39, 1:179–218.

Pettitt, Paul and Paul Bahn (2003) 'Current problems in dating Palaeolithic cave art: Candamo and Chauvet', *Antiquity* 77, 295:134–41.

—— (2015) 'An alternative chronology for the art of Chauvet cave', *Antiquity* 89, 345: 542–53.

Pike, Alistair W. G. *et al.* (2015) 'Dating Palaeolithic cave art: Why U–Th is the way to go', *Quaternary International* http://dx.doi.org/10.1016/j.quaint.2015.12.013.

Pirazzoli, Paolo Antonio (1991) *World Atlas of Holocene Sea-Level Changes*, Amsterdam: Elsevier.

Pizzorno, Alessandro (2010) 'The mask: An essay', *International Political Anthropology* 3, 1:5–28.

Pokorny, Julius (1959) *Indogermanisches etymologisches Wörterbuch*, Bern: Francke.

Popitz, Heinrich (2014) 'The concept of power', in G. Poggi (ed.) *Varieties of Political Experience*, Colchester: ECPR Press.

Powers, John C. (2012) *Inventing Chemistry: Herman Boerhaave and the reform of the chemical arts*, Chicago, IL: The University of Chicago Press.

Propp, Vladimir (1968) *Morphology of the Folktale*, Austin, TX: University of Texas Press.

Quiles, Anita *et al.* (2016) 'A high-precision chronological model for the decorated Upper Paleolithic cave of Chauvet-Pont d'Arc, Ardèche, France', *Proceedings of the National Academy of Sciences* 113, 17:4670–5.

Quinn, Bob (2005) *The Atlantean Irish*, Dublin: Lilliput Press.

Radin, Paul (1924) *Monotheism among Primitive Peoples*, London: Allen.

—— (1972) *The Trickster: A study in American Indian mythology*, with commentary by K. Kerényi and C. G. Jung, New York: Schocken.

Roman, Camil F. (2014) 'Walking and praying into the condition of the witness: Steps towards a non-sacrificial philosophical anthropology', *International Political Anthropology* 7, 2:59–78.

—— (2016) 'The French Revolution as a liminal process: Towards a political anthropology of radical social changes', PhD, University of Cambridge.

Rosenberg, Danny and Dani Nadel (2014) 'The sounds of pounding: Boulder mortars and their significance to Natufian burial customs', *Current Anthropology* 55, 6:784–812.

Rutherford, John (2000) 'Introduction' to Cervantes, *Don Quixote*, London: Penguin.

Sagona, Antonio and Paul Zimansky (2009) *Ancient Turkey*, London: Routledge.

Sandgathe, Dennis M. *et al.* (2011) 'On the role of fire in Neandertal adaptations in Western Europe: Evidence from Pech de l'Azé IV and Roc de Marsal, France', *PaleoAnthropology* 9, 216–42.

Sansoni, Umberto (1994) *Le più antiche pitture del Sahara: L'arte delle Teste Rotonde*, Milan: Jaca Book.

Santayana, George (1951) *Dominations and Powers: Reflections on liberty, society, and government*, New York: Scribner.

Schirmer, Wulf (1990) 'Some aspects of building at the "Aceramic-Neolithic" settlement of Cayönü Tepesi', *World Archaeology* 21, 3:363–87.

Schmidt, Klaus (2000a) '"Zuerst kam der Tempel, dann die Stadt": Vorläufiger Bericht zu den Grabungen am Göbekli Tepe und am Gürcütepe 1995–1999', *Istanbuler Mitteilungen* 50:5–41.

—— (2000b) 'Göbekli Tepe, Southeastern Turkey: A preliminary report on the 1995–1999 excavations', *Paléorient* 26, 1:45–54.

—— (2011) *Costruirono i primi templi 7000 anni prima delle piramidi: la scoperta archeologica di Göbekli Tepe*, Sestri Levante: Oltre.

Schmitt, Carl (2002) *Terra e mare*, Milan: Adelphi.

Simpson, J. A. and Weiner, E. S. C. (1989) *Oxford English Dictionary* (vol. VI), Oxford: Clarendon Press.

Slavin, Sean (2003) 'Walking as spiritual practice: The pilgrimage to Santiago de Compostela', *Body & Society* 9, 1:1–18.

Solnit, Rebecca (2001) *Wanderlust: A history of walking*, London: Verso.

Soukopova, Jitka (2012) *The Round Heads: The earliest rock paintings in the Sahara*, Cambridge: Cambridge Scholars.

Szakolczai, Arpad (2000) *Reflexive Historical Sociology*, London: Routledge.

—— (2003) *The Genesis of Modernity*, London: Routledge.

—— (2007) 'Image-magic in *A Midsummer Night's Dream*: Power and modernity from Weber to Shakespeare', *History of the Human Sciences* 20, 4:1–26.

—— (2009) 'Liminality and experience: Structuring transitory situations and transformative events', *International Political Anthropology* 2, 1:141–72.

—— (2013a) *Comedy and the Public Sphere: The re-birth of theatre as comedy and the genealogy of the modern public arena*, London: Routledge.

—— (2013b) 'In liminal tension towards giving birth: Eros, the educator', *History of the Human Sciences* 26, 5:100–15.

—— (2013c) 'Thinking as testing the limits of friendship: On the Voegelin-Schütz correspondence', in *VoegelinView*, 23–30 January.

—— (2016a) *Novels and the Sociology of the Contemporary*, London: Routledge.

—— (2016b) 'Processes of social flourishing and their liminal collapse: Elements to a genealogy of globalisation', *British Journal of Sociology* 67, 3:435–55.

—— (2017a) *Permanent Liminality and Modernity: Analysing the sacrificial carnival through novels*, London: Routledge.

—— (2017b) 'Permanent (trickster) liminality: The reasons of the heart and of the mind', *Theory and Psychology* 27, 2.

Thomassen, Bjørn (2014) *Liminality, Change and Transition: Living through the in-between*, Farnham: Ashgate.

Thoreau, Henry David (1962) *Walden and Other Writings*, New York: Bantam.

Turello, Mario (1993) *Anima artificiale: il teatro magico di Giulio Camillo*, Tricesimo: Aviani.

Turnbull, Colin (1968) *The Forest People*, New York: Simon & Schuster.

Turner, Christy G. (2008) 'A dental anthropological hypothesis relating to the ethnogenesis, origin, and antiquity of the Afro-Asiatic language family: Peopling of the Eurafrican-South Asian triangle IV', in J. D. Bengtson (ed.) *In Hot Pursuit of Language in Prehistory: Essays in the four fields of anthropology*, Philadelphia: John Benjamins.

Turner, Victor W. (1967) 'Betwixt and Between: The liminal period in *Rites de Passage*', in *The Forest of Symbols*, New York: Cornell University Press.

—— (1969) *The Ritual Process*, Chicago, IL: Aldine.

Turner, Victor W. and Edith Turner (1978) *Image and Pilgrimage in Christian Culture*, New York: Columbia University Press.

Valladas, Hélène *et al.* (2001) 'Radiocarbon AMS dates for Paleolithic cave paintings', *Radiocarbon* 43, 2B:977–86.

van Andel, Tjeerd H. and Curtis N. Runnels (1995) 'The Earliest Farmers in Europe', *Antiquity* 69, 481–500.

van Eck, Caroline (2010) 'Living statues: Alfred Gell's *Art and Agency*, living presence response and the sublime', *Art History* 33, 4:642–59.

van Gennep, Arnold (1960) *The Rites of Passage*, Chicago, IL: Chicago University Press.

Voegelin, Eric (1974) *The Ecumenic Age*, vol. 4 of *Order and History*, Baton Rouge, LA: Louisiana State University Press.

—— (1990) 'Equivalences of experience and symbolization in history,' in *Published Essays: 1966–1985*, Columbia, MO: University of Missouri Press.

—— (1998) *Revolution and the New Science*, vol. 6 of *History of Political Ideas*, Columbia, MO: University of Missouri Press.

Wallerstein, Immanuel (1974) *The Modern World System*, New York: Academic.

Warburg, Aby (1998) *Il rituale del serpente*, Milan: Adelphi.

Watkins, Trevor (1990) 'The origins of house and home?', *World Archaeology* 21, 3:336–47.

Weber, Max (1968) *On Charisma and Institution Building*, S. N. Eisenstadt (ed.), Chicago, IL: University of Chicago Press.

—— (1992) *The Protestant Ethic and the Spirit of Capitalism*, London: Routledge.

Whitman, Walt (1990) *Leaves of Grass*, Oxford: Oxford University Press.

Wydra, Harald (2015) *Politics and the Sacred*, Cambridge: Cambridge University Press.

Yates, Frances (1964) *Giordano Bruno and the Hermetic Tradition*, London: Routledge.

—— (1975) *The Rosicrucian Enlightenment*, London: Paladine Books.

—— (1979) *The Occult Philosophy in the Elizabethan Age*, London: Routledge.

—— (1992) *The Art of Memory*, London: Pimlico.

Zeder, Melinda A. (2011) 'The origins of agriculture in the Near East', *Current Anthropology* 54, S4:221–35.

—— (2015) 'Core questions in domestication research', *Proceedings of the National Academy of Sciences* 112, 11:3191–8.

Zeder, Melinda A. and Bruce D. Smith (2009) 'A conversation on agriculture: Talking past each other in a crowded room', *Current Anthropology* 50, 5:681–91.

GLOSSARY

Character The stable essence of any concrete being. It has a general aspect, concerning how it is formed; and a concrete part, concerning how it is different in its given form from similar others. It is captured well in the famous fragment of Heraclitus, *Ethos anthropoi daimon* ('the character is man's inner essence', or 'conscience is man's character').

Enchantment Entrapment through a particular modality of tricking, where the trickster gains the consent of the fooled one by creating an aura of great power or talent. According to Alfred Gell, art, magic, enchantment and technology are interconnected.

Gift relations Central term in the anthropology of Marcel Mauss. While for a time supporting Durkheim about the foundational significance of rituals of sacrifice, after WWI Mauss came to realise that societies are based on the giving, receiving and returning of 'total services', in everyday life and through communal participation. Formalised exchange threatens such foundations, but can never replace them.

Imitation In the philosophy of Plato and Aristotle imitation is the central feature of man, coming before and working beyond consciousness. Modern rationalistic philosophy denies the significance of imitation in mature adults, generating a dualism not only between body and mind, but also adults and children. The significance of imitative processes was reasserted by Tocqueville, Tarde, Deleuze, Latour and especially René Girard, discussing 'mimetics of desire', 'scapegoating' and 'sacrificial mechanism'.

Infantilisation/senilisation Two sides of the same process, where entities are enticed to give up their character, thus regressing – in an advanced age – to a mode of behaviour characteristic of an earlier stage in the life cycle. It combines the immaturity of childhood with the rigidity of old age.

Infantile senility implies loss of memory and mental capacities, a changed brain activity, infertility, infirmity, fatigue, dizziness, insomnia and the inability to look after oneself.

Liminality The term was introduced by Arnold van Gennep in his 1909 classic on rites of passage, but only gained wide acceptance from the mid-1960s, when Victor Turner recognised the significance of the concept. Liminality helps to capture and analyse, with a degree of precision, what happens under ambivalent, ephemeral and fluid conditions of transition. This can best be seen through the three stages of rites of passage, performed in moments of transition in the life cycle or the cycle of seasons, where initiands, like adolescents to become adults or a couple to be married, are first separated from their families, then publicly perform a test demonstrating their maturity, and finally are reintegrated into the community in new roles and identities. The central theoretical issue concerns the potentially transformative aspect of the middle stage of the ritual, when somebody is literally 'on' the limit. The ambivalence of liminality implies that such situations can be purposefully evoked and manipulated.

Permanent liminality The paradoxical situation when a temporary suspension of the normal, everyday, taken-for-granted state of affairs becomes lasting, generating a loss of reality, even a sense of unreality in daily existence, and an ensuing disempowerment and confusion. The problem is not deviating from 'the' norm, understood in a universalistic sense, but from whatever people living at a given time and place were taking for granted as normal and ordinary in their lives. This is bound to happen in particular when the liminal situation is artificially incited. Under conditions of permanent liminality and generalised enchantment the value of consent is undermined, becoming identical to failing to recognise the trick.

Representation The bringing of something absent into presence. If it is done by means of art or knowledge, it can be easily turned into transgression, by enticing a confusion between the genuine and the fake, for example by creating representations that conflate aspects of real beings. It can also be used to generate possession, for example by the wearing of masks.

Schismogenesis A term developed by Gregory Bateson, based on fieldwork in the early 1930s in Papua New Guinea. Through observing frequent repetitions of violent and highly imitative rituals, the idea came to him that in this network of societies at a certain historical juncture meaningful human order must have broken down, interlocking the various segments into a series of dualistic relations and producing a stalemate or permanent conflict which they could not escape. The central idea is that the identities of the fragments into which the entity was decomposed are not given, but become formed, mutually, through self-definition, other-labelling, and reactions to such labelling. Bateson distinguished between symmetrical and complementary schismogenesis, the former implying a competition between the fragments, while in the latter elements are forced into a system of hierarchical subordination, reversed only during specific rituals.

Subversion   The enticing of a concrete entity to give up its character. This can be done through the ideologisation of metamorphosis, based on a misapplication of the idea of change. Genetic mutations happen, but are extremely rare; a caterpillar is indeed transformed into a butterfly, but not into a sparrow. Subversion ignores the enormous stability in nature, and the resistance of entities to give up their character.

Transgression/Regression   Transforming character through the purposeful destruction of limits. It brings about exhaustion by infantilisation/senilisation.

Trickster   A term introduced into anthropology by Paul Radin, based on his fieldwork among the Winnebago Indians, before WWI. In ethnological stories, folktales and mythologies, the trickster is a wandering outsider, not belonging to any community, who becomes accepted as a harmless prankster, but can gain influence, even power in situations of crisis. This is because the trickster, not participating, is not touched by emotional involvement, thus can insinuate himself at the centre of attention, pretending to offer a solution while being only interested in proliferating confusion, as his power is conditional upon the rest of the population being kept in a state of limbo. Such figures include Hermes and Prometheus in Greek mythology, Loki in Scandinavian mythology, the leprechaun of Irish folktales, Reineke the fox in medieval stories, the coyote of the prairie or various West African spider, rabbit or monkey quasi-deities.

Unreality   A feature of the void, and of permanent liminality. It is generated by enticing concrete beings to transform themselves into something else than their character, or to exchange something concrete for an artificial construct.

Void   An empty space with no stable and concrete entities present, generating an enormous emotional charge for anyone entering it.

NAME INDEX

Abgar (King of Edessa) 154
Agamben, Giorgio 67, 68
Agnel, Georges 22
Agnew, Jean-Christophe 42
Alexander the Great 84
Alinei, Mario 31, 36
Anaximander 70, 150
Anthony, St. 156
Apelles 84
Argyrou, Vassos 3, 131
Aristotle 44, 46, 72, 149, 164, 168,
    181, 182
Arsuaga, Juan 55
Augé, Marc 146
Augustine, St. 44
Aujoulat, Norbert 22, 23
Azéma, Marc 38, 61, 68, 75, 79, 80, 84

Bachofen, Johann 145
Bacon, Francis 40, 41
Bahn, Paul 51, 83
Bakhtin, Mikhail 33–5, 53, 121, 138, 139,
    156, 171
Balter, Michael 54, 108
Balzac, Honoré de 156
Banning, Edward 94, 96, 113
Bar-Yosef, Ofer 88, 93, 94, 96, 110,
    111, 113
Basil the Great 154
Bataille, Georges 25, 47, 52–5, 57, 95,
    103, 126
Bateson, Gregory 3, 12
Baudelaire, Charles 14–5

Bauman, Zygmunt 180
Bédier, Joseph 156
Bednarik, Robert 26, 84
Belfer-Cohen, Anna 90
Bellavite, Andrea 170
Beltrán, Antonio 24, 26
Bertolotti, Maurizio 53, 109
Blakely, Sandra 141
Blanchot, Maurice 25
Bocquentin, Fanny 96, 98
Boland, Tom 3
Bolzoni, Lina 43, 45, 46, 84
Bonaventure, St. 155
Borkenau, Franz 42, 69, 157–8
Braidwood, Linda 108
Braidwood, Robert 108
Breuil, Henri 62
Broch, Hermann 143
Brown, Peter 79
Bruno, Giordano 46
Buddha 15, 21
Bunyan, John 156
Burckhardt, Jacob 79

Calasso, Roberto 15, 35, 39, 40, 45, 84,
    101, 146
Callot, Jacques 15, 138
Calvin, Jean 156
Camillo, Giulio 43–6, 84
Canguilhem, Georges 166, 168
Carbonell, Eudald 56
Cartailhac, Émile 26
Cauvin, Jacques 90, 92, 94, 108

Cervantes, Miguel de 62
Char, René 25
Chatwin, Bruce 14–5, 169, 180
Chauvet, Jean-Marie 22, 56
Childe, V. Gordon 86, 113, 116, 126
Christ *see* Jesus
Citato, Pietro 106
Clottes, Jean 25, 34, 38, 51, 56, 65
Cocteau, Jean 176
Coencas, Simon 22
Constantine the Great 155
Copernicus, Nicolaus 158

Dante, Alighieri 176
Darwin, Charles 15, 54, 113, 144
Davis, Julian 171
Deleuze, Gilles 19, 131, 140, 142, 143, 146
Derrida, Jacques 131
de Mortillet, Gabriel 26
Descartes, René 15, 17, 28, 41, 157, 158, 163
Détienne, Marcel 3
Dickens, Charles 18, 20, 21, 73, 106, 156
Diogenes Laertius 150
Djoser 130
Doi, Kiyomi 13, 14
Dostoevsky, Fyodor 106
Douglas, Mary 67–8
Dupront, Alphonse 152
Durkheim, Émile 35, 67, 68, 98

Eisenstadt, S.N. 74, 84
Eisner, Kurt 79
Eliade, Mircea 10, 67, 68, 97,
    100, 104, 121
Elias, Norbert 84, 157–8, 168
Emerson, Ralph W. 17
Engels, Friedrich 113
Erasmus, Desiderius 45

Faustus, Dr 43
Ferguson, Harvie 170
Ficino, Marsilio 46
Florio, John 40, 47
Foucault, Michel 2, 8, 25, 27, 36, 37, 38,
    39–42, 47, 52, 53, 54, 58, 50, 80, 83,
    84, 93, 100, 157–8, 159, 166, 176
Francis, St. 15, 156, 169
Francis I (King) 43
Frangipane, Marcella 114
Frank, Roslyn 53, 108, 150
Frankfort, Henri 133
Franklin, Benjamin 18
Freud, Sigmund 93, 163, 170
Frey, Nancy 13, 14

Gadamer, Hans-Georg 40
Gandhi, Mahatma 18
Garrod, Dorothy 88
Gell, Alfred 119, 140
Gernet, Louis 71
Giesen, Bernhard 10
Gimbutas, Marija 145
Girard, René 3, 35, 72, 91, 98, 152
Glory, André 22–3
Goethe, Johann W. 25, 72, 106, 112, 117,
    176, 181, 182
Goring-Morris, Nigel 90, 111, 112, 120
Gregory of Nazianzus 154
Gregory of Nyssa 154
Griaule, Marcel 129
Gros, Frédéric 8, 16–21, 25, 27, 36, 54,
    156, 158, 159, 171, 179
Grosman, Leore 54, 93, 94, 96, 97, 100
Guattari, Félix 131, 140, 142, 143, 146

Hachid, Malika 132, 133, 134, 146
Hadot, Pierre 159
Hallier, Brigitte 139
Hallier, Ulrich 139
Hegel, Georg W.F. 20, 54, 99, 131,
    157, 159
Heidegger, Martin 16, 31, 69, 73, 93
Heraclitus 25, 168, 181, 197
Herzog, Werner 4, 14, 37–8, 56, 175
Hippias of Elis 44
Hitchcock, Don 75, 77, 78, 84
Hitler, Adolf 79
Hobbes, Thomas 74
Hodder, Ian 97, 114–26 *passim*, 129, 145, 149
Hofmannsthal, Hugo von 1, 143
Holliday, Trenton 91, 92, 98
Hönigswald, Richard 158
Huizinga, Johan 32–3, 40, 53, 54
Husserl, Edmund 131
Huyge, Dirk 90, 92, 104, 130
Hyde, Lewis 4, 72

Ignatius de Loyola, St. 30, 46, 156
Ingold, Tim 8, 16–7, 25, 31, 34, 47, 54,
    61, 113, 157, 158

Jean Paul 131
Jesus 15, 152–3, 159, 171
John the Baptist, St. 152
Joyce, James 176

Kafka, Franz 85, 112, 162, 168
Kant, Immanuel 15, 17, 25, 28, 73, 74, 82,
    157, 158, 159, 161, 163, 182, 183

Kantorowitz 40, Ernst
Kelsen, Hans 158
Kenyon, Kathleen 111
Kerényi, Károly 112, 117, 141
Kierkegaard, Søren 15, 19, 54, 157, 159, 184
Koselleck, Reinhart 8
Kurosawa, Akira 87

Lao-Tse 15
Latour, Bruno 81, 100, 179
Le Bon, Gustave 78
Le Quellec, Jean-Loïc 127, 129, 136
Leonardo da Vinci 43
Leroi-Gourhan, André 60, 62, 64, 65, 81
Lessing, Gotthold E. 44
Lévi-Strauss, Claude 120
Levinas, Emmanual 131
Lewis-Williams, David 23, 25, 34, 86, 119–20, 129
Lhote, Henri 127, 132
Lorblanchet, Michel 62–70, 83, 85, 146
Luther, Martin 43, 156, 163

Magritte, René 40
Mair, Victor 31, 132, 144–5, 146
Mallarmé, Stéphane 39
Mann, Thomas 112, 170
Margueron, Jean-Claude 149
Marsal, Jacques 22
Martínez, Ignacio 56
Marx, Karl 113, 116, 177
Mauss, Marcel 27, 35, 118, 173, 180, 181
McCandless, Christopher 14
McNamee, Eugene 34
Merleau-Ponty, Maurice 158
Michieli, Franco 162–70
Milton, John 138, 153, 176
Mitchell, Stephen 31, 154
Mithen, Steven 89, 93, 94, 104, 110, 111, 112, 118, 124, 149
Mohammed 15
Monney, Julien 56
Montelle, Yann-Pierre 38, 61, 79–81
Mori, Fabrizio 127, 129, 132, 133
Mosquera, Marina 56
Müller, Hans-Peter 25, 112
Mumford, Lewis 42, 69, 93
Munro, Natalie 54, 97, 100
Mussolini, Benito 79
Muzzolini, Alfred 127, 139

Nansen, Fridtjof 170
Newton, Isaac x, 9, 15, 43, 47, 73, 138, 139, 161
Nietzsche, Friedrich 2, 9, 15, 39, 40, 42, 52, 54, 57, 76, 82, 99–100, 122, 123, 125, 143, 145, 157, 158, 159, 176

Olsen, Daniel 13
Ortega y Gasset, José 73

Parmenides 21, 182
Pascal, Blaise 16, 18, 161, 170
Patočka, Jan 98
Paul, St. 154
Peter, St. 154
Picasso, Pablo 25, 70, 84
Pico della Mirandola, Giovanni 46
Pizzorno, Alessandro 40, 135
Plato xi, 1, 10, 16, 19, 25, 44, 54, 60, 67, 71, 79, 82, 107, 118, 131, 138, 146, 149–52, 153, 155, 156, 161, 163, 164, 165, 167, 170, 173, 176, 181–3
Pollaiuolo, Antonio 101
Popitz, Heinrich 73
Proclus 152
Propp, Vladimir 33–5, 36, 150

Quinn, Bob 145

Radin, Paul 3, 72, 73, 133
Raphael 43, 107
Ravidat, Marcel 22
Riesman, David 73
Rilke, Rainer M. 17
Roman, Camil 8, 19, 20, 25, 56, 73, 171
Rousseau, Jean-Jacques 18, 157, 159

Sagona, Antonio 108, 118
Santayana, George 166
Sanz de Sautuola, Marcelino 24
Schachner, Richard 85
Schmidt, Klaus 103–11 *passim*
Schmitt, Carl 16
Schutz, Alfred 157
Shakespeare, William 42
Sieveking, Ann 63–6, 83
Simonides of Ceos 43–4
Socrates 151, 152, 165, 181
Solnit, Rebecca 25, 152, 159
Stalin, Joseph 79

Tarde, Gabriel 19
Tarkovsky, Andrei 175

Thales 70, 150
Thomassen, Bjørn 3, 166
Thoreau, Henry David 17, 27, 101
Tiepolo, Giambattista 70, 84
Tocqueville, Alexis de 73
Tolkien, J.J.R. 175
Tolstoy, Lev 156
Tonatto, Diletta 146
Turello, Mario 43, 45, 46, 84
Turnbull, Colin 149
Turner, Christy 91, 98
Turner, Victor 3, 35, 67, 84, 85, 166

Valla, François 88, 93, 94, 96, 115
van Eck, Caroline 141
van Gennep, Arnold 3, 67
Velazquez, Diego 70, 84
Vergunst, Jo L. 16
Vernant, Jean-Pierre 3
Viglius Zuichemus 45
Vitruvius 46

Voegelin, Eric 40, 42, 61, 79, 157–8,
    159, 183
Voltaire 159

Wallerstein, Immanuel 108
Warburg, Aby 18
Watkins, Trevor 88, 96
Weber, Max 2, 9, 12, 39, 69, 74, 78, 79,
    83, 84, 99, 117, 143, 156, 163, 166,
    170, 176, 183
Whitman, Walt 7, 51
Wilson, Peter 96
Wright brothers 18
Wydra, Harald 3

Yates, Frances 37, 38, 39, 42–6, 47,
    80, 84

Zeder, Melinda 108, 109, 113, 160
Zimansky, Paul 108, 118
Zizioulas, John 160

SUBJECT INDEX

Abacus 127
Abraham 111, 112, 167
absence 58, 139
'absolute literature' 39
absolutism 159
absorption 75, 76, 77, 144
abstract/ion 62, 126, 136, 137, 138
absurdity 62, 126, 143
Abu Hureyra 109–10
Acre 94
actor(s) 32, 41–2
adaptivity 4
'Adoration of Magi' 145
aesthetic 44, 53
affirmation of life 57
Africa 87, 89, 90, 91, 98, 129;
    Southern 105
aggressiveness 79
agriculture 16, 86, 88, 92, 102, 105,
    107–10, 116, 119, 129, 135, 145, 160,
    168, 177; see also domestication
Aguirre the Wrath of God (Herzog) 4
Ahmarian culture 90
'Ain Ghazal 111, 112, 113, 115
Alaska 14
alchemy 16, 20, 42, 44, 46, 84, 126, 137,
    138, 163, 183
Aleppo 102
'Alexander the Great and Campaspe in the
    Studio of Apelles' (Tiepolo) 84
alienation 131, 133, 134, 138
Alps 164, 165
Altamira cave 24, 25, 56, 69, 81, 85

alteration 1, 33, 38, 60, 69, 73, 80, 146
alterity see other/ness
Altopascio 173
Amazon 96
ambivalence 80, 85
America 14; Northern 105
ammoniac liquid 68
amphitheatre 38, 45
Anatolia 115, 118, 121, 122, 124, 125, 129,
    130, 145
Anatomy of Restlessness (Chatwin) 14
annihilation see destruction
Annunciation 153
anthropology 2, 8, 65, 66, 71, 79, 82, 112;
    fundamental (Huizinga) 32–3; political
    1, 172
Antioch 154
Antiquity 151
apeiron 70
apocalypse 112, 139
apparition 37
Apulia 90, 177
Arabia 128
archaeology xiii, 2, 8, 11, 15, 24, 71, 86,
    87, 91, 99, 102, 112, 113, 116, 124
Ardèche River 12
Arles 94
arrival (walker's) 14, 36
arrogance 14, 17, 18, 53, 70
arrow 76
Arslantepe 102, 129
l'art pour l'art 137
artefact 4, 73, 76, 82

artificiality 16, 19, 33, 35, 39, 59, 60, 61,
    65, 70,73, 74, 182, 183
artist 24, 53, 58, 59, 64, 69–70, 71
Art of Memory, The (Yates) 38, 42
Arudy 34
ascetic planet 125
ascetic priest *see* priest: ascetic
asceticism 126, 155
Astorga 178
Asia 87, 89, 145
Asia Minor 31
Assisi 15, 84
Aswan Dam 92, 104
Atapuerca cave 3, 55–6, 61, 62
Athens 151
Atlantic 86, 89, 98, 104–5, 150, 156
atonement 183
Augustinians 156
Aurignacian culture 90
auroch 75, 105
authenticity 33, 38, 166, 169, 179
authority 31, 35, 83
autonomy 159, 170
avant-garde 39
axial age 9
Azilian culture 90, 103

Babylon 113
bacchanalia 138
Balkans 13, 121, 125, 145
Batek 16, 170
Battle of Thymbra 150
bear 123, 150; cave 52
beauty xiii, 11, 16, 24, 25, 43, 44, 53, 57,
    58, 69, 79, 100, 101, 105, 106, 107,
    122, 138, 150, 151, 152, 155, 163,
    164–5, 168, 170, 175; lover of 151
Bedeilhac cave 34
Belgrade 173, 176
Benedictines 178
Berber 145
Berlin 162
bestiality 141
bestiary 68–71, 102, 105, 106, 109,
    118, 122
Bible 25, 84, 112, 113, 163, 171, 178
'big bang' 74
Bingöl 102
bipolarism 134
bird(s) 175
Bithynia 154
bizarre 93
Birth of Tragedy (Nietzsche) 52
bison(s) 60, 64, 104

bizarre 11, 93, 115, 121, 135, 136, 137
boar(s) 105, 106
Bølling-Allerød interstadial 89, 94
Bologna 43
bone(s) 55; hyoid 56; incision 74–8; mid-
    ear 56; leopard 122, 136
Book of Friends (Hofmannsthal) 1
boredom 19, 173, 177
boulder mortars 97
boundaries 73, 74, 172; artificial 74, 97;
    destruction 78, 82
bovine(s) 75, 76, 78
break 76, 80, 81, 131, 134, 137, 138
Breslau 158
Brindisi 173, 176
Britain 165
Bronze Age 102, 112, 129, 144
brutality 136
Budapest 176
'Building Dwelling Thinking'
    (Heidegger) 16
bull 106
bull-roarer 82
bungee diving 166, 169
bureaucracy 14
Burgos 61, 176, 178
burial practices 55, 67, 92, 95, 96, 98, 103,
    112, 113, 115, 120; dead under houses
    11, 95
Byzantium 44, 46, 90, 152, 155

Cabala 42
Cabeira 31
Cabeiri 126, 141
Cafer Höyük 110
Cagliari 113
Camino de Santiago 1, 7, 8, 13–4, 20, 56,
    155, 172–8
Canada 104
Canterbury 13, 156
capitalism 9
Cappadocia 102, 115, 120, 124, 128,
    154, 160
care 92, 109, 120, 121, 150, 173
care of the self (Plato/Foucault/Hadot) 27,
    36, 159
carnival 34–5, 121, 150, 156
Carolingians 44
Castellón (Spain) 90
Castelperronian 53
catacombs 155
Çatalhöyük 65, 73, 82, 100,103, 107, 113,
    114–26, 128, 129, 132, 144, 145, 146,
    149, 154

Catholicism 156, 160
cattle 110, 121, 122
cave xiii, 10, 37, 38, 144, 162; accessible
58, 66, 67, 79, 80, 161, 175; art/painted
xii–iii, 10–2, 21–4, 37, 45, 51–85, 86,
98, 109, 119–20, 128, 132; secret 67;
visiting 12
Cave of Forgotten Dreams, The (Herzog) 37,
38, 56
Çayönü 54, 110, 118, 124, 125
Celts 154
ceramics 129; Banshan 144, 145; Machang
144, 145
cervid(s) 64, 69, 122, 160
Chaldean astronomy 70, 150
chaos 18, 68, 69, 70
character 3, 10, 36, 71, 72, 74, 75, 76, 77,
78, 82, 130–140, 143, 144, 146, 176,
179–83, 197
charis 83, 173
charisma 74, 78–9, 83, 143, 156, 181, 183
Charybdis 20
chatter 16, 17
Chauvet cave 4, 12, 22, 23, 38, 51–61, 62,
67, 68, 69, 79, 80, 81, 83, 84, 85, 94,
99, 100, 102, 103, 120, 145, 157
child/hood 18, 19, 169
chimpanzee 56
Christmas 56
China 144–5
Christianity 9, 99, 102, 145, 154–6, 167,
169; early 154; Eastern 17, 171
Christmas 56
chronotope 86
Church 44
Cilicia 154
cinema 38, 61, 75, 79–80, 84
civilisation xiii, 3, 15, 32, 87, 88, 137,
154, 155, 166, 168; agricultural 125; its
masks 18; Minoan 152; modern 19, 175
(settled 173); as taming (Nietzsche) 122;
urban 128
civilising process (Elias) 157
classical age/ episteme (Foucault) 8, 9, 40,
41, 47
climate change 88–9, 94, 95, 117, 129, 130
cloning 77
Cluj 173
Côa Valley 26
Cobra Verde (Herzog) 4
Cold War 61
Collège de France 8
coincidence 62, 89, 110, 130, 165, 170
commercialism 11
communication 85; artificial 133
communism 2, 34, 79, 131, 164, 178

concept art 137
conception 134, 135, 167
conceptual history 28, 30
concreteness (of being/s) 40, 72, 181
conflict 74, 92, 113, 150; inter-
civilizational 98; permanent 198
conquest 79, 94, 97, 98, 125
consciousness 21, 54, 126, 164, 173; altered
state 65, 69
contagion 139
contentment 7, 30, 32, 38, 57, 67, 68, 76,
83, 99, 104, 179–83
contesting (Huizinga) 32, 54
conversion 20, 21, 22, 155, 165, 172, 175,
182, 183
Cordes Mountains 94
corruption 60, 152
corruptness 18, 156, 157, 166
cosmopolitanism 151
cosmos 18, 164, 170
Cosquer cave 94, 101
Cougnac cave 80, 85
courage 164
court society (Elias) 168
Cratylus (Plato) 181
crawling 63, 68, 70, 71, 75
creation 45, 60, 68–70, 138;
divine 24; myth 68; of the world 20,
60, 68
creator (of the world) 69, 70, 82, 100
crisis 3, 72, 74, 78, 108; perpetual 73
Critias (Plato) 152
critic(s) 153
critical theory 107
Croatia 175, 177
cross potent 144, 146
crowd(s) 78–9; psychology 78
crowding 111, 122, 162, 178
cruelty 176
culling 93, 109, 124
cult 103, 108, 110, 113, 114, 129, 145;
death 110; of ancestors 119
culture 55, 99, 137; cave art 86, 89, 90,
103; Christian 9; of death 93, 97,
106, 107, 109, 110–2, 118, 119, 124;
European 39, 149; Greek 71, 76, 126;
origins of 35; youth 13
curiosity 168, 170
cynicism 106, 133, 134, 152, 159
Cyprus 154, 160

danger 35, 38, 60, 63, 64, 104, 105, 107,
110, 122, 136, 166, 167
Danube 90
Dark Ages 155

Dasein (Heidegger) 31
dating methods 51, 52, 104; BC-BP 61, 127; carbon 83, 104; OSL 104
death 93
Death in Venice (Mann) 170
decadence 142
decay 103, 107, 176
deer *see* cervid(s)
Delphi 154
democracy 177, 184; mass 176
demon(s) 70, 119, 136, 141, 143, 183; of winemaking 141
depersonalisation 20, 32, 69, 70, 103
depravity 156
depression 10, 64, 111
deprivation 73, 74, 117, 134, 139, 144, 183
Derinkuyu 120, 128
Dersu Uzala (Kurosawa) 87
desert 10, 127, 128, 162, 176
desire 4, 15, 58, 70, 72, 77, 107, 134, 136, 137, 139, 141, 163–4, 167, 170, 178
destruction 69, 71, 77, 131, 136, 139, 144, 149, 159, 176
dialogue(s) 16, 32; Plato's 44, 149–52, 153
Dialogues (Rousseau) 159
Diktean cave 152
Diotima 152, 165
dirt (out of place) 67–8, 119, 122
Discipline and Punish (Foucault) 100, 157
disempowering 119, 198
disproportionality 64, 65
distancing 28, 80, 133, 136, 138, 150
distrust 70
divinisation of man 43, 46
divinity *see* god(s)
divine xii, 9, 10, 12, 46, 53, 67, 76, 78, 124, 134, 138, 150, 156, 157, 161–2, 163, 169, 182, 184
division 75
doe *see* cervid(s)
dog 93, 96, 160
Dogon 129
Dombey and Son (Dickens) 20
domestication 38, 77, 92, 93, 96–7, 99, 107–10, 122, 124, 179; of man 4, 96, 107
donkey 153
Don Quixote 30
Don Quixote (Cervantes) 62, 101
Dordogne 62, 75, 128
Drakensberg Mountains 129
dream(s) 57, 80, 104, 135
dualism xiii, 15, 149, 158–9, 163; object-subject 28; rationalist 30
Duino 164

Earth 7, 16, 18, 21, 54, 113, 128, 182
East Göllü Dag 115
economics: logic 89; neo-classical 11, 158; 'new' 17
Edessa *see* Urfa
Edinburgh 15
egg 139–43
Egypt 31, 65, 104, 129, 130, 133, 149, 155
eidos 60, 131
einkorn *see* wheat
Ekain cave 56
elders 125
elective affinity 117, 159, 164
electricity 10, 116
Elias (prophet) 94
eloquence *see* rhetoric
El Wadi 96
emmer *see* wheat
emotion(s) 3, 10, 33, 73, 76, 136, 143; high 53
emotional charge *see* void
empire(s) 79, 155; -building 74, 92; Roman 90, 154, 155
emptiness 10, 53, 68, 70, 74, 78, 79, 128, 133, 140, 143; *see also* nothingness; void
enchantment(s) 19, 119–23, 177, 197
encyclopaedia 43
energy 4, 16, 18, 75, 76, 138, 167, 176; kinetic 84
enframing (Heidegger) 93
entrapment 118, 178
England 8, 156, 157; Stuart 42
engraving(s) 60, 62–74, 83, 101, 104, 106, 130, 132
Enlightenment 9, 18, 24, 25, 43, 47, 117, 127, 159
entanglement (Hodder) 123, 124
entrapment 4, 95, 100, 118, 119, 123, 164, 177, 178
envy 97, 99
epiphany 10, 152, 153, 162; *see also* apparition
episteme (Foucault): classical 40, 41; modern 157
equids 105
Eros 165
eroticism 136
error 134, 166, 167
escapism 14
esoterism 42, 43
essence 7, 11, 19, 20; divine 25; inner 164
Esztergom 13, 173
eternity 19; preparing for 57, 58, 104, 107
etymology 15, 18, 28–31, 57, 58, 70, 71, 72, 99, 101, 135, 158, 173, 177, 181; German

18; Greek 29, 168; English 18, 28, 53;
Hungarian 29, 84, 85, 95, 170; Indo-
European 28, 29, 31, 84, 144, 173; Latin
18, 28, 83–4, 85, 101, 110, 113, 126, 146
Eucharist 40
Euphrates 108, 110
Europe 12, 17, 38, 46, 55, 86, 89, 90, 104,
150, 157, 167, 175, 177; Eastern 90, 178
Evenki 31, 87
Every Men for Himself and God Against All
(Herzog) 4
event 9, 23, 32; original 33
evil 18, 107, 159, 169, 184; absolute
(Citati) 106; etymology 18, 71
evolution/ism 2, 19, 22, 24, 51, 56, 58, 86,
88, 107, 113
excarnation 103
excess 19, 70
exchange 32, 40, 72, 102
exchangeability 136, 172, 179–83
excrements 11, 116, 122
exile 34, 154
existence 9, 181; divine 10; imitative 73;
material 10; void 10
exousia (authority/ presence) 24
experience(s) 3, 7–26, 19, 37, 53, 57,
58, 59, 79, 84, 130, 157, 167, 168,
169, 174, 175, 172–9; of children
169; death 151, 162, 163, 165, 166;
divine 33; equivalence (Voegelin) 57,
61; etymology 28–9; foundational 79;
of home 30; of joy 150; lived 16, 32;
modern vs. archaic 167; Palaeolithic
104; participation 19; personal 11, 14,
57, 157, 172–9; presence 19; religious
12, 79; unity 159; unmediated 157
experiment 12, 66
extreme sport 14

fairs 40
fake 4, 32
Fall 156
family 73
fantasy 135
Faust (Goethe) 25, 72, 112
feast 32, 54, 94, 95, 97, 121
feminine 18, 145, 152
Fertile Crescent 87, 108, 115, 124, 129
Finistère (France) 89
Finis terrae (end of world) 89
finiteness 182
fire 70–1, 116, 126
fish 74, 78
Fisterra (Spain) 89
flâneur 151

Florence 43, 84, 155
fluidity *see* flux
flute 82
flux 73, 87, 138, 173, 182
flying 75
folktale(s) 33–5, 37
folklore 74, 106, 150
Fontvieille 94
fool: holy 171
Forest People (Turnbull) 149
formalism 34
fox(es) 65, 105, 106, 119, 160
fracturing 76
fragmentation *see* fracturing
France 22, 51, 156
Franciscan(s) 17, 155, 170
Frankfurt School 157
freedom 7, 17, 20, 73, 125, 170
friendship 53, 137, 180, 182
Fulani 91
fundamentalism 9

Gabillou cave 60, 80
Galatia 154
Galilee 86, 88, 98, 101, 112, 154; Sea 152
Garden of Eden *see* Paradise
Gargas cave 81
gazelle 93, 105, 109
genealogy xiii, 2, 43, 52, 53, 60, 157
Genealogy of Morals (Nietzsche) 82,
99–100, 145
geography 158
geology 24, 128
geometrical 64, 66, 90, 158
Germany 51, 157
gift (relations) 17, 23, 36, 44, 51, 57, 83,
117, 118, 155, 173, 176, 178, 180, 181,
185, 197
Gift (Mauss) 181
given 17, 36, 51, 57, 66, 131, 176
Giza 130
gladness 181
global 88, 131, 184: city 149, 156,
167, 175, 176–7; village 114, 115, 156;
world 184
globalisation 12, 175
Gnosticism 42, 46, 126
goat 105, 109–10, 121, 141, 143, 160
Göbekli Tepe 62, 65, 100, 102–113, 114,
115, 118, 119, 121, 122, 123, 124, 125,
126, 135, 144, 145; as warning 106,
107, 118, 119, 122, 124
god(s) 31, 46, 104, 107, 109, 122–3,
129, 150, 156, 170; Hindu 145;
Olympian 117

gôes (trickster) 71, 125
Golden Age 19, 119, 121, 123, 125, 138, 149, 150, 156, 168; Spanish 156
golem 111
goodness 173, 179
good feeling see contentment
Gorgias (Plato) 151
Gospel(s) 153, 156
Gothic cathedral(s) 155
grace 11, 19, 38, 58, 67, 100, 105, 107, 122, 145, 150, 173
Gran Dolina (Atapuerca) cave 56
Grand Tour 165
gratification 181
Great God of Sefar 133–5
Great Goddess 121
Greece 125; classical/Ancient 53, 71, 76, 149, 151, 154
Greenland 88
Grizzly Man (Herzog) 4, 14
grotesque 68, 134, 138, 178
Grotta dei cervi cave 90
growth 4, 73, 134, 139, 166; population 108; unlimited 143
guilt 100

Halaf culture 110, 114
handaxe 55, 61; Excalibur 55
handprints 81, 83
happiness 51, 182, 184
Harifian culture 98
harmonia mundi 167
harmony 16, 25, 39, 101
Harran 102
Hasan Dag 115
hatred 99, 139
Hausa 91
health 163, 176, 180, 184
heart 7, 12, 16, 18, 162, 170; reasons of (Pascal) 18
Heaven 153
hedonism 126
Hell 119, 139
Hellenism 84, 126
Hephaistos 126
hermeneutics 81, 82
Hermes 45, 72, 75, 116
Hermetism 42, 46
hermit 155
Hermitage (St. Petersburg) 34
heron 64, 65
Hestia 116
hesychasm 17, 171
hide and reveal 45, 97, 123
hieros gamos 138

higher: existence 9; feeling 57; forms 32; impulses 182; order 33, 36; powers 17; reality 33, 44
Hippodrome of Clayton 112
history 128, 130; origin and meaning xiii
Holocene 91
Holy Spirit 154
home 30, 35, 97, 150, 152, 166, 170, 180, 183
homelessness 19, 153
Homo antecessor 3, 156
Homo clausus (Elias) 157
Homo economicus 32
Homo faber 32, 53, 54
Homo heidelbergiensis 55
Homo ludens 32, 53
Homo Ludens (Huizinga) 32–3
Homo sapiens 37, 53, 54, 85, 90, 100
horizon 73, 91, 125, 167
horse(s) 30, 56, 64, 65, 69, 104
house(s) 11, 30, 87, 88, 95, 96–7, 114–23; society 120
hubris 14, 18, 70–1, 113, 126, 154, 155, 168, 169
humankind 52, 54, 86, 95, 119, 128, 167
humiliation 17, 136, 145
humility/humbleness 14, 17, 18, 24, 53, 168, 171
Hungarian Pilgrimage Road 13, 173
Hungary 175, 177
Huns 145
hunter-gatherers 15, 16, 98, 103, 149
hunting 85, 93, 109
hybrid 76, 77, 136, 139, 141, 176
hyper-modernity 8, 12, 14
hypocrisy 11, 109

Icarus 18
Ice Age xiii, 88, 89, 102, 109, 129, 156
'Idea of the theatre, The' (Camillo) 43
idealism 159
identity 9, 11, 13, 20, 44, 72, 76, 131, 179; formation 13, 125
ideology 11, 15, 60, 65, 91, 96, 125, 131, 164
'iguana' position see sacred display
Iheren 135, 139–43
Ik 149
illusionality 135
image(s) 25, 37, 38, 39, 40, 43, 45, 46, 57, 60, 70, 72, 76, 80, 132, 137, 146, 162, 182; contagious 57, 84; fantastic 63, 134; frightening/shocking 57–8, 60, 71, 80, 105, 119, 122, 135; graven (Bible) 84, 131; instrumentalisation 81; -magic 79
imaginary beings 60, 64, 67, 70

imagination 10, 33, 46, 60, 80, 104, 162;
poetic 65; scientific 82
imitation 3, 27, 32, 42, 60, 72, 74, 84, 91,
98, 182, 197
impotence 99
in-betwenness 75, 141, 179, 182, 183
incommensurable 53, 57, 59–60,
138, 139
inconvertibility 179, 180, 183
incubator 124, 125, 127, 130, 139
indestructible 11, 168
India 31
individualism 126; atomised 15, 168; mass
119, 145; modern 20
industrialism 131, 175, 176, 177
infantilism 25, 123, 124, 134, 164, 176,
185, 197–8
infection *see* contagion
infiltrating 75
infinity xii, 4, 58, 72, 138, 163, 170, 182
initiation 45, 67, 69, 132, 145; rite(s) 3, 35,
67, 81, 123, 126
inner force 156, 165, 166, 169
innocence 99
inspiration 11, 30, 32, 71, 100
intactness *see* integrity
integrity 75, 78
intellectual(s) 152, 159, 185
intensity 76, 77, 78, 163
interest(s) 15, 153
internalisation 99
International Political Anthropology (IPA) 3
Into the Wild 14
intruder 22, 24
intrusion 74, 177
invasion 77, 84, 97, 98, 134, 175;
Barbarian 155
Iran *see* Persia
Iraq 87
Ireland 145
'iron cage' 69, 178
Iron Curtain 7
Isturitz cave 77
Italy 38, 90, 155, 156, 175

Japan 129
jealousy 99
Jebel Sahaba 91, 92, 98, 101
Jericho 82, 92, 104, 108, 109, 110–3, 114,
115, 118, 119, 124, 125; Tower 110–3;
Wall 110–3
Jerusalem 13, 153
Jesuit(s) 17, 24
Jordan Valley 109
Joseph and his Brothers (Mann) 112

joy 22, 27, 30, 58, 81, 105, 106; of
existence/ living 19, 181
Judean desert 111
judgement 11, 12, 44, 173; educating 12
jumping 74, 75, 105, 144
Jupiter 45
justice 137, 150

Karacadağ Mountain 102, 108
Kaymakli 120, 128
Kebara 96, 101
Kebaran culture 90, 91, 92, 100
kenosis 171
Kenya 92, 128
Kfar HaHoresh 112, 113
Kolozsvár *see* Cluj
Kostromskaya 34
Knossos 84, 152
knowledge 4, 12, 17, 19, 39–46, 53, 69,
71, 80, 81, 118, 123, 138, 140, 150,
153, 164, 175, 181, 185
Konya 154

Laetoli (Tanzania) 54
Lajja Gauri 145
Lake Turkana 92, 98
Lake Van 102
Land and Sea (Schmitt) 16
language(s) 8, 27–32, 39; Afro-Asiatic 91,
98; agglutinative 29; Celtic 31; Chinese
144–5; English 8, 27, 28, 29, 30, 31,
40, 84; French 27, 28, 29, 30, 36, 53;
German 29, 30, 31, 163; Greek 29,
31, 53, 116, 117, 174; Hungarian 28,
29–32, 36, 47, 84, 95, 116, 146, 170;
Indo-European 29, 31;
instrumentalisation 39; Italian 27, 29,
30, 40; Latin 28–9, 31, 116, 173, 181;
Old Church Slavonic 31; Persian 144;
Russian 8, 30; Semitic 91; Turkish 31
Lapponia 164, 166
Larrasoaña 175
Lascaux cave 12, 22–3, 25, 52–5, 57, 59,
60, 68, 69, 79, 80, 81, 83, 85, 102, 126;
Hall of Bulls 23, 145; Shaft Scene 60,
80, 121, 122, 132, 145
Las Meninas (Velazquez) 84
Last Glacial Maximum 89, 90
Laugerie-Basse cave 75, 84
laughter 33, 135
La Vache cave 84
Law 54; divine 182; Roman 181
Laws (Plato) 149, 152
leader(s) 78–9
learning to see 17

Leaves of Grass (Whitman) 7, 51
Lemnos 126
Leon 176, 178
leopard(s) 122, 123, 126
Lepenski Vir 145
Les Fieux cave 85
Les mots et les choses see *Order of Things*
Levant 86, 87, 88, 89, 90, 91, 102, 110, 118, 128; Spanish 90, 129
'Life: experience and science' (Foucault) 166
liminality 3, 10, 16, 33, 34–6, 43, 44, 73, 74, 80, 81, 84, 86, 87, 89–91, 94, 111, 123, 128–30, 137–9, 143, 162, 173, 174, 179, 180, 182, 183, 198; forced/artificial 125; instrumentalisation 74; permanent 58, 94–5, 198
liminoid (Turner) 166
limitlessness 58, 65, 71, 72, 74, 138
limivoid (Thomassen) 166
links: archaeology-modernity 8; archaeology-myth 116; art-magic-technology xiii, 4, 81, 119; BC-BP dating 61; bison-female (Leroi-Gourhan) 60; body-soul 16, 116; business-warfare-piracy (Goethe) 72; charisma-trickster 74, 79; cosmos-chaos 18; dead-living 55, 95, 103, 111, 113, 116, 124; death-sexuality 54, 97; divine-void 10, 161–2; divine-human 10, 30, 70, 137, 146; egoism-altruism 131; elementary-useful 17; existent-non existent 181–2; good-evil 149, 183; hands-feet 15–6; hospitality-hostility 150; image-sign 25, 52, 81; infinite-finite 182; liminality-marginality 115, 128, 130; man-world 18; modernity-walking 8, 12–4; Neanderthal-Cro Magnon 52, 53, 54, 60; painting-poetry 44; painting-engraving 71; play-imagination 33; presence-absence 40; public-private 120, 126; rationality-imitation 72; reality-unreality 65, 71, 76, 161; religion-magic 79–81, 119, 123; ritual-theatre 80; sacred-secret 67; sacred-profane 26, 67, 120; science-religion xii, 9; sea-sky-snow 170; senility-infantilism 134, 176, 197–8; subversion-representation 4, 58, 131, 136; theatre-sign 42, 45, 80, 81; void-transformation 78; walking-talking 16, 34, 56; words-things 4, 39, 45; zero-infinity 23, 137–8
Linton Panel 146
lion(s) 38, 56, 80, 90, 105
liquidation see destruction

liquidity/liquefaction 20, 73, 144
Lisbon 156
lithophone(s) 85
Lo and Behold (Herzog) 4
logical positivism 158
London 177
Lord of the Rings (Tolkien) 175
Los Dogoes cave 90
Los Casares cave 74
Lot river 63
Lot region see Quercy
love 53, 150, 151, 152, 170; divine 97, 145, 162

machine 72. 93, 176, 177
madness 56; Platonic 71
Madrid 175
Magdalenian 63, 64, 74, 75, 77, 78, 79, 84, 86, 89, 91, 104
mage 125, 141, 144, 146; Renaissance 42, 43, 46
magic 21, 40, 42, 46, 76, 84, 99, 164, 165; hunting 106
magician see sorcerer
Magic Mountain (Mann) 170
magus see mage
Malatya see Arslantepe
Malaysia 16, 31
Mali 129
Malta 102, 129, 130, 145
Maltese cross 146
mammoth(s) 104
man as measure (Protagoras) 150
Man Makes Himself (Childe) 126
Manu 31
Marcher: une philosophie (Gros) 27
Máriagyűd 13, 173
market economy 176, 177
Marseille 94
Marsoulas cave 80
Mas d'Azil 34
mask(s) 18, 19, 21, 111, 129, 135; stone 111
mass(es) 82
mass society 73, 119, 145
materialism 11, 24, 26, 51, 113, 116
maternal heartbeat 18
mathematics 40
matriarchy 145
matrix 68, 84
matter 113, 116
maturity 25, 131
meaning 31, 51, 70, 82, 183; absent 139; altered 28, 122; of art 70; secret 80
meaninglessness 178
measure 71, 82, 86, 96, 104, 150, 172

mechanisation 40, 177
media 17, 169, 184, 185; *see also* press
mediation 131, 156, 157
Meditations (Descartes) 158
Mediterranean 127, 129; Eastern *see* Levant
megalith(s) 102–11, 120, 130
Meliddu *see* Arslantepe
Melite *see* Malta
Melitene *see* Arslantepe
memory 31, 44, 119, 120, 121, 122, 123, 125, 130–2, 146; arts of 42–6, 80; guardians of 122, 125
Mēn 31
Menes 31
Mercury *see* Hermes
mercy 23, 67
merging 76
Mesolithic 77, 103, 129, 135, 137
Mesopotamia 110, 111, 125, 129, 133, 149
message 80, 85
Messak 127
metallurgy 35, 135, 141, 183; cold hammering 118
metamorphosis 3, 8, 13, 20, 33, 40, 46, 67, 69, 71–9, 84, 115, 116, 122, 123, 135, 137, 139–44, 179, 182, 183; will 140
metaphysics 183
Metaphysics (Aristotle) 164
metaxy (Plato) 183
mice 119, 120
microliths 90, 103
Middle Ages 40, 44, 106, 146, 156, 169
Middle East 104, 130, 132
mimesis *see* imitation
Minoan Crete 31, 152
Minos 31
miracle(s) 53, 57, 152, 165
mnemotechnics 43, 44, 80, 81
Möbius strip xii
modern world *see* modernity
modernisation 8
modernism 2, 107, 131, 164
modernity xii, 2, 7, 8, 43, 69, 73, 74, 108, 136, 137, 156, 157, 160, 167, 175, 176, 177, 178, 182, 185; alchemic 164; anti-modern 8, 9, 15, 157; civilizational dead end 2; liberal democratic 7; multiple (Eisenstadt) 9; post-Christian 9; as problem 7; its rise 2; secular 9
moderno-centrism 11, 107
modes of being (Latour) 81
monasticism 155, 156
monotheism 133, 160
monsters 31, 35, 79, 80, 119, 136; of Pergouset 60, 62–9, 71, 83, 115, 121

Monte Sant'Angelo 173
moon 21, 31, 169
morality 122
Moravia 90
Mordor 175, 176, 177
mortuary practices *see* burial
motherhood 119, 121, 145
mouflon 134
Mount Carmel 88, 94, 101, 102
Mount Kailash 20
Mountain People (Turnbull) 149
mouse 93, 101
Mousterian culture 128
mud 63, 68, 71, 115–6, 121, 128
Mureybet 108
music 82, 84
mutant 135
mutilation 81
Mycenaean-Minoan civilisation 90
mystery 25, 41, 118, 122, 160, 163, 164, 165, 170, 183
myth/ology 68, 69, 117, 126, 144, 150, 152; of Atlantis 150, 152; Greek 18, 141; 'true' 150

Nahal Hemar cave 111
Nativity 153
Natufian culture 54, 73, 82, 86–101, 102, 103, 106, 107, 109, 110, 111, 113, 115, 119, 120, 121, 124, 125, 135, 154, 155
nature 14, 16, 44, 69, 76, 150, 152, 154, 159, 163, 164, 165, 167, 168, 169, 170, 182, 185; animated 169; philosophy of 167, 169
Nature 92
Nazareth 112, 153
Neanderthal 37, 52, 54, 55–6, 60, 90, 96, 100, 117, 128, 156; fire use 117; speech 56
Near East 86, 87, 91, 129
Negev desert 111
Nenezi Dag 115
neo-Kantianism 54, 158
neo-liberalism 113
Neolithic 73, 77, 86, 87, 88, 91, 94, 106, 109, 112, 114, 115, 116, 119, 125, 126, 129, 139, 145, 160; PPNA 106, 108; PPNB 106, 110
Neoplatonism 42, 152, 182, 183
Nepal 169
Netherlands 51
Nevali Çori 108, 109, 113, 118
New Stone Age *see* Neolithic
New Testament 21, 24, 101, 149, 169; Acts 154; Book of Apocalypse 112; Letter to the Ephesians 166; Letter to

the Galatians 154; Luke 169, 171; Mark 169; Matthew 169, 171
New Zealand 169
nihilism 15, 123
Nile 104; Valley 90, 91
nobility 15
nomad(s) 14, 15, 150, 179, 180
Normal and the Pathological, The (Canguilhem) 166
normal(ity) 166, 168
Not-Being 4, 67
non-reality *see* unreality
Nosferatu the Vampyre (Herzog) 4
nostalgia 105, 131
nothingness xii, 20, 37, 53, 54, 55, 59, 68, 83, 138–9, 140
novel(s) 33–5, 37, 156
Nubia 91
nulla see nothingness
nullity *see* nothingness
numbers: seven 44; thirty-seven 164; forty-nine 44

objectivity 65–6
obsession 131, 169; with death 93
obsidian 92, 98, 102, 103, 115, 120, 121
occult 44, 137
Odyssey (Homer) 36
Old Stone Age *see* Palaeolithic
Old Testament 24, 106, 112, 150; Isaiah 116;
omnipresence 68
omphalos 20, 61, 104, 146, 156
O Pedrouzo 174
open female *see* sacred display
optics 17
Optics, Geometry, and Meteorology (Descartes) 158
ordeal 35, 59, 80, 81, 82, 100, 153, 174, 176
orgy 97, 136
origin(s) 71; absolute 73; of agriculture 86, 107; of art 38, 52, 53; of Christianity 152–6; of cities 87; of civilisation 87, 99; of comedy 101; of culture 98; of humankind 52, 54; of language 59; of life 68, 69; mythology of 68, 69; of philosophy 150–2; of religion 52; of speech 55–6; of world 70
order 25, 27, 164; collapse of 39; higher 36; of universe 43, 44, 46, 73
Order of Things (Foucault) 38, 157
other/ness 72, 81–2, 97, 131
other directedness (Riesman) 73
out-of-ordinary (Weber) 79, 143
outsider 141, 150, 199

Padua 44, 45, 156
painting(s) xii–iii, 1, 38, 52–61, 71, 104, 125, 127, 129, 132, 145, 146
Palaeolithic xii, 8, 11, 22–6, 33, 34, 38, 51–85, 86, 87, 88, 89, 90, 91, 92, 100, 101, 103, 104, 105, 115, 118, 119, 121, 122, 124, 125, 130, 131, 137, 138, 145, 150, 156, 170, 173
Palazzo Strozzi (Florence) 84
Palestine 86, 88, 108, 110
Papua New Guinea 96
Paradise 138, 155, 168
Paradise Lost (Milton) 153
paralysis 72
parasite/ism 4, 12, 97, 119, 138, 144, 149, 151, 175, 176, 177
Paris 34, 158
Parmenides (Plato) 152
participation 19, 20, 21, 32, 58, 81, 167–8, 181
passage(s) 81
patience 14, 167, 168
Patti Birch collection 34
Pech de l'Azé cave 117
Pech-Merle cave 63, 85, 118, 146
penis *see* phallic
Pensées (Pascal) 102, 161
people of god 93, 235
perception 10; divine 182; sense 28
performance: sacred 32
performative speech act 157
Pergouset cave 4, 60, 62–70, 79, 80, 83, 100, 103, 115, 121, 132, 145, 146; headless animals 69, 121, 126; headless man 65, 69, 122, 134; monsters *see* monsters: Pergouset
permanent/ce 58, 95, 166; liminality *see* liminality: permanent; settlement 87, 96
Persia 109, 110, 144–5, 150
person(ality) 3, 44, 70, 72, 74, 83, 145
personal integrity 75, 78, 159
Phaedrus (Plato) 25, 151, 182
phallic 65, 74, 75, 105, 122, 126, 134, 135, 136
Pharisees 152
philology 99
philosophy 1, 15, 60, 70, 79, 131, 150–2, 153, 154, 157–9, 164, 166, 168; analytical 158; of beauty 151; classical 3, 168; natural 167; peripatetic 16, 158; transcendental 161
Phrygia 31
physics 113, 161
pig 110, 118, 160

pilgrimage xiii, 2, 7, 12, 13, 16, 20, 35, 35, 56, 86, 87, 152–3, 155–6, 170, 173–80
pilgrim Church 160
Pilgrim's Progress (Bunyan) 156
plaster 112, 115, 116, 120, 121, 126
Platonic year 56
play 27, 32, 54, 136; divine 27
Play in Sand (Herzog) 37
pleasure 19, 62, 78, 94, 95, 166, 173, 181
Pleistocene 55
poetry 43
political science 82
Politics (Aristotle) 149
Pontus 154
Pool of Abraham 111
pornography 136
Porto Badisco 90
Portugal 155
possession 33, 75, 84, 135, 139, 163
'post-' 131
pottery *see* ceramics
power 74, 77, 78, 123, 173; emotional 79; first 74, 82–3; fluxional 83; human 126; inner 73, 74, 167, 179, 181; second 74, 82–3; transformative 76, 78, 82, 141, 143; transcendental 83, 143; of the void 82, 143
Prague 162
prayer/ing 18, 20, 65, 70, 134, 135
pregnancy 68, 134, 135
presence xiii, 4, 10, 19, 22, 24, 32, 37, 38, 53, 58, 59, 67, 72, 79, 80, 81, 10, 128, 141, 162; divine 33, 156
Presocratics 44
press *see* media
priest(s) 125, 145, 150, 151, 152, 153, 156, 179; -artist 82; ascetic 82, 99–100, 122, 125, 145; Brahmanic 67; Levitic 67; secret 81
problematisation 85, 107, 151
Process (Kafka) 85
profit-making 25, 180
progress 14, 21, 24, 25, 90, 125, 167, 175, 176, 177, 185; evolutionary 2
projection 76
Prometheus 18, 70, 117
prophet(ess) 94, 152
Protestant Ethic (Weber) 157, 163
Protestantism 9, 14, 143, 156–7, 160
pulsation 74, 95, 97, 122, 135, 136, 139, 143
Puritanism 24, 156
Pygmies 149
pyramid(s) 102, 111, 130
Pyrenees 174, 175

quantification 40
Quercy 62, 85
Qurta 92, 98, 104

radiation 10, 177
ratio 138, 183
rational choice 11, 159, 168
rationalism 11, 15–6, 28, 39, 157–9, 163, 164, 170, 183
rationality 2, 11, 15, 17, 42, 65, 72, 73, 82, 84, 91, 109, 113, 131, 172; instrumental (Weber) 12, 13, 39; trickster 178
Raymonden cave 78
realism 57
reality 1, 4, 10, 12, 20, 21, 24, 32–3, 39, 40, 60, 75, 76, 82, 131, 135, 139, 169, 175, 179–82; altering 38, 67, 82, 162, 173, 179, 181–3; flight from 135; higher 44; leakage of (Brown) 79; loss of 69; out of 136; trust in 104; unreal 75
reason of state 159
rebel 14, 19
recognition 79, 80, 152–3, 177
recognisability 38, 57
redemption 154–6
Reformation 43, 156–7
refuge 117, 167
regression 140, 199
religion 9, 22, 80, 123, 133, 150–5
Renaissance 8, 38, 39, 43, 46, 59, 145, 155, 156, 169, 170
renewal 9, 12, 20, 56, 153–9, 157, 159
repetition 19, 36
representation xiii, 4, 12, 25, 32, 37–42, 58, 69, 81, 88, 99, 100, 105, 107, 127–42, 157, 198; divine 32–3; duplicated 41, 80–1; human 135; of self 137; of transgression 137
representing (Huizinga) 32, 33, 54
Republic (Plato) 67, 149, 151, 155, 165
res 173, 181, 183
resentment 99
resignation 72
responsibility 9, 134
retaining 179, 182
revaluation of values 82, 92, 100
revelation 69, 83, 163, 164
revolt *see* rebel
revolution(s) 73, 92, 108; agricultural 86, 108, 109; French (1789) 22, 73; industrial 108; scientific 39
rhetoric 45, 46, 84
Rhône 94
rhythm 16, 19, 178
Richard III (Shakespeare) 42

ridicule 135
Rift Valley 128
Rig Veda 31
risk 35, 165, 166, 167, 170
Rites of Passage (van Gennep) 198
rites of passage 35, 67, 180
ritual(s) 3, 18, 22, 27, 35, 38, 66, 67, 80, 84, 100, 105, 109, 119, 123, 172, 179, 183
Roc de Marsal cave 117
rock-art 60, 66, 92, 104, 129, 130
Romania 175
Romanticism 8, 15, 28, 149, 157, 159, 169
Rome 13, 14, 154, 155, 173, 176
Roncesvalles 174
Roque Saint-Christophe 128
Rosicrucian Enlightenment, The (Yates) 42
Rouffignac cave 84
ruler(s) 154, 166; our 16
rupture *see* break
Russia 34, 35

'sacred display' 132, 135, 136, 144, 145
sacrifice xiii, 3, 18, 33, 35, 40, 54, 72, 77, 94, 96, 97, 98, 125, 151, 159, 183; child 111, 121; foundational 121, 159; human 121; origins 117; self- 70
sacrificial mechanism 33, 72, 98
Sadducees 152
Sahara 127, 128, 129, 132, 137, 143, 145
Sahel 91
Sainte-Eulalie cave 63
Saint-Jean-Pied-de-Port 173, 174
salvation 12
Samaria 152
Samothrace 126
San (Bushmen) 90, 129
sanctuary 100, 103, 108, 110, 118, 120, 130, 152, 153, 183; secret 63, 67
Sanliurfa *see* Urfa
San Miniato (FI) xii
Sanskrit 31
Santa Irene 174
São Paulo 177
satisfaction 173
Sattelzeit (Koselleck) 8
scandal(s) 58, 139
scarcity 95
scapegoat(ing) 72, 98
schism 81, 111, 158
schismogenesis (Bateson) 3, 12, 20, 126, 131, 151, 153, 166, 198
scholasticism 28, 44
science 12, 21, 40, 44, 46, 47, 51, 65, 82, 159; distrust in 42; Newtonian xii, 9; official 24

scorpion 105, 106
Scribes 152
Scripture 156, 160
Scylla 20
Scythia 34, 145
sea level(s) 88, 89, 103
secrecy 46, 69, 80, 97, 107, 132
secularism 9, 12, 83, 131
seduction 72, 81, 182, 183
self/hood 13, 20, 21, 74, 82, 131, 135, 172, 180, 183; authentic 20
self-abandonment 27
self-assertion 14, 20
self-confidence 134, 165, 167, 168
self-consciousness 11, 20, 80, 99, 130–2, 134, 145, 146
self-destruction 20, 131, 144, 168
self-hatred 9
self-interest 107
self-overcoming 76
self-negation 9, 20
self-portrait 70
self-presentation 133
self-realisation 159, 169
self-reflection 135, 137
self-sameness 182
self-transformation 135
self-understanding 102
senility 32, 134, 137–9, 176, 197–8
sense of distance 18
sense of reality 32
serenity 14, 19
Sermon on the Mount 152
serpent 105, 106
settlement xiii, 1, 4, 15, 72, 73, 84, 86–103, 108, 111, 114–26, 135, 145, 149, 151, 154–6, 160, 168, 176, 179, 183
sex(uality) 93, 126, 136, 164, 169
shadow(s) 58, 77, 78
Shaft Scene *see* Lascaux
shaman(ism) 15, 31, 34, 51, 53, 60–1, 65, 76, 80, 83, 100, 122, 129, 144
Sheela na gig 145
sheep 109–10, 121, 160
shrine visitation 179
Siberia 34
siege mentality 4, 79
sign 25, 39–42, 45, 52, 64, 80–1, 173
silence 16
simplicity 17, 19, 21, 162
Sistine Chapel 57
skull cult 11, 96, 111, 120, 121–2, 126
slavery 100; of impulses 83
sleep 163, 175, 178, 185

Smithsonian 61
sociability 16
social flourishing 114, 118
social theory 13, 84, 183
socialisation 21
socialism 7
sociology 1, 2, 8, 9, 79, 157, 163
soliloquy 17
solitude 16, 70
Solutrean 85, 90
Sophist (Plato) 10, 67, 161, 162
Sophists 18, 44, 71, 150, 151, 159, 169;
    Byzantine 46
Sorbonne 158
sorcerer/y 60, 76, 77, 79, 80, 85, 97, 122,
    125, 141, 142, 144
soul 15, 16, 22, 24, 44, 51, 73, 75, 82, 83;
    -fetching 74
South Africa 129
Spain 13, 16, 24, 56, 89, 155, 156, 175, 177
spectacle 20, 40, 46, 165
spectator(ship) 45–6, 81, 165
spear 85, 100; thrower 34
speed 18, 19, 25, 76, 112; velociferic
    25, 112
spell 141
spider 106
spiral 41, 72
spirit(s) 16, 22, 24; communication of 53;
    community of 4; of conquest 4
spirituality 9, 15, 17, 18, 61, 99, 118, 125,
    156, 179; Christian 153; Eastern 20,
    163; New Age 169; Orthodox 160;
    Palaeolithic 145
sport: extreme 14, 166, 169
stability 76
Stages on Life's Way (Kierkegaard) 184
Stalinism 61
Stalker (Tarkovsky) 175
stamp(ing) 58, 182, 183
standing reserve (Heidegger) 93, 100
statues: clay 111
sterility 4, 73
stress 95
storytelling 16, 34, 37
Stroszek (Herzog) 4
structuralism 34
struggle for survival 74
sublime 44, 165
submission/ submissiveness 75, 136
substitutability 32, 40, 45, 72
subversion 4, 58, 71, 72, 73–9, 82, 84, 125,
    130, 131, 136–8, 199
suffering 70, 74, 78, 174
Sumerian culture 110

sunflower 177
supernatural 74
super-real 76, 136, 162, 169
surmodernité 146
surplus 180, 181
surrealism 135, 137
survivor 74, 176
suspicion 97
synthetic 74
symbol 18, 45, 55, 68, 69
Symposium (Plato) 151, 165, 170
Syria 108, 155

table 39–44 *passim*
Tabula Smaragdina 42–3
Tadrart 125, 127
Tahiti 31
Tale of Two Cities, A (Dickens) 73
taming 99–100, 122, 123
Taoism 21, 144
Tarsus 154
Tarxien 145
Tassili 65, 79, 91, 105, 107, 109, 115, 123,
    125, 127–46; Bubaline/Wild Fauna 129,
    130, 132, 137; Caballin/Camelin 135,
    139; pastoral *see* Caballin; Round Head
    65, 104, 128, 129, 130, 132–6, 137,
    139, 146 ('Martians' 132, 133)
taste 11
tears of joy 23, 25, 33, 38, 56
technology(ies) 11, 16, 18, 21, 42, 46,
    69, 77, 83, 86, 93, 100, 157, 166, 168;
    of enchantment 119, 123; pyro- 112,
    116; scientific 176; subversive 73, 77;
    transformative 123, 124
telegraph 18
telephone 18
terror 73
Teyjat cave 104
thaumazein 53, 79
theatre 17, 38, 40, 42, 43, 44, 61, 79;
    Elizabethan 42; memory (Camillo) 43
theatricalisation 81, 82
theatricality 18, 19, 81; archaeology of 80;
    prehistoric 79–82
theatrum mundi 45
Theaetetus (Plato) 44
theology 40, 150, 153, 154, 160;
    Trinitarian 154, 160
Thessaly 43, 125
Three Graces 45
thought 157, 183; ancient/ archaic 76,
    182; European 153, 183; magical 145;
    modern 16, 40; mythic/ symbolic 18;
    rational 72, 84, 158

Tibet 20, 103
Timaeus (Plato) 53, 79, 146, 150, 152, 163
Titan(ism) 14, 18
tophet 111
tourism 13, 17, 20, 38, 158
tradition 8, 151, 180
trance 129
transcendence xii, 10, 54, 74, 161;
   religious xii
transcendental xii, 3, 75–6, 82, 141, 142, 182;
   situation 73, 74 (*see also* crisis, liminality)
transformation *see* metamorphosis
transgression xiii, 47, 52, 53, 54, 58, 67,
   68, 82, 96, 104, 123, 139, 143, 199
transition 35, 69, 87; Pleistocene-
   Holocene 130
Transylvania 173, 174; Carpathians 173
travel 8, 15, 34–5, 158
trial *see* ordeal
tribulation *see* ordeal
trick(s) 19, 44–5, 74, 81, 100, 117, 120,
   122–3, 177
trickster 3, 4, 24, 71–9, 84, 102, 106, 107,
   109, 117, 119, 122, 125, 129, 133, 144,
   150, 183, 199; Land 175, 177, 178
   (*see also* Mordor); life 176, 177; logic
   124; as sacrificer 73; techniques 176
Trinity 44, 160
Trois Frères cave 60, 80, 85
trust 72
Tuc d'Audubert cave 85
Tungusic *see* Evenki
Turin 165
Turkey 87, 108, 109, 110, 115
Tuscan-Emilian Apennines 173

Ucraine 132
ugliness 62, 175
Ulysses (Homer) 36
underground 120, 154, 155; caves 38, 59,
   104; cities 124, 128; imagination 104;
   river 63;
United States 8, 9
universalism 4, 73, 82, 113, 185
unlimited *see* limitless
unreality 1, 3, 10, 60, 69, 75, 76, 134, 143,
   199; of modernity 21; real 175
Ur (Mesopotamia) 167
Urfa (Turkey) 102, 111, 154, 167
uterus 140–1
utility 11, 172, 180, 185
utopia 20

vampire 4
vanity 70

Vatican 14
Vedas *see* Rig Veda
vengeance 144
Venice 43, 44
Ventimiglia 164
Veronica image 154
Vesta 116
Via Francigena 13, 14, 156, 173
victim(hood) 98, 176
victimage mechanism *see* sacrificial
   mechanism
Vienna 142, 158
violence xiii, 60, 72, 79, 84, 90, 91, 92, 97,
   98, 99, 101, 125
virtue 138, 139, 140
vision 58, 60, 100, 175; of beauty
   100, 106, 152; of history 87–8; of
   knowledge 43; of Madonna 22; of
   modernity 13, 172
visuality 17
vocation 163
void xii, 4, 9, 10, 12, 15, 20, 24, 37,
   53, 54, 55, 58, 59–60, 67, 68, 70,
   71, 74, 75–6, 78, 88, 97, 104, 130,
   133, 137–8, 161–70, 173, 179, 181–2,
   199; absolute 72; in algebra 137–8;
   alliance *see* union; its emotional charge
   xii, 10, 25, 53, 57, 59–60, 65, 78, 105,
   122; experiencing 163; hermeneutic
   82; involvement *see* union; leap
   into 185; liminal 35, 76, 123, 162;
   manipulation 140; merging with 74;
   representing 161; sympathy with 107;
   union with 134, 135; transformative
   potential 82
voiding 75
voidism 86
vulgarity 136
vulture(s) 103, 119
vulva 68

Wadi Djerat 128, 136
Wadi Halfa 92
Wadi Natuf cave 88
Walden (Thoreau) 27
wall(ing) 87, 99, 100, 111, 128–9
war(s)/fare 22, 91, 92, 97
water 63, 68, 70–1, 115, 174, 175
We Have Never Been Modern (Latour) 179
wheat 102, 177; einkorn 102, 108, 160;
   emmer 102, 108, 160
wild/ness 110, 122, 126; man 150
witchcraft *see* sorcery
witness 20
womb 68

world: building (Popitz) 73; foundation
129; as given 17; history 99; order
(settled 151); vision 38, 45, 57, 58, 59,
60, 68, 81, 122 (alchemic-technological
159; Greek/ anti-technological 117;
life-affirming 150; medieval 39; modern
15; Newton-Kantian 161; paranoid 82;
Platonic 53; sacrificial 167; scientific
9, 10, 15, 16, 161; technological 167;
walking 164)
World Youth Day 175
Woyzeck (Herzog) 4

Younger Dryas 89, 94, 97, 98
YouTube 90

Zagros Mountains 102, 109
Zarathustra (Nietzsche) 57, 76, 159
zero 37, 137, 138–9, 143
Zeus 117, 152
Zone (Tarkovsky) 175
Zoroastrism 159
Zubiri 175
Zürau 162
Zürau Notebooks (Kafka) 168